Reprinted with the permission of the Original Publishers

JOHNSON REPRINT CORPORATION
New York • London
1972

Library of Congress Catalog Card Number: 77-38878

This volume was reproduced from an original copy in
the collection of the New York State Library, Albany.

First reprinting 1972, Johnson Reprint Corporation

Johnson Reprint Corporation   Johnson Reprint Company Ltd.
111 Fifth Avenue   24/28 Oval Road
New York, N. Y. 10003   London, NW1 7DD, England

Printed in the U.S.A.

The Industrial Worker in Pennsylvania

1800 - 1840

By WILLIAM A. SULLIVAN

COMMONWEALTH OF PENNSYLVANIA

•

PENNSYLVANIA
HISTORICAL AND MUSEUM COMMISSION

HARRISBURG, 1955

PREFACE

A T THE BEGINNING of the nineteenth century such a term as "workingman" rarely if ever appeared in public print. The industrial worker as such was unknown. But by the decade of the 1830's, the "workingman" represented a novel but indeterminate force in the American community. He was a product of the Industrial Revolution which, in this first half of the century, was subtly transforming the whole mode of American life.

It was not until the late nineteenth century that the social upheaval brought on by the Industrial Revolution and its impact on the workingman attracted the attention of serious scholars. In 1886, Richard T. Ely, of Johns Hopkins University, published the *Labor Movement in America*. This study, although admittedly inadequate, opened up for the students of American economic and social history a vast, unexplored field for inquiry.

John R. Commons and his Associates at the University of Wisconsin undertook the enormous but exciting task of unearthing the manuscript materials which would disclose the role of labor in shaping the course of American history. Their efforts resulted in two monumental publications: the first being a ten-volume collection of manuscript materials referring to American labor entitled *Documentary History of American Industrial Society;* and the second being the most exhaustive and significant study of the American labor movement to date—a four-volume project entitled the *History of Labour in the United States.*

Since the appearance of the latter study, all subsequent histories of the American labor movement, especially those referring to the first half of the nineteenth century, have been, with rare exceptions, little more than "generalized summarizations of what had been presented in detailed fashion in the *History of Labour in the United States.*"[1]

Two exceptions to this generalization are the following: first is Professor Richard B. Morris' brilliant study of *Government and Labor in Early America,* an original and comprehensive investigation of labor in the Colonial period; and the second is Dr. Norman Ware's challenging history of *The Industrial Worker 1840-1860.* Dr. Philip S. Foner has undertaken an ambitious project entitled *History of the*

[1] Philip S. Foner, *History of the Labor Movement in the United States* (New York, 1947), p. 10.

iii

Labor Movement in the United States. The first volume of this pro-
jected two-volume study appeared in 1947, and its originality, particularly in its treatment of the labor movement in the first half of the
nineteenth century, lies largely in interpretation rather than in new
materials uncovered.

Since the vast panorama of American labor history has attracted the
attention of some of America's outstanding scholars, and the general
history of the American labor movement has been told, the aim of this
project is a narrower theme. The individual states have always been
a significant factor in American history, and the writer in this volume
undertakes a comprehensive study of the situation of the industrial
worker in Pennsylvania from 1800 to 1840.

In the following chapters the writer has examined the impact of the
Industrial Revolution on the Pennsylvania wage earner and his reaction
to it. His sources have been, primarily, manuscript account books
(day books, ledgers, journals and receipt books) which have been preserved in the numerous repositories throughout Pennsylvania. In
addition, contemporary newspapers have been used extensively, especially for tracing the development of the trade union movement. These
newspapers were invaluable and almost the only sources of information
for the discussion of labor-management relations and the numerous
strikes which broke out as a result of the inability of these two groups
to reconcile their differences. They also provided indispensable leads
to the politics of the workingman.

Without the aid of numerous individuals this study would never have
been possible. To Dr. S. K. Stevens, State Historian, and to the Pennsylvania Historical and Museum Commission, whose generous financial
aid has made publication possible, I am deeply obligated. At this time
I also wish to thank Donald H. Kent, Associate State Historian,
and Mrs. Autumn Leonard, Research Assistant, for editorial advice
and for aid in reading the proof. I shall always remember how
graciously Henry Howard Eddy, Chief of the Public Records Division
of the Commission, kept offices open after hours and assisted me in
other ways too numerous to mention. To the staffs of the numerous
historical societies scattered throughout Pennsylvania, I am especially
indebted. I shall remember with kindness Barney Cheswick of the
Ridgway Branch Library, who never tired of answering the innumerable requests of this writer.

To Dr. J. Martin Klotsche, President of Milwaukee State Teachers
College, I am indebted for first having suggested to me a study of labor
in the Jackson era. Nor can I forget the patience with which Professor

John A. Krout listened to my papers and assisted me through the doctoral seminar in which this paper was begun. I must also acknowledge the generosity of Professor Arthur C. Bining of the University of Pennsylvania, who shared with me his notes on the iron industry of Pennsylvania in the nineteenth century. To Dean Harry J. Carman of Columbia University I am indebted for having generously consented to read this entire manuscript.

Above all I am grateful to Professor Richard B. Morris of Columbia University. Throughout all my graduate studies he has patiently guided and assisted me. He has been generous with his time and criticism. His suggestions have been numerous and invaluable throughout the whole course of this project, both as to investigation of the sources and the preparation and revision of the manuscript. And finally to Betty whose assistance was indispensable, my deepest gratitude.

Whatever errors appear in this manuscript, errors of fact or interpretation, of omission or commission, are mine.

WILLIAM A. SULLIVAN

TABLE OF CONTENTS

I

THE INDUSTRIAL SETTING

THE YEARS from 1800 to 1840 form a convenient unit for a study of the industrial worker. During these years the status of the worker was undergoing a subtle but profound transformation. The introduction of steam-driven machinery and the growth of the factory system menaced the preëminent position of the skilled artisan, and brought unskilled hands, and women and child wage earners into direct competition with him. These same decades witnessed, too, the emergence of labor as an organized and active force in the economic and social life of the nation.

Pennsylvania, during these first four decades of the nineteenth century, provides an excellent locale for the study of the labor movement. Probably no other state could match its wealth in natural resources. Its fertile valleys, its wooded mountains, its almost inexhaustible deposits of coal and its beds of iron ore provided a firm foundation for a well-integrated economy. In the East two magnificent waterways, the Delaware and Chesapeake Bay, promised ready access to world markets for its products from the earth, the field and the forest. And beyond the mountains, the Ohio River carried the produce of the western country to the outside world.

Both as colony and commonwealth, Pennsylvania attracted wage earners of a variety of trades and occupations from the Old World. A generous land policy, a liberal frame of government and a bold advertising campaign made Penn's colony the most cosmopolitan settlement in English North America. German emigrants, the greater part of whom were mechanics and weavers, arrived shortly after the colony was founded.[1] Throughout the eighteenth century they came in ever increasing numbers, settling on the rich farm lands in Lancaster County. Welsh settlers arrived early, establishing themselves in Chester and Philadelphia counties. The Scotch-Irish came in alarming numbers. Contemptuous of land titles and disregarding the Indian treaties, they squatted on the unsettled lands of the frontier. Decades

---

[1] J. Franklin Jameson (ed.), *Original Narratives of Early American History: Francis Daniel Pastorius, Circumstantial Description of Pennsylvania, 1700,* printed in *Narratives of Early Pennsylvania, West New Jersey and Delaware 1630—1707* (New York, 1912), pp. 207 ff.

before the Quaker colony was established, the Swedes and the Dutch had planted settlements along the Delaware. This richly-endowed colony with its heterogenous population was destined to assume a commanding position among the English settlements in North America. Throughout the eighteenth century, its commerce and industries held a preëminent position in British America, and Philadelphia, its capital, was unquestionably the cultural and intellectual center of the thirteen English colonies.

When the nineteenth century opened, Pennsylvania still retained the position of industrial and cultural supremacy. Neither the War for Independence nor the subsequent years of uncertainty impaired its standing in this respect.[2] With a population of 602,548 in 1800, it was one of the most populous states in the Union.[3] No other state could match its industries in number and variety.[4]

Since the predominance of Pennsylvania was in no small measure due to the skill and industry of its mechanics and artisans, the industrial setting in which they worked and lived would seem to be worth considering. A rough accounting of American industries was made in 1810. Although the data collected was incomplete, it did give a fair representation of the nation's industrial development. Pennsylvania's annual production was reported to be $44,292,093 or one third greater than the production of New York, its nearest competitor. In the production of iron and steel, distilled liquors, hides and leather products, paper and hats, Pennsylvania led all the other states in the Union; in glass, it was second; and in textiles, third.[5]

Since the middle of the eighteenth century its leadership in the iron industry went unchallenged.[6] Shipbuilding and its allied industries prospered in the first decade of the nineteenth century and although Pennsylvania declined in importance as a shipbuilding center,

[2] Victor S. Clark, *History of Manufactures in the United States 1607-1860* (New York, 1929), I, p. 215 ff.

[3] Samuel Hazard (ed.), *The Register of Pennsylvania* (Philadelphia, 1828-1833), I, April 1828. p. 266.

[4] Tench Coxe, *A Statement of the Arts and Manufactures of the United States for the Year 1810* (Philadelphia, 1814), p. 7-8; see also John Bristed, *The Resources of the United States of America* (New York, 1818), p. 64; also J. Leander Bishop, *History of American Manufactures from 1608-1860* (Philadelphia, 1861), II, p. 172-173.

[5] Tench Coxe, *op. cit.*, p. 7; see also Malcolm Eiselen, *Rise of Protectionist Sentiment in Pennsylvania* (Philadelphia, 1932), p. 33.

[6] Arthur C. Bining, *Pennsylvania Iron Manufacture in the Eighteenth Century* (Harrisburg, 1938), p. 23 ff.

it long remained famous for the quality, the speed and the trim of its vessels.[7] The textile industry flourished there. And the inventive genius of Oliver Evans coupled with the native iron industry was to make Pennsylvania the home of the heavy machine industry.[8]

INDUSTRIAL CENTERS

There were in Pennsylvania at this time only two communities with a sufficient concentration of capital and labor to make possible the development of the factory system. As it had been in the past, Philadelphia continued to be the first city of the land. It was the banking and financial center of the nation. The Bank of North America was located there; and it was the home of Stephen Girard's Banking House and the Bank of Pennsylvania.[9]

The predominance of Pennsylvania in these formative years of the republic was due in a large measure to the financial and industrial pre-eminence of Philadelphia. According to the census of 1810, over one third of the manufactures of Pennsylvania was returned by this city.[10] The contributions of the mechanic and artisan toward this development have never been fully assessed. That outstanding historian of American manufactures, Victor S. Clark, asserts that in Philadelphia at this time there "resided the largest population of hereditary operatives and artisans, with probably the highest average level of manual skill in the United States."[11] One contemporary observer noted that[12] "There is no part of the world, probably, where in proportion to its population, a greater number of ingenious mechanics may be found than in the city of Philadelphia and its immediate neighborhood . . ." This concentration of skilled wage earners explains the predominance of Philadelphia at this time.

---

[7] Edward P. Cheyney, *Ship-Building on the Delaware*, p. 54c., printed in *Annual Report of the Secretary of Internal Affairs Pennsylvania;* Part III, *Industrial Statistics,* (Harrisburg, 1892), XIX; see also Charles L. Chandler, *Early Ship-Building in Pennsylvania 1683-1812* (Philadelphia, 1932), p. 36. Clark, *op. cit.*, I, p. 470.

[8] Greville and Dorothy Bathe, *Oliver Evans: A Chronicle of Early American Engineering* (Philadelphia, 1935), p. 219 ff.

[9] See Philip S. Klein, *Pennsylvania Politics 1817-1832* (Philadelphia, 1940), p. 22.

[10] Coxe, *op. cit.*, p. VIII; Bishop, *op. cit.*, II, p. 172-173, states: "The total value of Manufactures within the above limits /Philadelphia city and county/ was $16,103,869 and those of the whole state $44,194,740."

[11] Clark, *op. cit.*, I, p. 406.

[12] Bristed, *op. cit.*, p. 64.

Situated on the highway leading to the West was Lancaster, the second city of the State, and generally acclaimed to be the largest inland city in the United States.[13] Manufacturing thrived in this community which in 1800 had a population of 4,292 persons. It had long been famous for the excellence of its rifles, and the various branches of the iron industry located in this area enjoyed considerable prosperity. More tons of iron were worked at the various forges and furnaces scattered throughout Lancaster County, and the money value of the finished product was greater than that of any other county in the State.[14] Blacksmithing and carriage making prospered, and leather working provided employment for a large number of its citizens. In the vicinity of Lancaster there were sawmills in great profusion. The manufacture of hemp into fiber was an important industry, and the number of mills in operation was sixteen. Its early inhabitants were "pre-eminently tradesmen" who had come "from the region bordering upon the Low Countries and from the Rhine Valley—from the very heart and artery of European industrialism"—thus assuring the community of an experienced labor force.[15]

Although Pittsburgh in 1800 could scarcely be called a city, its potentialities as a future industrial community were already evident. The *Pittsburgh Gazette* in 1786 boasted that "this town must in future time be a place of great manufactory; indeed the greatest on the continent, or perhaps in the world." [16] In 1804, *Cramer's Almanack* noted with pride "that the aggregate value of the articles manufactured in Pittsburgh in 1803 amounts to upwards of $350,000." [17] Its location had made manufacturing inevitable. This village, strategically located at the confluence of the Allegheny and the Monongahela Rivers, was before 1860 probably the most important channel of migration and

---

[13] Fortescue Cuming, *Sketches of a Tour to the Western Country 1807-1809*, p. 31, printed in Reuben G. Thwaites (ed), *Early Western Travels* (Cleveland, 1904), IV. Bishop, *op. cit.*, I, p. 415.

[14] *A Series of Tables of the Several Branches of American Manufacture 1810* (n.p. n.d.), p. 50.

[15] G. D. Luetscher, "Industries of Pennsylvania after the adoption of the Federal Constitution with Special Reference to Lancaster and York Counties," *The American Ethnographical Survey, Conestoga Expedition 1902* (New York, 1911), p. 9, 11.

[16] The *Pittsburgh Gazette*, August 26, 1786, as quoted in George Fleming, *History of Pittsburgh and Environs* (New York, 1922), III, p. 468.

[17] *Cramer's Almanack*, 1804, as quoted in John Boucher, (ed.), *A Century and a Half of Pittsburgh and Her People* (New York, 1908), I, p. 320.

transportation between the Atlantic seaboard and the Trans-Appalachian West.[18] Settlers moving to the West found it to their advantage to secure the necessary manufactured goods from or through Pittsburgh.

No other city in the State grew as rapidly as this one. Pittsburgh in 1803, had a population of about 2,500. In 1820, this city had 7,248 inhabitants; ten years later it had 12,568, indicating a 73% increase; and by 1840, this city had a population of 21,115 making it the fifth city in the nation.[19] In a struggle that began over the control of this strategically located village the French lost an Empire.

While these were the major centers of industry in Pennsylvania in the first decades of the nineteenth century, they were by no means the only localities in which manufacturing thrived. Scattered throughout the State along the innumerable streams and creeks were countless fulling mills, saw mills, furnaces and forges employing capital and labor beyond calculation. Manufacturing was still in its infancy and the home was still an important center of production, making it impossible to ascertain with any degree of accuracy Pennsylvania's industrial development.

INDUSTRIAL PROGRESS

The industrial worker, when the century opened, made up a small segment of the total population of Pennsylvania. Agriculture engaged the attentions of most of the working people. But the force of events both at home and abroad during the first two decades of the nineteenth century was inexorably driving men and capital into industry and manufacturing.

The "development of industrial consciousness" was a force of immeasurable importance in the growth of a native industry. In a keen and incisive essay treating with the formative years of American industrial development, Samuel Rezneck observed that "it was the experience of the United States that the will to manufacture was born

---

[18] Louis C. Hunter, "Influence of the Market Technique in the Iron Industry in Western Pennsylvania up to 1860," *Journal of Economic and Business History,* I, 1929, p. 245; see also Solon J. Buck, *The Planting of Civilization in Western Pennsylvania* (Pittsburgh, 1939), p. 288 ff.

[19] Samuel Hazard (ed.), *United States Commercial and Statistical Register,* V. Sept. 1841, p. 108; *Pennsylvania House Journal,* December 6, 1831 to June 1832, II, p. 267; Samuel Hazard (ed.) *Register of Pennsylvania,* VII, March 1831, p. 172-173.

before manufactures were started, and, according to many, even before the ability to manufacture was present." [20]

Nowhere was this spirit more manifest than in the State of Pennsylvania itself. Organizations appeared to promote the cause of domestic manufactures and to educate the public to their importance. The Pennsylvania Society for the Encouragement of Manufactures and the Useful Arts was organized in 1787. Its primary purpose was the diffusion of knowledge relating to the technical processes of manufacturing which would enable the American-made products to compete with those of Europeans.[21] The difficulties which beset American industry in 1819 sharpened the interest in manufactures and brought about the revival of the Pennsylvania Society and the organization of the Philadelphia Society for the Promotion of National Industry.[22] "It is the cause of the Nation" for which it struggled, declared the Philadelphia Society. "It is the mighty question, whether we shall be really or *nominally* independent." And it dogmatically asserted, "if there be any truth in Political Economy more sacred and irrefragable than another, it is [that] the prosperity of Nations bears an exact proportion to the encouragement of their *Domestic Industry*." [23]

Far more effective in stimulating the growth of domestic industry was the commercial policy inaugurated in the last months of President Jefferson's administration, and later modified during the Presidency of James Madison. The Embargo and Non-Intercourse Acts came at a time when American ships were carrying a large share of the ocean's commerce.[24] Forced to abandon this lucrative trade, merchants with surplus capital turned to manufacturing as a profitable field for investment. This coincided with the closing of the American market to British-made goods. That perspicacious observer, Niles, noted that "since commerce has been embarrassed the manufactures have been increasing in the ratio of the troubles of commerce." [25] The Pennsyl-

---

[20] Samuel Rezneck, "The Rise and Early Development of Industrial Consciousness in the United States 1760-1830," *Journal of Economic and Business History*, IV, August 1932, p. 785.

[21] Bishop, *op. cit.*, II, p. 103; see A. H. Cole and W. B. Smith, *Fluctuations in American Business 1790-1860* (Cambridge, 1935), p. 20, 28.

[22] The *Aurora and General Advertiser*, Sept. 7, 1819; The *Lancaster Intelligencer and Weekly Advertiser*, Sept. 11, 1819.

[23] *Ibid.*

[24] Clark, *op. cit.*, I, p. 272; Bishop, *op. cit.*, II, p. 121, states that "the American tonnage employed in the foreign trade, as compared with that of all other powers so employed was in the proportion of more than twelve to one."

[25] *Niles' Register*, IV, May 15, 1813, p. 172.

vania press enthusiastically noted this shift of capital from commerce to industry. Without the development of manufactures declared the *Aurora*, "*freedom* and *independence* can never be perfectly secure." [26] Years later when American industry was suffering from the inundation of English-made goods, a House Committee on Commerce and Manufacture made the following report:

> Prior to the years 1805 and 1807, establishments for manufacturing cotton wool, had not been attempted but in a few instances, and on a limited scale. Their rise and progress are attributable to embarrassments to which commerce was subjected. . . . When external commerce was suspended, the capitalists throughout the union, became solicitous to give activity to their capital. A portion of it, as it appears, was likewise employed in erecting establishments manufacturing cotton wool.[27]

The second war with England, following closely on the heels of this restrictive commercial policy, gave an added impetus to the infant manufacturing establishments throughout the country. High prices and a steady demand for manufactured goods eased the translation of capital from commerce to industry. One individual identifying himself as A FRIEND TO MANUFACTURES sagely wrote:

> The contrary effect of the war upon the two countries, is striking; the commerce between them is, or ought to be, suspended; and the effects of this suspension, is to depress manufactures in that country, and encourage them in this. An interruption of our commercial pursuits, tends to a diversion of the capital and services thus employed, to the pursuits of manufactures, and this is done without sacrifice.[28]

Pittsburgh's beginning as a great manufacturing center is often traced to the War of 1812. Enterprising individuals, awake to the needs of the expanding communities in the West, took advantage of the lack of European imports and established manufactories to serve this crying need. Government orders gave an added spur to the industries of this city. This city provided much of the material for the fleet

---

[26] The *Aurora and General Advertiser*, June 28, 1811 and June 17, 1809; see also The *Democratic Press*, Feb. 14, 1812.

[27] The *Aurora and General Advertiser*, Feb. 27, 1819 quoting report of the Committee of Commerce and Manufactures, upon the subject of domestic manufactures, made to the House of Representatives. See also *American State Papers—Finance*, III, p. 82.

[28] The *Aurora and General Advertiser*, February 25, 1814; see Bishop, *op. cit.*, I, p. 178-179.

being constructed at Erie. "All the iron and cordage can be procured at Pittsburgh," wrote Isaac Chauncey, who was in charge of the ship-building program on the Lakes.[29]

The growing demands of the country called for greater production and necessitated improved techniques. Steam-driven machinery began to replace the water and horse-powered equipment of a former day and the consequences were revolutionary. Factory development was no longer restricted to the costly mill sites along the streams but enabled the entrepreneur to construct his mills in or near the towns where a much needed labor supply was always available.[30] Labor-saving machinery was exploited more extensively than ever before. Ardent champions of domestic industry in Pennsylvania had long argued that America with all its deficiencies could become a competitor of Great Britain in the industrial world through the development and use of machinery.[31] "Machinery is better adapted to the circumstances of this country than of most other countries," contended the *Aurora*, "because it performs the same quantity of labour, where the labour of men, and particularly of mechanics, is much dearer." [32] Women and children, otherwise idle, could attend this machinery and free men for more productive and patriotic endeavours.[33] "The war with the *power* of Great Britain," one commentator observed, "has created a war with her *interests*—and whatsoever may be the success of the former, it is certain that the latter cannot fail of advancing, in many respects the individual and national prosperity of this country." [34]

Nor was the blight which struck at the infant manufacturing establishments at the close of the war without its beneficial effects. There was a notable unanimity with which the varied economic interests throughout Pennsylvania supported the protective system. Early in 1815, some Philadelphia manufacturers, anticipating the losses to be incurred as a result of the cessation of hostilities, suggested that a convention of Philadelphia and New York manufacturers be held to

---

[29] Captains Letters, I, February 16, 1813, p. 78; also see George Fleming, *A History of Pittsburgh and its Environs* (New York, 1922), II, p. 54, and see Henry B. Fearon, *Sketches of America* (London, 1818), p. 202.

[30] *House Mscl. Document 4 Part 2, 47th Congress 2d Session*, p. 56.

[31] The *Aurora and General Advertiser*, March 19 and June 10, 1803.

[32] *Ibid.*, March 4, 1809, October 7, 1811, and May 11, 1812.

[33] *Niles' Register*, II, March 21, 1812, p. 36; see also *Cramer's Almanack*, 1817, p. 49; The *United States Gazette*, April 12, 1815, and The *Aurora and General Advertiser*, May 4, 1809 and November 12, 1814.

[34] The *Aurora and General Advertiser*, February 24, 1815.

urge some form of protection for American industries.[35] In the House of Representatives, one of the most effective voices raised in behalf of the protective system was that of Henry C. Baldwin, Congressman from Western Pennsylvania.[36] According to Eiselen, "the period of distress from 1818 to 1821 represented . . . a real turning point in the development of Pennsylvania protectionism." [37]

THE GROWTH OF THE IRON INDUSTRY

The most zealous partisans of the protective tariff were the iron masters from Pennsylvania. Since the iron industry was to become the pulse by which the economic life of the nation would be measured, it is necessary to survey briefly the progress and development of iron production in Pennsylvania to comprehend more fully the status of the workers who made so substantial a contribution to its growth. During the period under discussion, the iron industry experienced no significant changes, either in techniques used in smelting the ore or in the total volume of iron produced. It was not until the late 1830's that anthracite coal was used experimentally to replace charcoal in the smelting process, and it took another two decades before the output of anthracite iron production surpassed that of charcoal.[38] Nor had the railroads, whose impact was to be revolutionary, appreciably affected the iron industry prior to 1840.

Iron furnaces and forges were to be found in great profusion throughout the State. The heaviest concentration was located in the southeastern district. Berks County early became famous for its iron works. Its wooded hillsides and an abundant supply of magnetic ores free from phosphorus provided the two essential raw materials for a prosperous iron industry.[39] At the beginning of the nineteenth century there were six furnaces and forges in Berks County. An enumeration thirty years later revealed that there were then eleven furnaces which pro-

[35] *Ibid.*, March 2, 1815.

[36] *Niles' Register*, xviii, June 17, 1820, p. 288. See also John Boucher, *op. cit.*, I, p. 379-380.

[37] Eiselen, *op. cit.*, p. 51.

[38] *Hazard's United States Commercial and Statistical Register*, I, July 1839, p. 35 and November 1839, p. 352. See also the *Huntingdon Journal*, February 13, 1839, and the *Public Ledger*, February 19, and Oct. 29, 1839. And see Louis C. Hunter, *op. cit.*, p. 242-243.

[39] John B. Pearse, A *Concise History of the Iron Manufacture* (Phila., 1876), p. 151; Alfred Gemmell, *The Charcoal Iron Industry in the Perkiomen Valley* (Norristown, 1949), p. 15.

duced in a three year period 14,411 tons of pig iron and 3,587 tons of castings. The twenty-four forges located there made in a similar period 6,160 tons of bar iron and 5,150 tons of blooms. These iron works employed about 2,770 men.[40] According to the returns of the *Sixth Census* there was no increase in the decade from 1830 to 1840.[41] Undoubtedly the panic of 1837 contributed to this static condition.

Both Chester and Lancaster counties shared conspicuously in the advancement of the iron industry during this period. In the former county there were in operation two of the most extensive ironworking establishments in the State—the Lukens Rolling Mill, founded in 1810 by Dr. Charles Lukens and Isaac Pennock as the Federal Slitting Mill,[42] and the Phoenix Iron Company founded in 1790 by Benjamin Longstreth. An investigation of the iron industry of Chester County published in 1842 revealed that there were in this county four furnaces making annually 4,000 tons of pig metal and castings; five forges annually producing 1,800 tons of bar iron and blooms; six boiler mills with an annual production of 2,400 tons of boiler plate; and three sheet-iron mills making 600 tons of sheet iron yearly. In addition to these, the county boasted four nail factories, three foundries and three trip hammers.[43] One person out of every twenty-three in Chester County was dependent upon the iron industry for his livelihood.[44]

Lancaster had in these early decades of the nineteenth century probably the largest development of iron manufactures in the eastern district of Pennsylvania.[45] Located at Lancaster were the iron holdings of Judge Robert Coleman, reported to be one of the richest men in the United States.[46] In 1809, his furnaces and forges produced 2,000 tons of

---

[40] *Hazard's Register of Pennsylvania*, VIII, Nov. 1831, p. 297. See also Thomas F. Gordon, *Gazetteer of the State of Pennsylvania* (Phila., 1832), p. 45. And see *Documents Relative to the Manufactures in the United States* (Wash., 1833), II, p. 199, hereafter cited as *McClane's Report*.

[41] See the *United States Sixth Census (1840)*, p. 142.

[42] John S. Futhey, *History of Chester County Pennsylvania* (Phila., 1881), p. 349; see also James M. Swank, *History of the Manufacture of Iron in All Ages* (Phila., 1892), p. 195.

[43] *Hazard's United States Commercial and Statistical Register*, VI, January 1842, p. 54.

[44] *Ibid.*

[45] Swank, *op. cit.*, p. 196. Swank, in his description of the iron industry at the end of the third decade of the nineteenth century writes: "At this time Lancaster was the great iron centre of Eastern Pennsylvania."

[46] *Journal of Joshua Gilpin.* Sept. 16, 1809, p. 27. Handwritten copy in the Public Records Division of the Pennsylvania Historical and Museum Commission.

pig iron and 1,100 tons of bar iron annually. An enumeration of the county's iron industry in 1833 revealed that there were five charcoal furnaces annually producing 5,000 tons of pig iron; two rolling mills making five hundred tons of bar iron yearly; and eleven forges making 2,350 tons of bar iron annually.[47] According to the returns of the *Sixth Census,* the iron works of Lancaster County were surpassed in number and product only by those of Berks County in the eastern half of the State. Its eleven charcoal furnaces in 1840 made 6,912 tons of pig iron, and its three forges and one rolling mill made 2,090 tons of bar iron.[48]

Numerous iron works were to be found throughout the other counties in the eastern half of the State. Although Philadelphia was insignificant as a iron producing center, its ironworking establishments were both extensive and important to the industrial development of Pennsylvania. The Mars Works, the property of Oliver Evans, was located there.[49] In 1829, when there were but fourteen steel furnaces in the whole of the United States, three of them were located in Philadelphia. The heavy industries located there included the Baldwin Locomotive Works, and the Junction Car Works and Flue Mill, believed to be the largest of its kind in the United States, if not in the world.[50] Although furnaces and forges were to be found throughout the Lehigh District, it was not to assume a commanding position in the production of iron until after 1840 and the development of the anthracite furnace.[51] In addition, Montgomery, York and Dauphin counties had iron works of not insignificant proportions.[52]

As the settlers pushed on beyond the Alleghenies the demand for the products of iron—nails, shovels, axes, plates, etc.—increased rapidly. It was not long before furnaces and forges sprang up throughout the western half of the State. Fayette County was the scene of some

---

[47] Pearse, *op. cit.,* p. 219.

[48] *United States Sixth Census,* p. 130; see Pearse, *op. cit.,* p. 220.

[49] James Mease, *Picture of Philadelphia* (Phila., 1831), p. 75.

[50] Charles Robson, *Manufactories and Manufacturers of Pennsylvania* (Philadelphia, 1875), p. 5.

[51] Swank, *op. cit.,* p. 191.

[52] The *Lancaster Intelligencer,* June 13, 1826; *Hazard's Register of Pennsylvania,* I, April 1828, p. 221-222, Horace A. Keefer. *Early Iron Industries of Dauphin County* (Harrisburg 1927), p. 7. James M. Swank, *Introduction to the History of Iron Making and Coal Mining in Pennsylvania* (Phila., 1878), p. 33, 34. Israel D. Rupp, *History of Northampton, Lehigh, Monroe, Carbon and Schuylkill Counties* (Harrisburg, 1845), p. 32.

of the earliest iron enterprises in this part of the State. That Fayette County should have taken the lead in establishing iron manufactures in Western Pennsylvania was natural. The routes to the West cut across this county and it possessed all the natural advantages necessary for the production and manufacturing of iron.[53] By 1810, there were in this county ten furnaces, one air furnace, eight forges, three rolling and slitting mills, one steel furnace and five trip-hammers.[54] And throughout the first half of the nineteenth century Fayette County continued to be a great iron producing center.[55]

The richest ores and the most productive furnaces and forges in the western half of the State were located in the Juniata district.[56] "There are probably few counties in the State richer in valuable ores than Mifflin, Huntingdon and Centre," asserted John Wright, an iron-master.[57] Most of the blooms made here were sent to the mills at Pittsburgh instead of being rolled on the spot.[58] An estimate in 1817 placed the annual value of the product manufactured in Huntingdon County at about $400,000; in Centre County, about $300,000.[59] In 1826, it was reported that there were in the former county eight furnaces which made 6,000 tons of pig metal and castings annually, and ten forges producing about 2,850 tons of bar-iron, nails, sheets, etc., yearly.[60] Centre County at this time had "seven blast furnaces capable of producing 8,000 tons of metal, and annually producing 7,400, and employing 275 hands; and nine forges, capable of producing 2,490 tons, and actually producing 2,050 tons, and employing 230 hands." [61]   By 1835,

[53] Bining, op. cit., p. 237; George W. Hughes, "The Pioneer Iron Industry in Western Pennsylvania," Western Pennsylvania Historical Magazine, XIV, 1931. pp. 207-224.

[54] James M. Swank, History of the Manufacture of Iron in All Ages, p. 216; Hughes op. cit., p. 212.

[55] Ibid., p. 216; Hughes, op. cit., p. 212.

[56] John Melish, Travels Through the United States of America in the Years 1806 and 1807 and 1809, 1810 and 1811 (London, 1818, p. 205; see also James M. Swank, Early Iron Enterprise in Cambria, Somerset, Westmoreland and Indiana Counties (Philadelphia, 1900), p. 1.

[57] Documents Relating to the Manufacture of Iron in Pennsylvania. Published on behalf of the Convention of Iron Masters met December 1849 (Philadelphia, 1850) p. 47.

[58] Hazard's Register of Pennsylvania, I, January 1828, p. 42-43; Pearse, op. cit., p. 133.

[59] From the Bellefonte Independent Republican quoted in The Aurora and General Advertiser, January 17, 1817.

[60] Niles' Register, XXX, March 4. 1826, p. 3.

[61] Saturday Evening Post, December 22, 1837; The Berks and Schuylkill Journal, January 26, 1828; Pearse, op. cit., p. 174.

the output of these counties rivalled the production of the eastern district. And when the returns of the *Sixth Census* were published, it was revealed that the Juniata district was the leading iron producing center in the State if not in the nation. About $780,000 was invested in the iron works of Huntingdon County in 1840. Its twenty furnaces produced 13,855 tons of pig iron and its twenty-seven bloomeries, forges and rolling mills made 14,093 tons of bar iron.[62] These iron works employed 1,357 men. The Centre County iron industry exhibited a similarly expanding trend. Its seven furnaces produced 7,500 tons of pig iron and its nine rolling mills, bloomeries and forges had an annual production of 10,110 tons. These establishments employed 603 men, and the capital invested amounted to $398,000.[63]

In an ever-increasing stream the pigs and blooms from the furnaces and forges of the western counties flowed to the mills of Pittsburgh. No pig iron was produced in that city before 1859. At the beginning of the nineteenth century when Pittsburgh was a mere frontier village, its potentialities as a future iron manufacturing center were already manifest. In 1804, Joseph McClurg had erected the first iron foundry in that city.[64] Approximately a decade later four air foundries were in successful operation there. Anthony Beelen's foundry made 400 tons of castings annually. In conjunction with this plant was a mill for boring cylinders, air pumps and pipes for steam engines. According to *Cramer's Almanack*, "the castings executed in Pittsburgh are not excelled in point of clean casting and beauty by any in the United States."[65]

The value of the ironmongery manufactured at Pittsburgh in the first decade of the century was not inconsiderable. One estimate placed the annual value of the chisels, hatchets, drawing knives, shovels, tongs, jack-screws, hoses, chains, augers, adzes, hackles, locks, door handles, spinning-wheel irons, plough-irons, flat-irons, etc., made there between $12,000 and $15,000.[66] There were in Pittsburgh in 1807, three nail factories—Porter's, Sturgeon's, and Stewart's—which made about forty

---

[62] *United States Sixth Census.* p. 141.

[63] Louis Hunter, *op. cit.,* p. 244-245; see also Samuel Jones, *Pittsburgh in the Year Eighteen Hundred and Twenty Six* (Pittsburgh, 1826), p. 50-51.

[64] Bishop, *op. cit.,* II, p. 105.

[65] *Cramer's Almanack.* 1815, p. 64; see James Riddle, The *Pittsburgh Directory for 1815* (Pittsburgh, 1815), p. 50-51. Also see Russell J. Ferguson, *Early Western Pennsylvania Politics* (Pittsburgh, 1938), p. 217; *The Navigator,* 1817, p. 55.

[66] *Cramer's Almanack,* 1810, p. 53; *The Navigator* quoted in Swank, *History of the Manufacture of Iron in All Ages,* p. 227.

tons of nails annually. Within three years the annual production of
cut and wrought nails had increased to 200 tons.[67]

The overall picture of the iron industry in Pittsburgh and its vicinity
in the decades following the years of economic distress was one of
growth and prosperity. A survey of its iron works in 1825 disclosed
that there were seven steam rolling mills, eight air foundries, six steam
engine manufactories and an extensive wire factory. Weekly, these
mills converted into bars, sheets, rods, or nails about 130 to 140 tons
of pig iron.[68] One of these factories, the Union Rolling Mill, was
powered by two 100 horse power steam engines and employed about
100 hands. *Cramer's Almanack* reported that these mills in 1826 gave
"employment to upwards of 1,500 people, the value of whose labour
may be estimated at $1500 each per annum, or $2,250,000, while the
total product may be estimated at $3,000,000."[69]

New iron manufacturing establishments marked the steady progress
of industry in this city. Niles reported in 1828 that "the manufacture
of steel had been commenced with great success in Pittsburgh," and
stated that "specimens have been produced, said to be equal to the
best 'Crowley' steel."[70] In that same year, the Globe Plow Works
went into operation, and a large wire factory was erected at Beaver
Falls. The wire made here was said "to equal the 'best English' in
every respect." [71] The following year the Juniata Rolling Mill and
Nail Factory began operations. "They expect to roll 1,500 tons of
blooms into bar iron, boiler iron, sheet iron, etc. and to make four
hundred tons of nails annually," announced the *Pittsburgh Gazette*.
Fifty or sixty hands would be employed in this establishment.[72]

Throughout the decade of the 1830's, the iron industry centered
about Pittsburgh continued to grow.[73] Nor did the great panic of 1837

---

[67] *Ibid.*

[68] From The *Pittsburgh Gazette* quoted in *Niles' Register,* XXIX, November 19,
1825, p. 180.

[69] *Cramer's Almanack,* 1826, p. 67; Samuel Jones, *op. cit.,* p. 50-52; Sarah H.
Killikelly, *The History of Pittsburgh* (Pittsburgh, 1906), p. 164; Anne Royall,
Pennsylvania or Travels Continued (Washington, 1829), II, p. 91, 92, 94, 97, 98.

[70] *Niles' Register,* XXXV, October 11, 1828, p. 102.

[71] *Ibid.*

[72] The *Pittsburgh Gazette,* September 29, 1829; The *Mifflin Eagle and Lewistown
Intelligencer,* October 3, 1829; *Niles' Register,* XXXVII, October 17, 1829, p. 121.

[73] The *Berks and Schuylkill Journal,* October 17, 1829; W. G. Lyford, The *Western
Address Directory* (Baltimore, 1837), p. 69; The *Pennsylvania Reporter,* November
14, 1834.

seriously retard its growth. In 1840, in Pittsburgh and its vicinity there were twenty-eight furnaces for cast iron, making 6,584 tons of iron valued at $46,880. There were in addition twelve bloomeries, forges and rolling mills which produced 45,100 tons of bar iron and nails valued at $4,500,000. These establishments employed over 1,305 men, and the capital invested amounted to $1,931,000.[74]

A statewide inventory of Pennsylvania's iron works indicates the remarkable expansion the industry had undergone in these first four decades of the nineteenth century. When the constitution was adopted in 1789, Swank states that "there were fourteen furnaces and thirty-four forges in operation in Pennsylvania."[75] Approximately two decades later there were forty-four blast furnaces, seventy-eight forges, four bloomeries, eighteen rolling and slitting mills, six air furnaces, fifty trip-hammers, five steel furnaces and 175 naileries in operation in this State. These furnaces accounted for 26,878 tons of cast iron, or fifty percent of the domestic production; while the forges worked up 10,969 tons of bar iron, or forty-four percent of the total.[76] The returns of the *Sixth Census* disclosed that in 1840 there were in Pennsylvania 113 furnaces, making annually 98,395 tons of pig and cast iron; and 169 bloomeries, forges and rolling mills annually accounting for 87,244 tons of bar iron, etc. The capital invested in the iron industry of Pennsylvania amounted to $7,781,471, and the men employed by it numbered 11,522.[77]

The prime force which attracted capital to these hazardous enterprises was the profits to be derived from a successful undertaking. Iron was scarce, the prices high and the profits alluring. In 1818, for inferior bar iron Jacob Haldeman, an ironmaster of Dauphin County, received at Baltimore $100 per ton; for pig iron thirty-five dollars per ton.[78] The previous year he had sold to the United States Army

[74] *United States Sixth Census,* p. 141; *Hazard's United States Commercial and Statistical Register,* III, December 1840, p. 375.

[75] James M. Swank, *Introduction to a History of Iron Making and Coal Mining in Pennsylvania,* p. 34.

[76] Coxe, *op. cit.,* p. 52; James M. Swank, *History of the Manufacture of Iron in All Ages,* p. 231; see also Eiselen, *op. cit.,* p. 33.

[77] *United States Sixth Census,* p. 130; *Hazard's Register of Pennsylvania,* VI, January 1842, p. 54.

[78] Haldeman Papers, Letter to Jacob Haldeman from Ballard & Hall, his agents at Baltimore, May 26, 1818—in the Public Records Division of the Penna. Hist. and Museum Commission.

Arsenal at Harper's Ferry bar iron at $160 per ton.[79] That same year Swedish bar iron sold at Cincinnati for $200 to $220 per ton.[80] At Pittsburgh in the late 1820's bar iron sold for $125 to $140 per ton; blooms for $100 per ton.[81]

That there were profits to be made in this industry is incontestable. Thomas Bull, an ironmaster of Berks County, has left the following record of the profits reaped from the operation of a furnace, probably the Joanna Furnace, in the first decade of the nineteenth century:[82]

Proffitt [sic] in carrying on the furnace from
10th Jany 1798 till 1st Jany 1800 .... $18,000
    from 1st Jany 1800 till 1st Jany 1801 ....   9,471.94½
    from 1st Jany 1801 till 1st Jany 1802 12,000
    from 1st Jany 1802 till 1st Jany 1803 12,000
    from 1st Jany 1803 till 1st Jany 1804 ....   7,331.94
    from 1st Jany 1804 till 1st Jany 1805 .... 10,829.55
    from 1st Jany 1805 till 1st Jany 1806 ....   5,089.26
    from 1st Jany 1806 till 1st Jany 1807 .... 12,946.86
    and a former profit 2,744.17

Thus in a nine year period his profits totaled $90,443.72. For the year ending January 1, 1810, the profits for carrying on the furnace were $11,435.89.[83] An ironmaster of Venango County in 1829 informed the editor of the *United States Gazette* that "under proper management and good materials, a furnace will clear at present prices, *ten thousand dollars per annum*."[84] On a capital investment of $110,000, the Valentine and Thomas Iron Manufacturing Company of Centre County revealed its annual profits to be about $10,000.[85] Some Pennsylvania iron works reported profits as high as twenty percent, but

---

[79] Haldeman Papers, Letter from M. H. to Lloyd Beall, March 1817; compare Fearon, *op. cit.*, p. 183.

[80] The *Aurora and General Advertiser*, January 17, 1817.

[81] The *Miner's Journal*, August 22, 1829; The *Berks and Schuylkill Journal*, August 15, 1829. Compare Haldeman Papers, Letter from John Elder to Jacob Haldeman, August 21, 1829.

[82] Thomas Bull Esquires Book—Amount of Total Moneys gained in Carrying on the Furnace from the time John Smith went to live and under his management, p. 9, 12, 15, 17, 19, 22, 25, 32; in the possession of the Berks County Historical Society.

[83] Joanna Furnace Account Book, p. 276; in the possession of the Berks County Historical Society.

[84] The *Miner's Journal*, August 22, 1829; The *Berks and Schuylkill Journal*, August 15, 1829; Eiselen, *op. cit.*, p. 102.

[85] *McClane's Report*, II, p. 321, 322.

eight to ten percent was a fair average.[86]   In the spring of 1837, James L. Morris of Berks County noted in his diary that the "Hopewell furnace made this year clear of all expenses $40,773—the regular average for several years before was $17,000."[87]   From the evidence one must agree with the *Bedford Gazette* which declared that "the profit made by Iron-masters . . . is a fair compensation for their skill, capital, and enterprise."[88]

GROWTH OF THE TEXTILE INDUSTRY

Although in subsequent years the iron industry was the predominant force in the industrial life of Pennsylvania, if not in the nation, in the years from 1800 to 1840 the textile industry far more typified the factory system which was to characterize modern industrial society. Whereas technological change had little or no effect on the iron industry in this period, its effects on the textile industry were revolutionary. Where the relationship between worker and management was personal and relatively harmonious in the iron industry, in the cotton industry it was marked by strife and the clash of class interests.   Where the iron industry was scattered throughout the rural regions of the State, the cotton manufacturers tended to concentrate in the crowded urban centers.   Where the iron industry employed men almost exclusively, the textile industry exploited the labor of women and children extensively.

In these formative years of the Republic the textile industry underwent a great transformation.   Water and steam power supplanted the hand and horsepower of an earlier day, and the social consequences of these changes were momentous.   It meant the transfer of spinning and weaving from the home to the factory, the growth of cities and an increase in the number of landless wage earners.   The use of power-driven machinery, particularly in the textile industry, received a great stimulus from the restrictive policy undertaken by the Federal government during President Jefferson's administration.[89]   Machinery doubled in price during the war years but increased productivity and correspond-

---

[86] *Ibid.*, p. 205, 246, 249, 250. 252, 253, 257, 267, 268, 292, 293, 294, 308, 309, 321, 322, 325, 326, 327, 344, 345 and 365.

[87] James L. Morris Diary, I, May 20, 1837; in the possession of the Berks County Historical Society.

[88] The *Bedford Gazette*, July 25. 1834.

[89] The *Aurora and General Advertiser*, May 3, 1810; see also *American State Papers, Finance*, III, p. 82.

ingly high prices for cotton goods offset this disadvantage. "Those machines moderately worked," wrote John Baxter, a manufacturer of cotton spinning machinery, "will clear their expences [sic] in one year, besides accomplishing more than double the work . . ."[90]

Philadelphia's preëminence as a textile manufacturing center was largely attributable to her proximity to large supplies of cheap fuel, and the utilization of power-driven machinery. The expansion of cotton and woolen manufacturing was accompanied by the development of the textile machine industry, and the Quaker City even before 1820 was regarded as an important center for the production of this machinery. Peter Eltonhead of Philadelphia in 1803 informed the public that he was making cotton spinning machinery and would "set them to work in any part of the United States."[91] The following year he had established a machine factory in Pittsburgh.[92] Alfred Jenks, who for years had been a pupil of and had worked with Samuel Slater, established a manufactory near Philadelphia in 1810 for making cotton spinning machinery.[93] In 1830, he developed a power loom for weaving checks and first introduced it in the Kempton Mills at Manayunk.

Throughout the first half of the century the textile industry of Pennsylvania was centered largely around Philadelphia and its vicinity. It is true that during the period Pittsburgh's cotton and woolen manufactures made considerable progress, but the heaviest concentration remained in the eastern half of the State. It is impossible to determine the exact number of cotton manufacturing establishments in this area at the opening of the nineteenth century, but from contemporary accounts we do know of one mill of considerable size located here which suggests a trend toward factory development at this early date. The Kensington Cotton Mills employed eighty or ninety persons of different ages who worked 2,664 spindles and 1,080 throstles.[94] Niles in 1816 reported the construction of a large spinning mill near Philadelphia containing 5,000 spindles. A factory of this size would employ

---

[90] Letter from John A. Baxter to a person in Washington quoted in *Niles' Register*, VI, March 5, 1814, p. 16; The *Democratic Press*, November 14, 1813.

[91] The *Aurora and General Advertiser*, May 10, July 6, 21, 1803; Bishop, *op. cit.*, II, p. 100; Edwin T. Freedley, *Philadelphia and its Manufactures* (Philadelphia, 1867), p. 300.

[92] *Tree of Liberty*, March 17, 1804; The *Pittsburgh Gazette*, April 27, 1804; see also S. K. Stevens, *Pennsylvania: Titan of Industry* (New York, 1949), p. 92.

[93] Freedley, *op. cit.*, pp. 233, 300.

[94] Mease, *op. cit.*, p. 20.

approximately 250 hands.[95] Several years later when the ill effects of the great depression of 1819 had been dissipated and a general recovery was being made by industry, it was estimated that there were in Philadelphia thirty cotton mills averaging 1,400 spindles each and employing nearly 5,000 looms and 3,000 persons.[96]

One of the most remarkable examples at this time of the growth of the textile industry and the expansion of the factory system was the development of the manufacturing town of Manayunk. In 1820, there was only a toll house located in this village on the banks of the Schuylkill. Five years later there were "thirty or forty large manufactories, principally of cotton . . . employing upward of 500 hands," located in this village.[97] Its textile works in 1827 consisted of five cotton mills working 14,514 spindles and 210 power looms. The largest mill, that of Borie and Keating, had 4,500 spindles and 120 power looms. Two hundred fifteen men, women and children were employed in this factory. Weekly, it produced about 20,000 yards of cloth.[98] Manayunk, in subsequent years, continued to attract textile manufacturers, and mills on an extensive scale were constructed here.[99]

The disastrous consequences of the panic of 1837 on the progress of the textile industries in and around Philadelphia are difficult to determine with any exactitude. That it did restrict the city's growth is evident. If we accept the returns of the 1840 census as a measure of the relative growth of that industry, we must conclude that it had not expanded appreciably since 1824. In the greater Philadelphia area, there were forty-five cotton manufactories, equipped with 40,852 spindles and employing 2,903 hands. The value of the manufactured product was $3,157,119, and the capital invested amounted to $2,695,400.[100]

[95] *Niles' Register*, X, August 24, 1816, p. 431; according to a Report of the Secretary of Treasury on Manufactures, "800 spindles employ forty persons, viz., five men, 35 women and children," quoted in The *Aurora and General Advertiser*, May 3, 1810; see Bishop, *op. cit.*, p. 148.

[96] The *National Gazette*, Sept. 11, 1824; Bishop, *op. cit.*, II, p. 294; Freedley, *op. cit.*, p. 233.

[97] *Poulson's Daily American Advertiser*, April 21, 1825; *Niles' Register*, XXVIII, Aug. 20, 1825, p. 387; XXIX, Sept. 10, 1825, p. 21; also see Bishop, *op cit.*, II, p. 253.

[98] The *Annual Register*, 1827-28-29, III, p. 119; The *Berks and Schuylkill Journal*, Nov. 17, 1827; The *Miner's Journal*, Dec. 1, 1827; *Niles' Register*, XXXIII, Dec. 1, 1827, p. 211; *Hazard's Register of Pennsylvania*, II, July 1828, p. 14.

[99] *Hazard's Register of Pennsylvania*, II, July 1828, p. 14, 15; The *Pennsylvanian*, July 25, 1832; The *Public Ledger*, March 5, 1840.

[100] *United States Sixth Census*, p. 130.

The most distinctive feature of the Philadelphia textile industry was the persistence of the hand-loom weaving industry. As late as 1860, Freedley could write: "Philadelphia is truly the great seat of Hand-loom Manufacturing and Weaving in America." [101] This city experienced the rise of the factory system matched by a paradoxical growth in the number of hand looms in operation. Cloth making in Philadelphia was patterned after the English system. The spinner, the dyer, the weaver, and the printer and finisher were for the most part independent manufacturers, serving the cloth merchants. In the late 1820's, there were in the greater Philadelphia area 4,500 weavers and 200 dyers.[102]

Pittsburgh was the scene of much of the industrial development which took place in Western Pennsylvania. The trend toward factory organization which was coincident with the growth of the textile industry was confined almost solely to this area. At the beginning of the nineteenth century Peter Eltonhead and James Kerwin pioneered in the establishment of cotton mills in Pittsburgh and its vicinity.[103] In 1809, there were two cotton mills in this area; one working ninety spindles, and the other capable of working 230, manufacturing cords, chambrays, jeans, dimities, checks, tickings, girtings, etc., valued at $20,000 annually.[104]

Spurred on by the demands created by the War of 1812 the wool and cotton manufactures of Pittsburgh grew in number and size. Niles, assiduously recording the industrial growth of the nation, wrote in the spring of 1814 that "the *wool* and *cotton* manufactures [of Pittsburgh] had made handsome progress, and there are several valuable establishments; one of them very spacious, five stories high." [105] It was during the War or immediately afterwards that steam-driven machinery was introduced into the cotton mills in the western part of the State. James Arthur, whose woolen factory had in operation two jennies of

[101] Freedley, *op. cit.*, p. 233.

[102] *Hazard's Register of Pennsylvania*, I, June 1827, p. 28; VIII, August 1831, p. 128; *The American Sentinel*, April 26, 1828; *Niles' Register*, XL, May 21, 1831, p. 128; Clark, *op. cit.*, I, p. 395. For earlier years of that decade see *Niles' Register*, XX, Aug. 25, 1821, p. 403; XXI, September 15, 1821, p. 39; XXVIII, May 7, 1825, p. 159; XXX, June 3, 1826, p. 236; XXXI, October 21, 1826, p. 116; *Doylestown County Patriot*, May 2, 1825; *The Norristown Herald*, Sept. 11, 1822.

[103] *Tree of Liberty*, March 17, 1804; *The Commonwealth*, Nov. 20, 1805; *Cramer's Almanack*, 1806 quoted in George H. Thurston, *Pittsburgh Progress, Industries, and Resources* (Pittsburgh, 1886), p. 81.

[104] *Cramer's Almanack*, 1810, p. 53; *The Aurora and General Advertiser*, Sept. 14, 1809; *The Commonwealth* as quoted in Killikelly, *op. cit.*, p. 135.

[105] *Niles' Register*, VI, May 28, 1814, p. 208.

forty spindles each, one slubbing billy of forty spindles, two carding machines and eight looms, which daily carded about eighty pounds of wool, is generally accredited with being the first to utilize steam power in this part of the State.[106]

But the real development of the textile industry in western Pennsylvania did not occur until after 1822 when the panic had run its course. During the panic, the textile industry of Pittsburgh was completely wiped out. According to one report there were no mills in operation in 1819.[107] Late in 1822, the firm of Adams, Allen & Company went into operation, offering for sale cotton yarn from number ten to eighteen, guaranteed to be "of equal quality to any made in the United States."[108] The following year the Phoenix Cotton Factory was open for business. This plant had 500 spindles and eight power looms in operation, and an additional 1,000 spindles would be in operation before the year's end.[109]

Jones, in his *Directory of Pittsburgh for the year 1826*, belittled the progress of that city's textile industry. "The manufactures of cotton which in the eastern states and in Europe, employ so large a proportion of wealth, skill and industry, have, as yet, been established here, but to a limited extent," asserted the author of the *Pittsburgh Directory*. Actually, considerable progress had been made. The Phoenix Cotton Factory now boasted 3,000 spindles and sixteen looms in operation. It employed about 200 hands, principally boys and girls. The proprietors of this mill, Adams, Allen, Grant and James S. Craft, had plans for the erection of another factory which would employ 5,000 spindles and 160 power looms.[110] There were five other cotton factories in the city which employed 353 hands and whose product was valued at $160,488.[111]

Throughout the 1830's the cotton industry of Pittsburgh and the surrounding areas continued to expand. Nor did the severe shock which

[106] *Niles' Register*, VIII, April 29, 1815, p. 141; *Cramer's Almanack*, 1817, p. 50; Erasmus Wilson, *Standard History of Pittsburgh* (Chicago, 1898), p. 203; Stevens, *op. cit.*, I, p. 91.

[107] A statement of the comparative extent and value of the manufactures of Pittsburgh and vicinity in the year 1815 and 1819 in *Hazard's Register of Pennsylvania*, IV, Sept. 1829, p. 169; see also Lawrence Thurman, The *Cotton Industry in Pittsburgh 1800-1861* (unpublished Master's Essay, University of Pittsburgh, 1941).

[108] The *Pittsburgh Gazette*, December 27, 1822.

[109] The *Western Press*, January 14, 1823; *Niles' Register*, XXIII, January 25, 1823, p. 322.

[110] S. Jones, *op. cit.*, p. 62; The *Berks and Schuylkill Journal*, Nov. 10, 1827; The *Democrat and Farmers' Gazette*, Nov. 11, 1827; Anne Royall, *op. cit.*, p. 106.

[111] Jones, *op. cit.*, p. 66.

struck all branches of manufacture in the latter part of this decade reduce the money value of the total manufactured product of the textile industry. Despite an actual reduction in the number of men employed and in the number of spindles in operation, the value of the manufactured product increased. A longer work day and more efficient plant operation probably account for this increase. In 1836, there were in the greater Pittsburgh area six cotton factories which had in operation 28,900 spindles and employed about 1,030 operatives. The value of the manufactured product was estimated to be $500,000.[112] In 1840, there were five factories which had in operation 17,750 spindles and employed 730 persons. The value of the manufactured product was reported to be $551,200, and the capital invested amounted to $580,000.[113]

Pennsylvania's textile industry ranked with that of New Hampshire and New Jersey. It had more looms in operation than any other state except Massachusetts. But in spinning it ranked far below the great textile industries of Massachusetts and Rhode Island. There were in 1840 one hundred six cotton mills in the state; ninety-nine of them were located in the eastern portion, and seven in the western. These mills had in operation about 126,424 spindles, and employed 5,522 men, women and children. According to the *Sixth Census,* the value of the manufactured article was $5,013,007 and the capital invested amounted to $3,325,400.[114] The great demand for cotton and woolen goods and the opportunities for profit induced many adventurous individuals to invest their labor and capital in this branch of manufacture. In 1810, the capital required for each spindle was one hundred dollars. This included the fixed capital applied to the purchase of the millseats, and to the construction of the mills. This figure also applied to the capital required for the purchase of machinery, and to that employed in wages, repairs, raw materials, goods on hand and other contingencies.[115] By 1814, the amount of capital required had doubled. Despite this, and

---

[112] Lyford, *op. cit.,* p. 104; compare the statistics in Thurston, *op. cit.,* p. 89. For the year 1836 he states that there were 21,800 spindles in operation and 900 hands employed. The value of the product was $770,000.

[113] *Hazard's United States Commercial and Statistical Register of Pennsylvania,* III, December 1840, p. 375; *United States Sixth Census,* p. 148.

[114] *United States Sixth Census,* p. 148; *Hunt's Merchant's Magazine,* 3, 1840, p. 453; Clarke, *op. cit.,* I, p. 544, 552.

[115] The *Aurora and General Advertiser,* May 3, 1810; *American State Papers, Finance,* II, p. 427.

because of the general price rise and the greater productivity of machines and labor, expenses could be cleared in one year.[116]

It is virtually impossible to secure any dollar totals on profits for the textile industry, but *McClane's Report* does record the estimates of individual proprietors. Eight textile manufacturers of Philadelphia and its vicinity reported a return of about eight percent on their capital.[117] In the western half of the State there was a greater variation: some of the manufacturers reporting profits of twenty and twenty-five percent and others as low as four percent.[118]

OTHER INDUSTRIES

As the iron and textile industries grew more numerous and more complex, and new sources of power were developed, the manufacture of steam engines and other machinery became an important industry. During the Revolution, parts of the machinery essential to the manufacture of textiles, according to Freedley, were made in Philadelphia. Mention already has been made of the work of Peter Eltonhead and Alfred Jenks. Textile machinery sold in Philadelphia in 1814 at the following prices: a carding machine of the first quality, $200; a roving frame, fifty dollars; cards, a year ago only forty-five cents, now ninety cents; a machine of six spindles for spinning, only one hundred dollars and one for twelve spindles, one hundred fifty dollars.[119]

Since Philadelphia and Pittsburgh were the centers of industrial concentration at this time, it was inevitable and logical that the manufacture of steam engines should have been undertaken in these two cities. Undoubtedly, one of the most distinguished names in early American engineering was that of Oliver Evans. In 1803, he had organized the Mars Works at Philadelphia for the manufacture of steam engines on a plan which the *Aurora* stated was "superior to the English engines not only in the manner of using the steam and the great saving of fuel resulting therefrom . . . but in the construction and simplicity of all parts of the machinery." [120] The decade of the 30's saw the establishment in Philadelphia of two large concerns for the construction

---

[116] *Niles' Register*, VI, March 5, 1814, p. 16; James Montgomery, *Practical Detail of the Cotton Manufactures of the United States of America and the State of the Cotton Manufactures of that Country Contrasted with that of Great Britain* (Glasgow, 1840), pp. 126, 138.

[117] *McClane's Report*, II, p. 200, 201, 204, 205, 206, 207, 213.

[118] *Ibid.*, pp. 339, 400, 441, 442, 446, 465.

[119] *Niles' Register*, VI, March 5, 1814, p. 16.

[120] Mease, *op. cit.*, p. 17, 76; *Niles' Register*, I, Feb. 1, 1812, pp. 406, 407.

of locomotives—the Baldwin and the Norris Locomotive Works. The Junction Car Works and Flue Mill went into operation at this time.[121] During the years 1833 and 1834, the Baldwin Works built five engines. In the following year, it constructed fourteen locomotives, and in 1836, the number had increased to forty. The panic of 1837 seriously curtailed its operations and in 1840, only nine engines were built.[122] The Norris Works during five years of operation—from 1834 to 1839—had constructed seventy-eight locomotives and tenders. Engines made at this shop had been shipped to Canada, Cuba, England, Germany and Austria. In 1839, it had an order from England for nine engines; from Austria, for three; from Prussia and Hungary, for two. Over 300 mill hands were employed by this firm.[123]

Not long after the establishment of the Mars Works in Philadelphia, steam engines were being made in Pittsburgh. By 1814, three large plants for making steam engines were located in this city. One, the Pittsburgh Steam Engine Company, constructed them on Oliver Evans' plan; another, the Mississippi Steam Engine Company, made them on Fulton's plan; and Thomas Copland, the proprietor of the third, manufactured them according to the plan of Bolton and Watt.[124] Twelve years later the number of engine factories had doubled, and in 1826, there were thirty engines made, worth approximately $152,800. The Phoenix Iron Works situated near Philadelphia had at this time placed an order with the Pittsburgh firm of Stackhouse and Thompson for a hundred horse power engine.[125] Anne Royall, who wrote so glowingly of Pittsburgh and its industries, did not err too greatly in her impression of its capabilities in this branch of manufacture. "No place in the world," asserted this unusual woman, "can surpass Pittsburgh as to the means and materials for manufacturing these powerful machines." [126] Just prior to the collapse in 1837, the production of its iron foundries and its engine and machine shops was surpassed in value only by the proceeds of its rolling mills. There were in the city at this time eighteen factories employing upwards of 1,000 hands, and whose product was valued at $2,130,000.[127]

---

[121] Charles Robson, *op. cit.*, pp. 6, 18; Freedley, *op. cit.*, p. 306, 309.

[122] *Ibid.*

[123] *Hazard's United States Commercial and Statistical Register*, I, July 1839, p. 46; see also *Niles' Register*, LII, Dec. 9, 1837, p. 240.

[124] *Cramer's Almanack*, 1814, p. 169; *Niles' Register*, VIII, April 29, 1815, p. 141.

[125] Jones, *op cit.*, pp. 59, 61; *Niles' Register*, XXIX, Nov. 19, 1825, p. 180.

[126] Anne Royall, *op. cit.*, II, p. 102.

[127] Lyford, *op. cit.*, pp. 17, 18, 96, 109.

Numerous other industries and trades in Pennsylvania prospered and grew in this first half of the nineteenth century, and although they were still in their infancy when this study ends, they pointed out the direction in which the economic future of Pennsylvania lay. The glass industry, relatively unimportant in the eastern half of the State, grew rapidly in the Pittsburgh area despite serious obstacles. Capital was scarce; skilled glass blowers and cutters were few on the frontier; and lastly, good clay had to be imported from other regions.[128] In 1810, there were in operation in and around Pittsburgh four glass works—O'Hara's, Bakewell's, George Robinson's, and one at New Geneva in which Albert Gallatin had invested some of his capital. Together they produced glass valued at $90,000 annually.[129] Four years later, Niles reported that in the western part of the State there were six or seven glass houses making goods valued at $200,000 to $250,000 annually.[130] Prostrated as were most of the industries in the State by the panic of 1819, it was not until 1826 that the glass industry recovered the position which it had attained in 1814.[131] According to Lyford, "four of the largest glass factories in the country . . . are located in Birmingham one mile from the city of Pittsburgh." [132] This industry continued to prosper and even the great panic of 1837 did not halt its progress. There were in operation in the western district of Pennsylvania in 1840, twenty-six glass houses and thirteen glass cutting establishments employing 699 men, and the total product of these plants was valued at $702,400. An estimated capital of $640,600 was invested in these factories. The eastern district returned only two glass houses and two glass cutting establish-

---

[128] Denny O'Hara Letter Book, Mss., pp. 27, 28, 37, 38; see also William J. Bining, *The Glass Industry of Western Pennsylvania* (unpublished Master's Essay, Univ. of Pittsburgh), pp. 24, 32.

[129] *Cramer's Almanack*, 1809-1810, p. 53; The *Aurora and General Advertiser*, September 15, 1809.

[130] *Niles' Register*, VI, May 28, 1814, p. 208.

[131] *Hazard's Register of Pennsylvania*, IV, September 1829, p. 169; *Niles' Register*, VII, November 5, 1814, pp. 130, 340-341; XXIX, November 19, 1825, p. 108; Jones, *op. cit.*, p. 71; Bining, *Glass Industry*, p. 80; *American State Papers, Finance*, III, pp. 641-642.

[132] Lyford, *op. cit.*, p. 101; *Cramer's Almanack*, 1826, p. 68. See also *Pittsburgh Gazette*, Nov. 7, 1834; *Berks and Schuylkill Journal*, Nov. 8, 1834; *Niles' Register*, XLV, Nov. 30, 1833, p. 217; XLVII, Nov. 8, 1834, p. 147; Statement of the Manufactures of the City of Birmingham and the South Sides of the Monongahela for the years 1836-1837, cited in Howard N. Eavenson, *First Century and A Quarter of American Coal Industry* (Pittsburgh, 1942).

ments, employing 736 men and the articles manufactured were valued at $70,000. The capital invested amounted to $73,500.[133]

The coal industry had its origins in these early decades of the nineteenth century and grew from insignificance into an industry employing thousands of men and millions in capital. Large deposits of both anthracite and bituminous coal were to be found in Pennsylvania; the bituminous deposits were almost exclusively located in the western part of the State. In 1818, the Lehigh Coal and Navigation Company was incorporated by the State legislature ostensibly for the improvement of the navigation of that river but actually for the exploitation of the rich anthracite deposits of the Lehigh district. The capital stock of this company was $325,000 in 1821, suggesting that its operations were to be on a grand scale.[134] The anthracite coal industry generally dates from the year 1820 when 365 tons of coal were sent to Philadelphia from the headwaters of the Lehigh.[135] Niles noted in the following year that "Lehigh coal, in considerable quantities is now arriving at Philadelphia," and declared, "when the 'navigation company's works' are completed, the supply promises to be abundant for all wants of that great city." [136] In 1830, about 181,000 tons of anthracite were sent to the market, and by 1840, the tonnage had increased to 628,370 tons. The anthracite mined in the whole State at that time was 859,686 tons, and 2,977 men, and a capital of $4,334,102 were employed in these operations.[137]

The bituminous industry had been confined solely to Pittsburgh and its vicinity in the first half of the nineteenth century. Although not as extensive as the anthracite operations, there were employed in this branch of the coal industry in 1840 a capital of $300,416 and 1,798 men. About 415,023 tons of coal were raised.[138]

---

[133] *United States Sixth Census*, p. 150; *Hazard's United States Commercial and Statistical Register*, III, December 1840, p. 375; see also Isaac Harris, *Business Directory of Pittsburgh* (Pittsburgh, 1841), p. 117.

[134] Lehigh Coal and Navigation Journal, Mss. pp. 1, 85; in the offices of the Lehigh Coal and Navigation Company, Phila. See also Alfred Mathews, *History of the Counties of Lehigh and Carbon* (Philadelphia, 1869), p. 48; and see Charles V. Hagner, *Early History of the Falls of the Schuylkill* (Philadelphia, 1809), p. 48.

[135] *Report to the Legislature of Pennsylvania Containing a Description of the Swatara Mining District* (Harrisburg, 1839), p. 33; *Niles' Register*, XXX, April 21, 1826, p. 138; Samuel T. Wiley, *Biographical and Portrait History of Schuylkill County* (Philadelphia, 1893), p. 43.

[136] *Niles' Register*, XX, March 24, 1821, p. 63.

[137] *United States Sixth Census*, p. 138; *Niles' Register*, XL, July 16, 1831, p. 342.

[138] *United States Sixth Census*, p. 143.

With rare exceptions capital flowed ceaselessly and in ever increasing quantities into the mills and factories of Pennsylvania. The possibilities for industrial expansion appeared unlimited. Two great financial panics could not halt its progress. The voices of industry grew louder and more persuasive. The press of the State sympathized and campaigned energetically in its behalf, and in the halls of the legislature its pleas were heard and occasionally acted upon.

In the twenty year period, from 1820 to 1840, the growth in Pennsylvania's manufactures was remarkable. Inaccurate as the returns of these early census may be they do provide a yardstick for a comparative measure of the progress being made by the industries of the State. Pennsylvania in 1820 was reported to have had a capital of $6,323,077 invested in the various manufacturing establishments throughout the State, and these various industries employed 8,875 men, women and children.[139] Twenty years later the capital invested was estimated to be $31,815,105 and approximately 87,722 men, women and children labored in the mills and factories of the Keystone State.[140] These statistics bespeak the prosperity and expansion of industry. Our concern is in determining the extent to which the workers who contributed so substantially to its development shared in its profits.

---

[139] *Digest of the Manufacturing Establishment in the United States and Their Manufactures* (Washington, 1823). See also *Senate Document No. 45, 1st Session 18th Congress,* and The *National Gazette,* March 6, 1824.

[140] *United States Sixth Census.*

II

THE WAGE EARNERS

INDUSTRIAL PROCESSES, revolutionized by the harnessing of water and steam, wrought transformations in our society whose ends are not yet in sight. Inexorably, with the advent of the factory system the geography of America was altered, and American life in its moods and its ideals underwent a profound change. Drab factories with their clusters of squalid tenements destroyed the serenity of the American countryside; shattered, too, was Jefferson's idyllic agrarian dream.

The promise of America—advancement and riches—was there for those of ambition and enterprise who would seize it. Especially was this true in Pennsylvania in the first half of the nineteenth century. Mills and factories grew in size and variety. Artisans, mechanics, and laborers of all kinds were in great demand throughout most of this period.

The mushrooming mining community of Pottsville, situated on the headwaters of the Schuylkill, suffered from a chronic shortage of labor. Men of all trades "may find constant employment and good wages" in this booming coal town, asserted the *Miner's Journal.*[1] Skilled artisans were urged to migrate here, but the greatest appeal was addressed to the common laborers who were wanted at the mine pits. As many as a thousand laborers were called for at one time, but fifty to one hundred was the usual number.[2] One mine operator near Norristown, obviously hardpressed for hands, made the enticing offer of an eight hour work day and twenty dollars a month in wages to those who would apply at his pits.[3]

But no other industry could match the demands for labor created by the transportation projects undertaken both under public and private auspices. Not hundreds but thousands of day laborers were needed for the construction of the Pennsylvania canal. In 1828, the *Schamokin Canal Boat* advertised for 7,000 day laborers. "There is work to be had for the entire year," this paper declared, "and good wages, in cash, are

---

[1] The *Miners Journal*, July 21, 1827.

[2] *Ibid.*, August 13, 1825, August 19, October 21, 1826, April 28, May 12, June 23, July 21, August 18, 1827; *Niles' Register*, XXXIV, Aug. 2, 1828, p. 276; The *Mechanic's Free Press*, May 30, 1829; The *United States Gazette*, April 18, 1835.

[3] The *Miner's Journal*, August 11, 1827.

paid weekly to all good workers. . . ."[4] Frequent notices appeared offering canal hands as much as fourteen and fifteen dollars per month and
found, and occasionally some contractors offered as much as twenty-
five dollars per month.[5] Even during the great panic of 1837 when unemployment was rife, and misery and want were everywhere, laborers,
stone masons and carpenters were very much in demand on the canal
and railroad projects throughout the State. "From 500 to 1,000 laborers
are wanted on the west branch division of the Pennsylvania canal,"
reported the *Public Ledger* in the summer of 1837. As an inducement
the *Ledger* added, "the Country is healthy, good wages are given, and
the work will continue for a year or two."[6] During the following summer when the depression was at its height, this paper reported that
"Two Thousand Laborers are wanted on the Gettysburg (Pa.) Extension Railroad, to whom constant work and the best of wages will be
given."[7] Similar notices continued to appear despite the prevailing
hard times.[8]

Nor were the services of the factory hands in less demand. One
manufacturer, testifying before a committee of the State Senate investigating factory conditions, declared that "the demand for labor
here in ordinary times is great," and this was confirmed both by the
frequent "men wanted" notices in the newspapers and in the reminis-
cences of foreign travelers.[9]

For the ambitious and thrifty American workingman, success appeared inevitable. Man could be the master of his own fate. If fortune
smiled upon him, it was of his own making; if he failed, the responsibility
was his alone. An article reprinted in *Hazard's Register of Pennsylvania*
gave credence to this idea when it asserted that "as a general rule, with
few exceptions, frugal industrious journeymen, unencumbered with

[4] The *Schamokin Canal Boat*, Feb. 2, 1828; typewritten transcript in the possession
of the Pennsylvania Historical and Museum Commission.

[5] The *Aurora and Pennsylvania Gazette*, June 16, 1828; The *Saturday Evening Post*,
August 16, Sept. 20, 1828; The *Lycoming Gazette*, May 20, 1829; The *Daily
Chronicle*, May 13, 1820, Sept. 12, 17, 1831; The *Pennsylvania Inquirer*, Sep-
tember 18, 1831; The *Juniata Telegraph*, October 19, 1831.

[6] The *Public Ledger*, June 1, 1837.

[7] *Ibid.*, June 1, 1838.

[8] The *Public Ledger*, July 31, 1829; The *Western Press*, August 9, 1839.

[9] *Pennsylvania Senate Journal*, II, 1837-38, p. 213; The *Aurora and Pennsylvania
Gazette*, June 17, 1828; The *Mechanic's Free Press*, August 7, 1830; The *Berks
and Schuylkill Journal*, June 25, 1831; The *Union Times and Republican Herald*,
July 1, 1831; The *Huntingdon Journal*, May 8, 1839; The *Public Ledger*, July 19,
1839.

families, may save so much of their wages, as in a few years, to be enabled to commence business on their own account on a moderate scale." [10]

There is often a large gap between appearances and realities. Although there were apparent signs of opportunity for the workingman to improve his status (and in many instances the opportunities were real), in actuality he shared but slightly in the general business progress of the first half of the nineteenth century. By the thousands workers flocked to the cities to meet the demands of new industries, and these urban manufacturing centers teemed with masses of landless, job-hunting wage earners.

THE FACTORY OPERATIVES

It is difficult to realize the immensity of the task confronting these industrial communities in absorbing the masses who came to fill the benches and tend the machines. From 1820 to 1840, the population of Philadelphia had increased from 63,802 to 93,615.[11] Its suburban development was even more pronounced. In 1820, the combined population of the city and its suburbs was 108,745; in 1840, it was 205,850.[12] This rapid growth resulted in almost indescribable congestion in every manufacturing city in the nation.

In the dark and filthy alleys and along the blighted streets, the poor somehow existed. An early Philadelphia social worker, Mathew Carey, has left his impressions of the poverty and wretchedness which prevailed among large segments of the factory population in that city.[13]

> I visited a room in Shippen street, [wrote M. Carey] where the M'Giffies live, which contained no furniture, but a miserable bed, covered with a pair of ragged blankets. Three small chunks lay on the hearth. The day was intensely cold. The occupant, a woman far too slenderly clad, had two children, one about five years old, the other about fifteen months. Both were inadequately dressed for the season, and were *destitute of shoes and stockings. The Younger Child had had its hands and feet severely frost-bitten, and the inside of the fingers so much cracked with the frost, that a small blade of straw might lie in the fissure!*

Nor was this an isolated account.

---

[10] *Hazard's Register of Pennsylvania,* VIII, July 1831, pp. 54, 55.

[11] *Fourth Census or the Enumeration of the Inhabitants of the United States in 1820* (Washington, 1821), p. 17; *United States Sixth Census,* p. 131.

[12] *United States Fourth Census,* p. 17; *United States Sixth Census,* p. 161.

[13] Mathew Carey, *Essays on the Public Charities of Philadelphia* (Philadelphia, 1830), pp. 5, 6.

In the summer of 1832, a citizens committee of Philadelphia, determined to awaken the social consciences of the City Fathers, investigated and made the following report of the living conditions which prevailed among large segments of the working class in Upper Delaware Ward:[14]

> The result of this investigation [the committee reported] shows, that the whole number of tenements is sixty-four; total number of inhabitants, four hundred and seventy-three. Of these, there are thirty tenements containing fifty-five families, and two hundred and fifty-three individuals, that have not the accommodation of a privy for their use! They are compelled to make use of vessels of various descriptions; the contents of which are daily thrown into the neighbouring docks or into the streets! It will be observed, that the buildings in this block (with one or two exceptions) occupy the whole ground belonging to the premises. The privies (of thirty-four) are situated either in the cellars, or in the vaults under the streets. Of the thirty tenements above mentioned, there are four with three and two with four, and two with six families in each.

The circumstances in which the poor of Pittsburgh lived were much the same as in Philadelphia. Poverty, wretchedness and squalor went hand in hand with the development of industries. A Pittsburgh physician called upon to testify before a Pennsylvania Senate Committee investigating factory conditions, disclosed the pitiable surroundings in which the factory children of that city lived.[15]

> Factory children generally, (Dr. Callaghan informed the Committee) live in confined, narrow, ill-ventilated lanes, alleys, and back yards, in the most densely inhabited portions of the city, and suburbs, and in the confined ill-ventilated rooms and cellars, among the poorest of the poor, in old frame houses where the atmosphere is peculiarly bad, highly impregnated with putrid miasmata, arising from the offals of a crowded and miserable population —each family having, in many instances, only a single room for all the purposes of life. As for example: I know a family consisting of a father, mother and six children, four

---

[14] *Report to the Select and Common Council of the City of Philadelphia by a Citizens Committee of Upper Delaware Ward.* Signed by Thomas Taylor, Daniel Barr, Samuel J. Robbins, William Rush, Powell Stackhouse, and John Perkins— Philadelphia, July 23, 1832. Cited in Thomas Brothers, *The United States of North America as They are* (London, 1848), Appendix V., p. 403. See also Mathew Carey, *Essays on the Public Charities of Philadelphia* (Phila., 1830), p. 27.

[15] *Pennsylvania Senate Journal*, II, 1837-38, p. 348.

of whom are employed in factories, living in a cellar. And again I know a frame house, twenty feet by thirty, two stories high, containing six small rooms, and in each a family of factory children: nor are these solitary examples.

Not only did the factory operatives live in crowded and unsanitary dwellings but rents, although low, absorbed a sizeable part of their incomes. At Whitaker's Mills in the northeastern section of Philadelphia two rooms above the dye house rented at the rate of twenty-five dollars a year.[16] Weavers in that city annually paid on an average from sixty to eighty dollars a year for rent. Their wages averaged about five dollars per week which meant that if they worked continuously throughout the year rent consumed at least one fourth of their annual income.[17] It was a general practice among many of the manufacturers to board their hands, and the profits therefrom were not inconsiderable. According to one observer, these manufacturers netted a profit of one dollar a week for each hand boarded.[18]

If his home surroundings were depressing, the conditions under which the factory operative labored were scarcely any better. The introduction of power machinery and the spread of the factory system had imposed upon the American worker a regimentation and a discipline which were both foreign and repugnant to him. In these mills propelled by steam, the engineer "regulates the speed of the machinery, and all the operatives, adults and children must keep pace with it."[19] The *New York American* declared that "the 'personel' [sic] of a large factory is a machine . . . any stoppage, even any irregularity in one department, deranges the whole. A strict and almost superstituous discipline is necessary to keep this vast instrument going for one single day."[20]

Much of the ill will which developed among the factory hands grew out of the regulations and methods adopted to enforce and maintain this discipline and insure the smooth operation of the plant. Charles V. Hagner, a cotton mill owner, confirmed this when he stated that "a frequent bone of contention between the employer and employed in manufactories, is certain rules, in the nature of a contract, established

---

[16] William Whitaker's Account Book, October to December, 1824, pp. 8, 9.

[17] *Hazard's Register of Pennsylvania*, I, January 1828, p. 28.

[18] Peter Neilson, *A Six Year's Residence* (Glasgow, 1830), p. 153.

[19] *Pennsylvania Senate Journal*, II, 1837-38, p. 324.

[20] From the *New York American* as quoted in *Niles' Register*, LII, August 19, 1837, p. 393.

in all well regulated mills, and which are chiefly indispensable for their good management." [21]

Arbitrary labor contracts, usually verbal in form but understood by all, enabled the entrepreneurs and the managers of the factories to maintain a rigid control over their employees. These rules and regulations were adopted and enforced by the employers without any consultation with their workmen. Mere acceptance of employment was an assent to the rules. The general rules which prevailed at the Silesia Factory are cited as typical: [22]

1. The hours of work shall be from sunrise to sunset, from the 21st of March to the 20th of September inclusively; and from sunrise until eight o'clock P. M., during the remainder of the year. One hour shall be allowed for dinner, and half an hour for breakfast, during the first mentioned six months; and one hour for dinner during the other half year; On Saturdays, the mill shall be stopped one hour before sunset, for the purpose of cleaning the machinery.

2. Every hand coming to work a quarter of an hour after the mill has been started shall be docked a quarter of a day; and every hand absenting him or herself, without absolute necessity, shall be docked in a sum doubled in amount of the wages the hand shall have during the time of such absence. No more than one hand is allowed to leave any one of the rooms at the same time,—a quarter of a day shall be deducted for every breach of this rule.

3. No smoking or spirituous liquors shall be allowed in the factory under any pretence whatsoever. It is also forbidden to carry into the factory, nuts, fruits, etc.; books or paper, during the hours of work.

7. Every hand (excepting those who rent a tenement belonging to this concern,) shall give at least two weeks' notice of his or her intention to depart from or to cease working in this factory, and the said hand shall continue to work in it, if required to do so, during and until the expiration of the said two weeks. In case of failure herein, the said hand shall forfeit all the wages which may be due to him or her at the time of leaving the mill.

---

[21] *Pennsylvania Senate Journal*, II, 1837-38, p. 326.

[22] The *Germantown Telegraph*, November 6, 1833. Compare with testimony given before the Pennsylvania Senate investigating committee; *Pennsylvania Senate Journal*, II, 1837-38, pp. 201, 296, 301, 309, 324, 330, 338, 353. See also *Daily Chronicle*, January 7, 1830.

Adam Smith was the prophet of the new order. In the laissez-faire ideal which he so brilliantly postulated, the emergent princes of industry found sustenance for their cherished belief of freedom of contract. To them, freedom of contract was one of those simple, ineluctable natural laws, which, if observed, would ensure progress and happiness for all mankind. When in 1837 the industrial peace of Philadelphia was threatened, the *Public Ledger,* one of the early penny newspapers, observed that recognition by labor and management of the contractual nature of their ties would go far toward eliminating friction and strife:[23]

> The relations between . . . proprietor or overseer and the operatives whether minors or of full age is [contended the *Ledger*] strictly one of contract, in which nothing beyond the terms of the contract can be required by either party. The one agrees to perform labor, the other to pay money; and so far they are on perfectly equal terms. If the operative agrees to labor for a certain price, and to conform to certain rules, the employer has no right to alter these rules without the consent of the other. If he do so alter them, the laborer is absolved from his part of the contract, and may depart immediately with the right to payment for labor already performed according to the price stipulated. This is the legal ground on which such contracts rest, and if it were generally understood, both by employers and operatives, many disputes, contentions, strikes and other proceedings mischievous to both parties would be avoided.

This idyllic interpretation of freedom of contract had little relation to the facts, for capital was hardly prepared to accept labor as its equal.

The mill hands bitterly resented the lopsided nature of the labor contract. Occasionally their smoldering anger flared into open rebellion. Especially critical were they of the rule requiring them to give their employers a two weeks' notice when leaving, but imposing no similar obligation upon the latter. "In some of the factories," one factory operative declared, "one of these rules is that if any of the hands leave the factories, the proprietors retain from one to two weeks of their wages, under the pretence that the hands must give two weeks' notice before leaving; but the proprietors discharge the hands without notice."[24] Some factory owners affirmed the charge. Others asserted

---

[23] The *Public Ledger,* June 1, 1837.

[24] *Pennsylvania Senate Journal,* II, 1837-38, pp. 296, 297. See also the *Allegheny Democrat and Working Man's Advocate,* October 21, December 9, 1836.

that if any of their hands were discharged without notice "they are entitled to a week's wages in advance," and several employees who had been summarily dismissed corroborated this.[25]

The blacklist was one of the most effective weapons which the employers possessed in disciplining their hands. Nor were they reluctant to use it. Although not a part of the wage contract, it was a tacit agreement among the various cotton mill owners not to hire any hands who could not produce a certificate of discharge from their previous employers.[26] William Blackstock, a Pittsburgh manufacturer, explained that the "reason for the establishment of this rule, [was] to prevent hands from leaving without notice, and to prevent tampering with hands, by the employers themselves." [27] Not only was a certificate of discharge made a prerequisite for securing another position, but the employers also made it a general practice of informing "all the employers in the vicinity, whenever a hand [had] been discharged." [28] So oppressive were these practices that the Committee investigating factory conditions in the Pennsylvania textile mills concluded that "these regulations, taken together leave scarcely an alternative to the operative, but unconditional submission." [29]

Collective bargaining, although not unknown, was hardly the accepted mode for formulating a wage contract. Management determined the wages, the hours and the general working conditions. Wage negotiations were carried on between the individual wage earner and the boss, leaving the worker free to accept the conditions proffered or move on.[30]

But he was beginning to resent the arbitrary character of these labor negotiations. The surge of democracy which swept America in this first half of the nineteenth century was partially an expression of the unrest and dissatisfaction which permeated the laboring masses. The "weavers . . . in America pay very little deference to their employers in general," noted an Englishman who was making a tour of the United States.[31] Even more important, the men were organizing into trade

---

[25] *Pennsylvania Senate Journal,* II, 1837-38, pp. 334, 345, 353.

[26] *Ibid.,* pp. 334, 342, 343, 344, 353. See also J. Lynn Barnard, *Factory Legislation in Pennsylvania: Its History and Administration* (Philadelphia, 1907), pp. 13, 14.

[27] *Pennsylvania Senate Journal,* II, 1837-38, pp. 334, 342, 343, 344, 353. See also J. Lynn Barnard, *Factory Legislation in Pennsylvania: Its History and Administration* (Philadelphia, 1907), pp. 13, 14.

[28] *Ibid.*

[29] *Pennsylvania Senate Journal,* II, 1837-38, pp. 334, 342, 343, 353.

[30] The *Germantown Telegraph,* October 30, Sept. 4, 1833.

[31] Neilson. *op. cit.,* p. 155.

unions and collectively voicing their protests. Strikes were becoming common and the factory hands were appointing committees to make their wishes known to the employers.

The employers met this threat with customary harshness. Two employees of William Blackstock's factory, who had been delegated to inform him that his hands desired the ten-hour system, were discharged without notice and proscribed. Mr. Blackstock observed that these two employees "had taken rather too efficient a part in the business." [32] At Samuel McBride's factory (Philadelphia), where a serious difficulty had arisen between labor and management because of the careless manner in which the warps had been handled, "three of his best hands" were dismissed "for taking an active part in favor of their fellow workers." [33] Thus, with these two formidable weapons, the right of arbitrary dismissal and the blacklist, the employers were able to maintain the initiative in their relations with their hired hands.

Indicative of the one-sided nature of the relations between labor and management was the system of fines and punishments devised by the mill owners to maintain factory discipline. Heavy fines were meted out for varying reasons, most commonly for lateness. It was a rule among most of the factories to deduct as much as one quarter of a day's earnings for those who failed to report within five minutes of the opening of the plant.[34] This issue played a prominent part in the protest of the citizens of Pittsburgh which led to an investigation of factory conditions throughout the State. "The [cotton factory owners] have been uniformly in the practice of deducting one quarter from each day's labour, when they were but five minutes late," complained the factory hands of that city.[35] Matthew M'Candless, an operative, charged that "if the hands come in more than five minutes after the bell, they are docked." Dismissal was the penalty for the repetition of this offense.[36]

Physical punishment as a disciplinary measure was confined almost solely to child workers, both male and female, but occasionally grown women felt the sting of the lash.[37] A factory girl from one of the

[32] *Pennsylvania Senate Journal*, II, 1837-38, pp. 344, 345.

[33] The *National Laborer*, October 1, 1836.

[34] *Pennsylvania Senate Journal*, II, 1837-38, p. 338.

[35] The *Allegheny Democrat and Working-Men's Advocate*, October 21, 1836.

[36] *Pennsylvania Senate Journal*, II, 1837-38, pp. 230, 324.

[37] See Richard B. Morris, *Government and Labor in Early America* (New York, 1946), p. 480 ff. for a discussion of physical punishments of servants in Colonial America.

Pittsburgh mills declared, "I have seen poor innocent females not only 'docked' of a half day's wages for going to work a few minutes after set time, but beat over the shoulder by a rope with knots on the end, until their backs were black and blue; and if they left on that account they would be docked a week's wages." [38] One of the witnesses before the Senate investigating committee asserted that "those superintendents who are severe are preferred by employers."

It was the children who suffered most from maltreatment by their employers. George Low, a thirteen-year-old factory hand, stated that he "was frequently punished by having [his] ears pulled; at one time the foreman pulled them until they bled." "I was punished because I could not take the laps off," this boy declared.[39] And in Northern Liberties, a suburb of Philadelphia, a superintendent of one of the cotton mills was haled into court and convicted for having unmercifully beaten a boy "for arriving too late in the morning." [40]

Though fines and punishments weighed heavily upon the factory worker, and though they often caused him considerable anxiety and actual hardship, they paled into insignificance when compared with the questions of hours and wages. Trending lower wages and interminably long hours convinced the factory operative of the degradation of his status in society. Seldom if ever were these wage and hour contracts in writing, and the employer's voice was as arbitrary in these matters as in the other factors affecting the conditions of employment.

The actual wage and hours records extant for the cotton factories are few and fragmentary, but those that are still available record the depressing story of the factory operatives. The accounts of the Whitaker Cotton Mill in the northeastern section of Philadelphia, which if typical, disclose an actual decline in wages and an increase in the hours of labor. In 1820, the weavers at this mill were paid one dollar per cut making tickings.[41] The price by 1832 had been reduced to seventy-five cents per cut, and in the following year it was cut to seventy cents. Late in the summer of 1837 the men struck work to restore the wage cut, but without success. By 1840 the price had been reduced to sixty cents per cut, and the hours of work had been increased. Those hands weaving cords suffered similar wage setbacks. They, in 1830, had been

---

[38] The *Allegheny Democrat and Working Men's Advocate,* December 9, 1836.

[39] *Pennsylvania Senate Journal,* II, 1837-38, p. 346.

[40] The *Public Ledger,* June 1, 1837.

[41] A one quarter cut was fifty yards long and thirty-six inches wide, and a seven-eighths cut was fifty yards long and thirty-one and one-half inches wide.

paid sixty cents per cut and ten years later the records reveal that they were being paid only fifty cents for the same work.[42]

Wage reductions throughout the 1830's caused considerable friction between the weavers and their employers. The employees of the Schuylkill Cotton Factory, whose wages averaged only three dollars a week, were threatened in the spring of 1834 with a twenty-five percent reduction in their wages.[43] In 1839, the handloom weavers of Mr. Corlies' Mill, faced with a twenty percent reduction in their wages, decided to appeal to the public to force their employers to desist from this action. In their attempt to elicit public sympathy, they disclosed the pittance which they had been receiving prior to this attempted reduction.[44]

> Eighteen yards of Superfine Check considered a day's work, which at $4\frac{1}{2}$ cents per yard, amounts to 81 cents per day, or $4.86 per week—out of which is to be deducted 75 cents per week for winding, leaving a balance of $4.11; for house rent, fuel, light, loom and tackling repairs, etc., 1.37\frac{1}{2}$ per week—leaving a balance of 2.73\frac{1}{2}$ for finding food and raiment for a family of four or five members. The proposed reduction being $1.08 per week, in exact ratio to the above, would reduce the amount for finding food and raiment for the family to $1.65 per week.

Nor did the decade of the 40's reveal any improvement in the status of the weavers. "God knows," wrote a Journal of the period, "some of the poor fellows had great cause to feel rebellious. Empty stomachs and empty purses are not the best advocates of good order. At the prices paid, some of them, we are told, a man and his wife, with constant and close application sixteen hours per day, could not earn over $2.50 per week." [45]

Declining wages and a longer work day were the lot, not only of the handloom weavers but of all other types of operatives in the textile industry. The mule spinners at Whitaker's Mill were in 1820 paid at the rate of thirty cents per one hundred hanks, and the highest wages of the best hands amounted to twenty-two dollars per month.[46] Niles in 1828, reported that "the mule spinners in the neighborhood of Phila-

---

[42] Whitaker Account Books, 1820, 1821, 1830, 1833, 1834, 1835, 1836, 1838, 1840.

[43] The *Man*, May 3, 1834; The *Pennsylvanian*, May 9, 1834. Compare with Neilson, *op. cit.*, pp. 152, 153, 157.

[44] The *Public Ledger*, August 30, 1839.

[45] *Pennsylvania Annual Report of the Secretary of Internal Affairs: Part III; Industrial Statistics 1880-81,* (Harrisburg, 1882). p. 268. See also *House Mscl. Doc. 4, Pt. 2, 47th Congress, 2d Session, p. 44,* and Norman Ware, The *Industrial Worker* (New York, 1924), p. 63.

[46] William Whitaker's Account Book, May 26, 1821.

delphia receive about two dollars per day" which would have meant
a considerable advance in their wages.[47] But in that same year the
spinners of that city went on strike against a proposed reduction of
their wages. They complained that even at the old prices a spinner
could make "from $7.50 to $8.50 per week for himself by working the
full period of twelve hours daily." [48] James Montgomery, a Britisher
who had a wide familiarity with the American textile industry, wrote
in 1840, that "the rate at which the mule spinners are paid in this
country [the United States] would average from eight to ten cents per
one hundred hanks." [49] If this assertion was true it would indicate a
substantial reduction in their pay rates.

But even more grievous than the general low level of wages was
the widespread exploitation in the textile mills of women and children,
who made up almost two thirds of the labor force in the cotton factories
throughout the State. The legislative committee investigating factory
conditions in Pennsylvania concluded that one third of the employees
in the cotton mills were men and two thirds were women.[50] As Edith
Abbott points out in her study of the employment of women in the
textile industry there was no initial displacement of men by women
nor any great prejudice against women in the mills. Until the introduction of the power loom, the early factories were spinning mills, and
spinning had always been "women's work." [51] More women, Tench
Coxe reported in his *Digest of Manufactures* prepared in 1814, were
turning to the occupation of the weaver while the men were taking over
the supervisory work. They worked the same long hours as the men
but their wages fell considerably below that of their male co-workers.
It is true that, as the records of the Whitaker Company reveal, some
women weavers boasted earnings which equalled and even surpassed
those of the men but these were exceptional cases. Listed below are
the monthly earnings of the seven highest paid workers in the card
room of the Whitaker Factory—all women.

---

[47] *Niles' Register*, XXXIV, June 28, 1828, p. 281.

[48] *Hazard's Register of Pennsylvania*, January 17, 1829 as quoted; John R. Commons,
History of Labour in the United States (New York, 1819), p. 418.

[49] James Montgomery, *Practical Detail of the Cotton Manufactures of the United
States of America and the State of the Cotton Manufactures of that Country
Contrasted with that of Great Britain* (Glasgow, 1840), p. 75.

[50] *Pennsylvania Senate Journal*, II, 1837-38, p. 323.

[51] See Edith Abbott, "Employment of Women in Cotton Mills," p. 603, *Journal of
Political Economy*, Nov. 1908, 16, pp. 602-621. See also Edith Abbott, *The
History of the Industrial Employment of Women in the United States: An In-
troductory Study*, p. 478. *Journal of Political Economy*, Oct. 1906, pp. 461-501.

	Ann Lord	Margaret McMillan	Susan McMillan	Sarah Neil	Mary MacMillan	Louisa Elkins	Sarah Elkins
1832							
Nov. 3—Dec. 1	$21.00	$21.75	$20.25	$15.75	$17.25	$15.00	$12.95
1833							
June 8—29	15.75	15.75	15.75	14.25	15.75	14.25	14.25
Sept. 4—30	7.00	—	17.50	11.20	11.20	14.00	15.40
1834							
Jan. 4—Feb. 1	10.50	—	18.20	15.40	17.50	15.40	14.70
July 12—Aug. 2	8.60	—	8.50	8.20	9.00	7.70	8.70
Dec. 6—31	10.50	—	11.70	7.70	8.40	7.70	9.10
1835							
July 11—Aug. 4	13.10	7.70	9.80	11.90	8.40	11.20	11.90
Sept. 5—Oct. 31	13.30	10.40	3.50	2.55	8.78	11.80	15.45
Dec. 5—31	15.40	11.20	13.60	—	9.10	13.80	14.35
1836							
Jan. 9—30	16.70	14.70	15.30	—	3.50	15.50	13.95
July 9—Aug. 10	15.40	12.60	14.40	13.50	11.20	14.90	13.50
Dec. 4—31	14.85	16.10	15.35	14.50	9.80	15.60	16.80
1837							
Jan. 7—Feb. 4	13.50	15.85	16.15	11.90	18.65	12.60	14.00
Aug. 5—Sept. 2	—	6.60	6.75	6.00	6.60	—	—
Dec. 9—30	—	7.35	7.35	5.70	6.00	—	—
1838							
Jan. 2—Feb. 3	—	12.00	13.50	12.00	7.80	—	—
July and Aug.	—	9.75	12.00	13.80	7.20	—	—
December	—	11.25	10.80	—	5.75	—	—
1839							
Jan. 2—Feb. 2	—	12.70	12.20	—	9.00	—	—
June 8—29	—	13.50	14.95	10.40	—	—	—
Dec. 7—31	—	9.10	14.95	—	—	—	—
1840							
January	—	14.00	12.35	—	—	—	—
June	—	—	8.00	—	—	—	—
December	—	—	13.80	—	—	—	—

Fragmentary as these records are, they still reflect the same general decline in wages which the men had experienced. For some inexplicable reason their lowest totals appear in 1835, a year of general prosperity. The complete absence of some of the names from the record books for the years 1837, 1838, 1839 and 1840 suggest that they were victims of the great depression and were among those swelling the ranks of the unemployed.

The wages of these women were not typical of the earnings of the average female worker in the cotton mills of Pennsylvania. The weekly and monthly earnings of the female worker were on the whole considerably less. According to the information supplied by the various mill owners throughout Pennsylvania in 1832, the wages of the female workers ranged from fifty cents per week to two dollars and sixty-two and one-half cents per week.[52] Other sources indicate that these estimates of the earning power of the women employed in the textile mills were in all probability correct. In the late 1830's, the women at Whitaker's Mill were averaging between one dollar and two dollars per week.[53] "The great object with all manufacturers in this country," surmised James Montgomery, "is to pay their help just such wages as will be sufficient inducement for them to remain at the work. Hence the greater the quantity of work produced the higher the profit, because paid at a lower rate of wages." [54]

Though the men and the women factory workers had suffered many indignities and though their losses were both material and psychological, no group suffered as grievously as did the children who made up a large part of the labor force in most of the textile mills. According to one estimate, one fifth of all the factory workers in Pennsylvania were children under twelve years of age.[55] "There can be no doubt that the introduction of machinery was at first extremely injurious to those whose means of living were affected," wrote an early student of the labor movement.[56] And this was especially true as it applied to the many young boys and girls who daily made their dreary way to take positions alongside the grown men and women.

---

[52] *McClane's Report,* II, pp. 206, 221, 337, 338, 394, 395, 396, 420, 421, 430, 431, 432.

[53] Whitaker's Account Book, October 1838, January 1839 and January 1840.

[54] James Montgomery, *op. cit.,* pp. 97-98.

[55] *Pennsylvania Senate Journal,* II, 1837-38, p. 323.

[56] William Trant, *Trade Unions—Their Origin and Objects* (Washington, 1915), p. 10.

They came to add their meager pittance to the family income. The mill owners often contended that they made no profit out of the children; and that they, the children, were forced on them by the poor, and in many instances worthless parents. Joseph Ripka, a mill owner declared: "I employ twenty-five children under twelve years of age and they are pressed on me by widows, or by mothers of dissipated husbands, and when I do employ them, it is more for charity than anything else." [57] Other mill owners made substantially the same assertions.[58] Undoubtedly it was true that needy and greedy parents did send their children to the mills at a very early age, nonetheless, the fact that many mill owners solicited for children would lead one to believe that their claim of not profiting from the employment of children was disingenuous. Occasionally advertisements for factory help announced that "a family that could furnish four or five hands, would be preferred." [59] This same Joseph Ripka who had stated that he hired children only out of charity, advertised in the *Public Ledger:* "Men with families who work either as Power loom weavers or Card Room hands, will be preferred." [60] In a letter to the *Mechanic's Free Press* an operative declared that he had known "many instances where parents who are capable of giving their children a trifling education one at a time, deprived of that opportunity by their employer's threats, that if they did take one child from there, (a short time for school) such a family must leave the employment . . ." And he asserted that he had known many instances when these threats were put into execution.[61]

Nor did the employers' contentions that there was no profit in the employment of children bear critical examination. Many of the witnesses before the Senate Committee investigating factory conditions in Pennsylvania pointed out that if the labor of children under a certain age were prohibited, "it would cost the employers more for larger hands, who could not be had without larger wages." [62] Robert Kerr, a factory hand, contended that the employment of minors "would

[57] *Pennsylvania Senate Journal,* II, 1837-38, p. 358.

[58] *Ibid.,* p. 302; Barnard, *op. cit.,* pp. 14, 15.

[59] *Mechanic's Free Press,* August 7, 1830; *Union Times and Republican Herald,* July 1, 1831; The *Huntingdon Journal,* May 8. 1839.

[60] The *Public Ledger,* July 19, 1839.

[61] The *Mechanic's Free Press,* August 8, 1830. See also The *Working-Man's Advocate,* March 24, 1832.

[62] *Pennsylvania Senate Journal,* II, 1837-38, pp. 283, 287, 291.

increase the wages paid by the factory owners as children over twelve
could not be had for wages as low as those under." [63]

It was the long hours of work and the pitifully low wages which drew
the attention of the public to the miserable status of the children in
the factories. One of the great humanitarian drives characteristic of
the Jackson era was the movement for free public education. Great
concern was voiced for the poor factory children who could not enjoy
the benefits of education, free or otherwise, because of the long hours of
work. Sunrise to sunset had been the traditional length of the work
day in America, and the practice of illuminating the factories with
lamps in the 1830's enabled the owners to increase the length of the
work day. At the Whitaker Factory during the late thirties, the men
began to work at 5:30 in the morning and remained at the job until
7:30 in the evening. The machines were stopped at seven A. M. allowing
thirty minutes for breakfast and again at noon, allowing thirty minutes
for lunch.[64] In 1839, the *Public Ledger* disclosed that the hours of labor
at the factories in Norristown were nearly fifteen in the summer months.
Although twelve hours was considered the usual work day, it was not
unusual for the factory operatives to work thirteen and fourteen
hours daily.[65] The working people of Manayunk, very much aggrieved
by the condition under which they labored, complained that they were
"obliged by [their] employers to labor this season of the year, from
five o'clock in the morning until sunset, being fourteen and a half, with
an intermission of half an hour for breakfast, and an hour for dinner,
leaving thirteen hours of hard labour." [66] Seventy-two hours was
considered to be the average work week in most of the mills throughout
the State. In its report concerning the time of labor in the factories
of Pennsylvania the legislative committee stated that[67]

> there is nothing which deserves the name of a system in
> the time of labor, in the factories in Pennsylvania, so far
> as the investigation of the committee extended. In the
> vicinity of Philadelphia, for instance, where the cotton

[63] *Ibid.*, p. 287.

[64] Whitaker Account Book, October 1838, Sept. 1839 and Oct. 1840.

[65] The *Allegheny Democrat and Working-Man's Advocate*, Oct. 7, 1836; The *Public
Ledger*, June 27, 1839; The *Germantown Telegraph*, August 28, 1833; The *Working-
Man's Advocate*, March 24. 1833; *Pennsylvania Senate Journal*, 1837-38, II, p.
338; Whitaker Account Book, January 1840; *McClane's Report*, II, pp. 204, 207,
225, 226, 450.

[66] The *Pennsylvanian*, Aug. 28, 1833; *Hazard's Register of Pennsylvania*, I, p. 157.

[67] *Pennsylvania Senate Journal*. II, 1837-38, p. 322.

mills are numerous, eleven hours of labor per day are exacted in some establishments and in one, at least, it has exceeded fourteen hours per day; the humanity or the cupidity of employers, being the only motive by which it is regulated.

One employer when queried by the committee as to the evils of the factory system as it then prevailed in Pennsylvania replied: "I know of no evil worth notice, except that which arises from the refractory, factious spirit of some of the men, and they are mostly foreigners." [68] Another, when asked if he thought that the hours of work were too long and the labor of children excessive, blandly replied, "far from it—it approaches nearer to amusement." [69] But such myopia was not characteristic of all the mill owners. It was generally agreed even among many of the employers that one of the greatest evils of the factory system was the long hours of work. Most of the ills associated with the textile industry, especially as they affected the child laborers, stemmed from the long work day. Their education was sadly neglected. Boys and girls entering the factories at the age of seven and eight had little opportunity for securing the advantages of a formal education. It was estimated that of all those under eighteen years of age employed in the cotton mills, not more than one third could either read or write. This, it was concluded, was "an effect of their early employment in factories, and the total neglect of their education afterwards." [70]

Though many of the mill owners frowned upon the employment of children under twelve, they were at the same time apprehensive of any reduction in the hours of labor or in the prohibition of child labor. John P. Crozer, a manufacturer, stated that "employers have not always encouraged education; small operatives have often been scarce, and employers were therefore desirous to retain the children in the factories." The State Senate Committee investigating factory conditions after sifting through the testimony of both the factory hands and the owners concluded that "the labor of children under twelve years of age, in factories, is not desirable or profitable; and that no injury would result to employers, by the enactment of a law to prohibit the employment of all children under that age." [71] One Philadelphia paper, ob-

---

[68] *Pennsylvania Senate Journal*, II, 1837-38, p. 353.

[69] *Ibid.*

[70] *Pennsylvania Senate Journal*, II, 1837-38, p. 323; see Barnard, *op. cit.*, p. 14.

[71] *Pennsylvania Senate Journal*, II, 1837-38, p. 324. See testimony of Samuel Riddle, an employer, p. 229, and that of Mr. Blackstock, p. 352

viously distressed by the deplorable conditions of the children in the factories, and especially by the neglect of their education, charged that "they are obliged at a very early age to enter the factories, to contribute to the support of the family—by which means they are reared in total ignorance of the world, and the consequences of that ignorance, is the inculcation of immoral and often times vicious habits." [72]

Critics of the factory system charged that, not only was the education of these children neglected, but their health and morals were also impaired by the long hours of work in an unwholesome atmosphere. The carding, spinning and picking rooms where they usually worked were poorly ventilated. The physicians who testified before the Committee were in complete agreement as to the ill effects of constant labor in the cotton mills. [73]

> A child placed in a factory, at from seven to twelve years of age, as many of them are, [Dr. L. Callaghan of Pittsburgh informed the Committee] gets its constitution utterly and irreparably destroyed for life. . . . They never acquire that buoyancy and hilarity of spirits, common to children of their age. . . . They are early attacked with rickets (Molitis ossium) and other diseases of the bone; the spine, the breast bone, with the bones of the lower extremities, become distorted; hence, the antagonistic classes of muscles lose their action, and the child is rendered disabled for life.

Dr. John F. Bullick of Philadelphia confirmed the pessimistic report of his Pittsburgh colleague. [74]

> I have known females in good health to go into the mills, and after being in for about twelve months [this physician declared] they have become pallid and complained of head-ache—settled nervous headache, and considerable affection of the stomach—the symptoms of dyspepsia, the regular course of nature, the menses cease.

It was the reasoned opinion of this committee that not only did they consider the shorter work day "essentially necessary for the preservation of their [children's] health," but felt that "ten hours of labor per day, is as much as the majority of adults can perform without ultimate injury to their health." [75]

---

[72] The *Pennsylvanian*, August 28, 1833.

[73] *Pennsylvania Senate Journal*, II, 1837-38, p. 349.

[74] *Ibid.*, pp. 317-318.

[75] *Ibid.*, p. 326.

What should have made life particularly wretched for these infants who labored through an intolerably long work day, in a dirty and dusty atmosphere, was the pittance they received in return for their labors. Their wages varied according to their age and some of them received only twelve and one-half cents day or seventy-five cents a week, which was roughly equivalent to a cent an hour.[76] Wages of the older children generally averaged from one dollar to two dollars per week. While the more highly paid workers, that is, the mule spinners, and those employed in the cardroom of the Whitaker Factory had suffered from a reduction in their wages, the records reveal no similar decline in the earnings of the children and lesser paid workers.[77]

From all that we have considered it would appear that the position of the factory operatives was an unenviable one. His oppressions were many, his wages low, and what proved particularly irksome to him was the difficulty he often experienced in collecting the actual wages due him. It was a practice among many of the mill owners to combine a store with their mill operations, and the wage contract occasionally stipulated that a portion of the wages were to be paid in store orders. One observer commenting on the contractual relations between the workers and their employers in the textile mills states that, "in general, the conductors of the factories keep a shop or store and it is stipulated that one half of the wages shall be paid in groceries, etc." [78] An embittered mechanic in a letter to the *Mechanic's Free Press* related the offensive practices of a factory owner in Marseilles, Pennsylvania.[79]

> There is an extensive manufacturer in Marseilles, Pennsylvania, [wrote this mechanic] who is in the habit of issuing promissory notes, "good for so much in merchandise, etc., if presented to my store." Those who are in his employ are not only necessitated to accept of this *garlick*, but it frequently happens, when they present it for 'merchandise,' that they cannot get such articles as they want; and even if he has the articles they want, they are obliged to give fifteen and twenty percent more than they could purchase elsewhere with current money.

Another manufacturer at Morrisville, Pennsylvania, paid his hands in store orders and his profit was reported to be ten to fifteen percent.

---

[76] Whitaker Account Books, 1820, 1821; see *McClane's Report,* II, pp. 200, 201, 206, 221, 430, 431. And see *Pennsylvania Senate Journal,* II, 1837-38, pp. 281, 283, 309, 311, 315, 319, 351.

[77] Whitaker Account Books, 1834-1837.

[78] Isaac Holmes, *An Account of the United States of America* (London, 1823), p. 201.

[79] The *Mechanic's Free Press,* April 10, 1830.

Others paid their hands in depreciated bank notes which meant at times a loss of at least ten percent of their wages.[80] In addition to this, the general practice of paying the factory hands only once in every four weeks and at the same time withholding a portion of their wages left the operatives in a continual state of financial insecurity.[81]

The American operative could derive scant satisfaction from the fact that his wages were better than those of his fellow workers in England and on the continent, for it was generally recognized that he worked harder than did his brethren across the seas. Harriet Martineau, who had been favorably impressed by the congenial atmosphere which prevailed in the American mills, dogmatically asserted that "there seems to be no doubt among those who know both England and America that the mechanics of the New World work harder than those of the old."[82] James Montgomery, who was thoroughly familiar with the operations of cotton factories in both countries, declared that "the manufacturers here can afford to pay higher wages than the British, because they run their factories longer hours, and drive their machinery at a higher speed from which they produce a much greater quantity of work." [83] And an operative who had worked in the mills in both countries stated, "I consider the operation of the factory system upon persons employed, is more oppressive in this country than in England." [84] The *Public Ledger* concurred in this opinion.[85]

> The great evil which laborers are subjected to in this country [the *Ledger* wrote] is the amount of work they have to perform. Though receiving a higher rate of wages than those of Europe, and better paid for their services, yet the length of the time they are obliged to keep at their work to receive this compensation makes the task they perform fall heavier upon them.

Operations which in England required the services of two and three individuals were performed here by a single adult worker. A conviction was beginning to pervade a large number of the factory hands

---

[80] The *Pennsylvania Reporter*, June 20, 1834; The *Mechanic's Free Press*, October 10, 1830; The *Germantown Telegraph*, April 15, 1835; The *Public Ledger*, June 8, 1837; and February 23, 1839.

[81] *Pennsylvania Senate Journal*, II, 1837-38, p. 297; The *Pennsylvanian*, June 6, 1835.

[82] Harriet Martineau, *Society and Manners in America* (New York, 1837), II, pp. 251-252. See also Montgomery, *op. cit.*, p. 126.

[83] Montgomery, *op. cit.*, p. 138.

[84] *Pennsylvania Senate Journal* II, 1837-38, p. 313.

[85] The *Public Ledger*, June 27, 1839.

that their situation was no better than that of the textile workers across the seas.[86]

In this dismal chronicling of misery and poverty one cannot ignore the thousands of poor tailoresses and seamstresses whose tale of suffering and oppression is the saddest of all. These unfortunate women who made "slops" for the ships and sewed shirts and pantaloons for the Army labored incessantly to obtain the barest necessities of life. Hunger and cold were their constant companions and their greatest exertions barely raised them above the status of paupers. In 1829, according to the researches of Mathew Carey, "the hardest working among them only earn fifty-eight dollars a year, out of which they pay for rent and fuel, thirty-nine dollars." A balance of nineteen dollars remained for food and clothing for themselves and their children for a whole year.[87] Expert seamstresses working early and late could make no more than one dollar twelve and one-half cents per week, from which fifty cents was deducted for lodging, leaving sixty two and one-half cents per week or nine cents a day for food and the other necessities of life.[88]

Some irresponsible critics charged that the widespread poverty and suffering among the poor was due "to their own extravagance, idleness and improvidence during the spring, summer and fall when work was plentiful.[89] But it was pointed out that "there is no male vocation however loathsome, however deleterious to health, however degrading, that is not sought after, and undertaken with thankfulness, often at shamefully low wages." [90] This assertion was equally applicable to the female workers. In refuting this argument and in demonstrating the industry of these women, Mathew Carey reported an occasion when 1,100 applicants sought employment at the Provident Society for making shirts at twelve and one half cents each—"although it was known that none could have more than four shirts." [91] This ardent champion of the poor, after having made his exhaustive investigations into the conditions of the oppressed of Philadelphia, agreed with the conclusions

---

[86] The *Pennsylvanian*, August 28, 1833; The *National Trades' Union*, December 19, 1835.

[87] The *Mechanic's Free Press*, February 14, 1829; The *Berks and Schuylkill Journal*, February 21, 1829.

[88] Mathew Carey, *A Plea for the Poor*, pp. 6-7.

[89] Carey, *op. cit.*, p. 1; see *Hazard's Register of Pennsylvania*, III, January 1829, p. 41.

[90] *Letter on the Condition of the Poor addressed to Alexander Henry, Esq.* By a Citizen of Philadelphia, 1836, p. 9.

[91] Mathew Carey, *Essays on the Public Charities of Philadelphia*, p. 7.

of the Police Commissioner of New York "that no inconsiderable portion of female distress, and female depravity, is to be attributed to the very scanty remuneration they receive for honest industry . . . there are many instances of young and even middle aged women, who are lost to virtue, apparently by no other cause than the lowness of wages, and the absolute impossibility of procuring the necessaries of life by honest industry." [92]

That the grievances of these artisans who worked in the mills and factories were real is obvious. But far more serious than all other grievances was that overpowering sense of degradation which was beginning to be felt by large masses of these working people. "The losses of the individual worker in the first half of the century," wrote an astute student of the labor movement, "were not comfort losses solely, but losses, as he conceived it, of status and independence and ·no comfort gains could cancel this debt." [93]

This theme was aired again and again at the meetings of the working people. "What," they were asked, "is the cause of [their] degeneracy?" And why should it be "more degrading to turn a spinning wheel in a factory, than a spinning wheel at home?" A growing pessimism permeated the minds of many; a feeling of frustration, a loss of hope, a conviction that there was no escape. "Those who are toiling day after day, spending their strength, and wasting their health in the production of wealth are doomed not only to poverty with all its attendant inconvenience, but even to contempt," gloomily predicted a mechanic of Philadelphia. [94]

Nor was this a matter of concern to the wage earners alone. When the rumblings of protest and discontent over hours and wages and all the other attendant evils of the factory system began to be heard throughout Pennsylvania, one of the conservative Philadelphia papers pointedly reminded its readers that although "labouring in the field or in a workshop cannot confer any distinction . . . it ought not to be a degradation." [95] This editorial struck closely to the heart of the issue since the problems of the working classes were social as well as economic, and

---

[92] *Letter from Mathew Carey to Messrs. English, I. A. Newton, R. H. Kelly, S. S. Steele, and W. Newton* cited in the *Pennsylvanian,* May 2, 1836, and The *Public Ledger,* May 4, 1836; see also The *National Laborer,* April 30, 1836.

[93] Ware, *op. cit.,* p. i. xi, xiv. See Sidney and Beatrice Webb, *The History of Trade Unionism* (London, 1911), p. 47 for a discussion of the situation of the factory workers in Great Britain at this time.

[94] *Philadelphia Mercury,* December 29, 1827.

[95] *Poulson's Daily American Advertiser,* August 18, 1830.

transcended the comparatively narrow struggle for better wages and shorter hours.

Long hours of work combined with the constant fear of unemployment and the depreciation in the value of human labor had a demoralizing effect upon the wage earner. It was the artisans who suffered most from the dislocations and the adjustments which beset American business in the early stages of the Industrial Revolution. During the great panic of 1819 unemployment reached epidemic proportions. Various estimates placed the unemployment in Philadelphia from 5,000 to 20,000.[96] In Pittsburgh, the number of employed had fallen from 1,960 in 1815 to 672 hands in 1819.[97] No enumeration of the unemployed, no calculation of the pecuniary loss to the nation could adequately reveal the heartrending tragedy inherent in this great panic. The story of the stirrings, the doubts, the fears, which gripped the hearts and minds of men was left untold. A Citizens' Committee of Philadelphia investigating the effects of the great crisis suggested that the losses were not material losses alone.[98]

> But who [the committee asked] can calculate the injuries of another description that flow from it? The demoralization that necessarily results from want of employment, and its attendant dissipation: the heart rending pangs felt by parents, whose prospects of supporting their families are blighted and blasted? the numerous estimable females accustomed to earn a subsistence by spinning, and other employments adapted to their sex, and whose wants and distresses may force them to a life of guilt and wretchedness.

By 1824, the panic had spent itself, but even at that late date mechanics found themselves on the brink of poverty and threatened with pauperism. In January of that year *Poulson's Daily American Advertiser* reminded its readers that unemployment was still a grave problem and deplored the general apathy of the public. "The scarcity of employment is ... subject of much regret," this paper declared, "and we lament that it is not more generally taken into serious consideration."[99] Several weeks later a group of public spirited citizens, among

---

[96] The *Aurora and General Advertiser*, July 22, 29, Oct. 5, 1819. See Mathew Carey, *Address Before Philadelphia Society for Improvement of Agriculture*, pp. 25, 26, 30. *Hazard's Register of Pennsylvania*, IV, Sept. 1829, p. 169.

[97] *Hazard's Register of Pennsylvania*, VII, April 1831, p. 280. See Erasmus Wilson, *Standard History of Pittsburgh* (Chicago, 1898), p. 217.

[98] The *Aurora and General Advertiser*, October 15, 1819.

[99] *Poulson's Daily American Advertiser*, January 7, 1824.

them Mathew Carey, met "for the purpose of taking into consideration the alarming increase of pauperism—the distressed state of numerous estimable individuals, destitute of employment—and the best means of remedying those evils." The following month a Provident Society was established and "230 applications were made for employment on the first afternoon of its opening." [100]

Insecurity and fear continued to plague the worker. A slight business recession in the summer of 1829 had precipitated another crisis. Unemployment was rife. From all over the State came the dismal reports of factory closings and the discharge of the operatives. It was reported the Globe Mills situated near Philadelphia had suspended operations entirely and about 400 hands were thrown out of work. Other factories which had continued in operation, had "notified their hands, that a reduction of wages must be submitted to, or the works be suspended." Four thousand looms which had been in operation the previous year were said to be idle.[101] The news from Pittsburgh—factory shut downs and the discharge of hands—was equally distressing.[102]

The winter of 1829 was a particularly cold and bitter one for the poor of Pennsylvania. Faced with unemployment or the threat of becoming jobless, the wage earner was also confronted with rising living costs. The price of wood in Philadelphia had doubled since the early fall when only the rich had sufficient funds to purchase it in abundance. Wood which formerly sold at $4.25 to $5.50 a cord now sold for eight to ten dollars a cord.[103] Flour, which in 1828 was quoted at $5.60 a barrel, was now selling at twelve dollars.[104] Thousands of laborers travelled "hundreds of miles in quest of employment on canals at sixty two and a half cents, seventy five and eighty seven and a half cents per day, paying one dollar and fifty cents and two dollars per week for their board." [105] Bleak indeed seemed the future for the working man.

Scarcely four years had slipped by before the workers were again threatened with a loss of their means of securing a living. The vindictive and shortsighted policy of the president of the Second Bank of

---

[100] The *United States Gazette*, February 12, 1824.

[101] The *Free Trade Advocate*, June 20, 1829, p. 399; *Niles' Register*, XXXVI, June 27, 1829, p. 281 and July 4, 1829, p. 297.

[102] The *Statesman*, July 22 and September 2, 1829.

[103] *Poulson's Daily American Advertiser*, February 27, 1828; The *Mechanic's Free Press*, May 9, 1829.

[104] *Hazard's Register of Pennsylvania*, II, October 1828, p. 221.

[105] Mathew Carey, *Essays on the Public Charities of Philadelphia*, p. 21.

the United States, Nicholas Biddle, in calling in loans threatened the country with financial ruin.[106] In September of 1833 Niles complained that "money is scarce," and a month later warned of the probability of a paralysis in business. The *Saturday Courier* reported that "shutting up shop is becoming the order of the day." [107] Manufacturers in and about Philadelphia were "discharging their operatives." [108] Misery and want were the common lot of all, both of common laborers and journeymen mechanics. "The present pressure of the times, is without known precedent," the *Germantown Telegraph* reported. "The whole country seems to be on the verge of one widespread distress and ruin." [109] Some large manufacturing establishments had suspended all operations and the hands were turned out "to suffer all the horrors of hopeless poverty." [110] The distress was appalling.

> I have been in business for many years [wrote a resident of Pottsville] but I have never saw [sic] such times. There is no business doing here. About 2,000 men are looking for work, and everything is at a stand. A great many men with their families have to go to the house of employment to keep from starving. Hands can be got for their boarding.[111]

The recession of '33 was but a prelude to the great debacle of 1837. Barely had the laboring classes recovered from the economic dislocations of the previous layoffs than they once again had to endure unemployment, privation and want. Property suffered as well as labor but as one student pointed out, "it is impossible . . . to measure comparably the degree and kind of loss which each class incurred." [112]

---

[106] See R. C. Catterall, *The Second Bank of the United States*, p. 321; Arthur Schlesinger, Jr., *The Age of Jackson*, p. 104; The *Columbia Spy*, September 21, 1833. For a more sympathetic appraisal of Nicholas Biddle see Bray Hammond, "Jackson, Biddle and the United States Bank," *Journal of Economic History*, VII (1947), pp. 1-23.

[107] The *Saturday Courier*, February 2, 1833.

[108] The *Pennsylvanian*, August 26, 1833; The *Bucks County Intelligencer*, December 20, 1833; *Niles' Register*, XLV, September 7, 1835, p. 17.

[109] The *Germantown Telegraph*, January 3, 1834.

[110] The *Crawford Messenger*, January 3, 1834; The *Bucks County Intelligencer*, February 17, 1834; The *Bedford Gazette*, February 21, 1834, *Niles' Register*, XLV, January 4, 1834, p. 309.

[111] *Niles' Register*, XLVI, April 5, 1834; The *Columbia Spy*, March 15, 1834; The *Berks and Schuylkill Journal*, August 30, 1834; The *Harrisburg Chronicle*, January 8, 1835.

[112] For the most penetrating short study of the great depression of 1837 see Samuel Rezneck, "Social History of an American Depression, 1837-1843," *American Historical Review*, vol. XL, No. 4, July 1935, pp. 662-687.

Early that year the sufferings of the poor began to command public notice. The problem of relief was acute. There were many and loud complaints of the "hardness of the times." The prices were high; the suffering great. James L. Morris of Berks County noted in his diary that "one now-a-days hears of nothing else but hard times—failure—scarcity of money and what is worse, breadstuffs." [113] Public committees were called into action to look into the cause for the high prices. Soup kitchens were set up to take care of the destitute. One of the soup houses in the western section of Philadelphia ladled out soup to 1,054 adults and children daily. Private relief agencies appeared, to devote their time and energy to ease the suffering of the hard-pressed. And a committee was set up in Philadelphia to beg for the poor who "were dying of want." [114]

Probably never before had the complacency of thinking Americans been so rudely shattered. "What is to be done?" queried the *Public Ledger.* "The pecuniary difficulties which have for some time afflicted our community continue in almost undiminished severity," reported the *Ledger* in the fall of 1839. What were to be its effects on the poor man who in his "daily struggle with want and penury . . . [knows] that even when he sleeps to gain strength for the toil of tomorrow; that the enemy he contends against is sleepless and never rests," inquired the troubled editor of this Philadelphia paper. [115] What could be more tragic than young men thrown back on the resources of their families and friends because there was no work. What could be more distressing than "workmen standing in the market place all idle, for no one will hire them." [116] Some even felt that the nation's economy had reached the peak of its expansive possibilities and saw little hope for improvement in the future. [117]

> There begins to prevail, among the more reflecting of our citizens [wrote the *Ledger* in 1839] an apprehension that the present troubles are not temporary in their nature—are not the eruptions of high health, but the settled symptoms of a cankered and cureless disease— are not mere ripples on the advancing tide of our national prosperity, but the agitations of a certain and rapid ebb.

[113] James L. Morris Diary, May 9, 1837.

[114] *Niles' Register,* LI, 401 ff., February 25, 1837; Thomas Brothers, *The United States as They Are,* p. 66; The *Pennsylvanian,* March 23, 1838; The *Germantown Telegraph,* April 26, 1837; The *Public Ledger,* May 13, 1837.

[115] The *Public Ledger,* September 20, 1839.

[116] *Ibid.,* September 21, 1839.

[117] *Ibid.,* September 19, 1839.

There can be no doubt that recurrent crises, bringing widespread unemployment and declining living standards, caused many men seriously to doubt the efficacy of the factory system. According to some of the workers it was merely a more effective means of robbing them of the fruits of their labor.[118]

> The factory system [complained one mechanic] is that system by which, with the aid of *machinery*, a small company of men, possessing a large stock of money and sometimes aided by legislative enactments, are enabled to avail themselves of the labor of hundreds and frequently thousands of men, women, and children, to increase the wealth of the *company*, while the men, women, and children are generally worked to the utmost possible number of hours a day and paid for their work the smallest possible compensation which will enable them to keep life in the body and sufficient strength to return to their daily task.

The factory system, more than any other single factor, convinced the workers of the degradation of their social status. They bitterly resented the willingness of some of the mill owners to equate human labor with that of the machine, and in the machines they found a cause for their oppression and degeneration. When one statistically-minded individual estimated that "Philadelphia lost $1,000 every time the mechanics quit to go to dinner," the *Public Ledger* denounced him as belonging to "that hard hearted school which considers man a mere labouring machine, whose value is to be estimated by the amount of labour which can be forced from him." [119]

The *Mechanic's Free Press,* a paper which claimed to speak for all the working men of Philadelphia, gave considerable space to a discussion of the relative merits of labor-saving machinery. But readers were not left in the dark about its own attitude. It was extremely hostile. "Who shall estimate the immense injury, to the mind and body which machinery inflicts on the young labourers?" queried one of the contributors to this paper. And in reply to his inquiry stated, "the injury to the *boy* may be estimated, in the diminished stature, shrunken muscles, and cadaverous looks; but the injury to the mind can never be appreciated." [120] It was generally recognized that great progress had been made and that civilization had advanced through the introduction of labor-saving machinery, but it was felt by many that

---

[118] The *Working Man's Advocate,* March 24, 1832.

[119] The *Public Ledger,* January 23, 1837.

[120] The *Mechanic's Free Press,* November 21, 1829.

all this had been accomplished at the expense of the wage earner. Some went so far as to question the worth of the new machinery.[121]

> It is the almost universal belief of working men [contended the *Mechanic's Free Press*] that their situation is annually growing worse; and . . . in a matter depending on personal experience, we may allow the working men to be pretty good judges. . . . Now, if, in spite of the operation of labour-saving machinery, our condition is deteriorating, why should we wish for any new invention, that will produce great derangement in a given calling, without (judging from past experience) at all benefiting the mass of productive labourers?

Man and machine were becoming indistinguishable and it was the conviction of the one who purported to speak for the working classes that the effect of the establishment of manufactories was "to sink and degrade the actual manufacturer into a necessary piece of machinery." "In a great manufactory the laborer is only qualified to be what he is—a part of the machinery," this same individual declared.[122] Manayunk, a small manufacturing community just outside of Philadelphia, was pointed out as a deplorable example of the oppressive and degrading effects of machinery on the productive classes.[123]

> We will now take a hasty glance at the condition of the labourers employed, as living appendages to our principle machinery. Look at Manayunk—the heart sickens to behold the remorseless system of infant labour obtaining foothold upon our soil! . . . Look at some of our city machinery—young girls are earning a scanty pittance, by standing many hours in a day attending the monotonous motion, till their faculties of body and mind are in a fair way of being benumbed. Alas! what a price do they pay for their existence! . . . Here, then, we have abundant evidence, *so far*, the effect of machinery has been to impose burdens on sex and age, not necessary in former periods; whereas the effect of machinery to be truly beneficial to the productive classes, ought to be, diminished exertion and increased remuneration.

It was difficult to convince the working men of the beneficial aspects of machinery when they experienced greater hardships than ever before. He was not yet willing to listen dispassionately to the argument that machinery would greatly reduce the costs of manufacture and

---

[121] *Ibid.*, November 7, 1829.

[122] The *National Laborer*, April 23, 1836.

[123] The *Mechanic's Free Press*, November 7, 1829.

spread its benefits to all. The disproportionate cost of the manufactured article and the final selling price convinced the wage earner that he was not receiving an equitable share of the wealth which he had helped to create. Articles of clothing which cost the purchaser five dollars were manufactured at a total cost of two dollars to the proprietor. According to the *Mechanic's Free Press,* the cost of the material was one dollar and seventy-five cents, the cost of labor, seventy-five cents, and the cost of the article to the purchaser was five dollars. "The difference in the cost of material and the price of the article must be the value of labour," continued this journal.[124] "We see," complained a critic of labor-saving machinery, "that the more assistance our Mechanics and Working Men derive from machinery, and consequently, the more rich and comfortable they *ought to be,* the *less* rich and comfortable they are." [125]

The factory operative, along with most of the other wage earners of Pennsylvania, was deeply disturbed. He had seen the machine make threatening inroads on his way of life. His hours of work had increased but his wages had not increased proportionately, and more and more he saw women and children entering into occupations which formerly had been monopolized by men. He searched frantically for a solution to his dilemma but in vain. Recurrent crises swept away the few gains which he had won through stubborn struggle and left him to flounder among the forces which were transforming America into a great industrial nation.

---

[124] The *Mechanic's Free Press,* May 8, 1830.
[125] *Ibid.*

III

THE WAGE EARNERS—PART II

The Iron Workers

WHILE THE FACTORY operative was experiencing all the stresses and strains which modern industrial society imposes upon the wage earner, the stolid worker on the iron plantations was isolated from the main stream of American life. He lived on the huge holdings of the ironmaster and found his life more closely akin to that of the medieval serf than the industrial worker. He looked to the ironmaster for his job and his home; made his purchases at his store, and often found himself heavily in debt and his freedom seriously circumscribed by his obligations to him.[1]

None of the turbulence which characterized the relations between labor and management in the textile industry was in evidence among the iron works scattered throughout the State. His hours of work were long, equally as long as those of the factory hands. The nature of his work was hard and gruelling, physically far more strenuous than that of the operative.[2] Working in minepit, and forest, or at furnace and forge was "man's" work and the names of women rarely appeared on the ironmaster's pay roll. However, boys were frequently employed.

The ironworker's was a rural existence and probably here lay a partial explanation for the comparative peace which prevailed in the iron industry in the first half of the nineteenth century. Although hardship and poverty were his lot, he was never as completely at the mercy of those fickle economic forces which brought so much misery and unrest to the city worker. In contrast with the factory hand who lived more often than not in crowded and unsanitary dwellings, the ironworker and his family were sometimes provided not only with a home but with a sizable plot of land for gardening, pasturing his animals, and firewood. The labor contract which defined the relations between the ironmaster and his workmen, especially with the more highly skilled—the founders, the fillers, the guttermen, the coalers,

---

[1] James M. Swank, *History of the Manufacture of Iron in All Ages* (Philadelphia, 1892), p. 189.

[2] Arthur C. Bining, *Pennsylvania Iron Manufacture in the Eighteenth Century* (Harrisburg, 1938), p. 19.

etc.,—was often committed to writing and covered, not only the all-important issue of wages, but occasionally dealt with such fringe issues as housing, rent, board, firewood and pasturing.

These workers lived, as a rule, in the tenant houses belonging to the ironmaster. Since there was no one at that time who concerned himself with the poverty among these rural workers, as had Mathew Carey with the factory operatives, the actual circumstances in which they lived are not known. Whether their dwellings were crowded and dirty is a matter for speculation. But hunger and cold were never as great a threat to them as to the city worker. In addition to housing for themselves and their families, the ironworker often was provided with a barn for his cow and the right to firewood from the master's land.[3] William Harner's contract with the Joanna Furnace was typical of the many drawn up between these men and their masters. "William Harner," the contract stipulated, "to Receive $14—to have houz [sic] with firewood—the wood to be cut and hauled by him—and to have houz [sic] for one cow." [4] Some of these workers kept hogs and turkeys to supplement the family larder, as David Reed's contract with the Joanna Furnace would suggest. He was to receive a "home and firewood . . . with houz [sic] and pasture for one cow [but] to have no hogs here or turkeys running at large." [5]

The rents varied considerably from plantation to plantation and from worker to worker so that it is difficult to generalize as to these costs. Wage earners at the Joanna Furnace in the second decade of the century paid rents varying from eight to sixty dollars per year. As would be expected, the more highly skilled paid the higher rents, and the lesser workers the lower rents. Thomas Kenny, a founder, paid fifty dollars annually, while Francis King, a coal stocker, paid only eight dollars a year for rent. Edward Hawk, a coaler, paid sixty dollars a year, but the majority of the hands paid rents varying from twenty to forty dollars yearly.[6] For the skilled hands these rents were modest and eminently fair. Edward Hawk had in 1812 earned $1,341.67, and Thomas Kenny, an ore raiser, received in that same year $1,369.17, which indicates that not even a twentieth part of their annual income

---

[3] Joanna Furnace Journal, Mss., April 1, 1833. Memorandum of Tenant houses belonging to the Joanna Estate.

[4] *Ibid.*, Jan. 16, 1833.

[5] *Ibid.*, Memorandum of Bargains made with the hands at the furnace. June 1, 1833.

[6] *Ibid.*, December 21, 1810, December 30, 1813.

was consumed by rent.[7] On the other hand, the common laborer whose earnings were small and seldom paid in cash paid proportionately a far greater share of his wages for rent. During the years 1833 and 1834 when business was listless and depressed, rents ranged between twenty and forty dollars annually at the Joanna Furnace. But more often the rents were made an integral part of the wage contract for many of the workers, and at the above iron works during these years, many workers were listed as living "rent free." [8]

The situation at the Joanna Furnace was representative. The houses were usually the property of the master, and as the century advanced the rents were included in the wage bargain. In 1830, when the Cumberland Works of York County hired Samuel Neiman as forge carpenter, Jacob Haldeman, the ironmaster, agreed to pay him sixteen dollars a month and "to find him a House and firewood." [9] At the Juniata Forge, "all the hands connected with the Forge receive[d] a house with a stove in it, rent free." [10] Where rents continued to be a separate charge, they could not under any circumstances be considered as one of the more oppressive features of the iron workers' life. John Koch, a coaler, at the Cumberland Works, who was paid thirty cents for every cord coaled, agreed to pay "$35 rent for the house and premises occupied." [11] A rollerman at the Triadelphia Iron Works who was engaged for one year at the rate of one dollar and twelve and a half cents per day was "obligated to pay in four equal quarterly payments the sum of twenty-five dollars rent." [12]

Far more taxing were the charges for board. Since the work around the iron establishments was "man's" work, it was necessary for the ironmasters to provide boarding facilities for their unattached hands. Board varied only slightly from one furnace to another, and was substantially the same in 1840 as in 1800. It ranged from one to two dollars a week depending entirely on the particular furnace or forge. At the Birdsborough Forge in 1810, the men were paying seven shilling

---

[7] Juniata Furnace Journal, Memorandum of Bargains made with the hands at the Furnace, December 21, 1811.

[8] *Ibid.*, April 1, 1833.

[9] Agreement made between Jacob M. Haldeman and Samuel Neiman, January 8, 1830, Haldeman Paper, Mss.—Uncatalogued.

[10] Juniata Forge and Mary Ann Furnace Notebook, Mss., June 24, 1850.

[11] Agreement between John Koch and Jacob M. Haldeman, July 23, 1831, Haldeman Papers, Mss. (Uncatalogued).

[12] Blotter and Payroll of Triadelphia Iron Works, Mss., May 1837 to December 1850, Article of Agreement between Jas. Yearsley and Brs. and David Welsh, January 24, 1848.

six pence or one dollar a week for their board.[13] An employee at the
Charming Forge, who in 1820 received only $100. in wages, paid nine
shillings a week or slightly more than one half his wages for board
alone.[14] Some of the men employed by H. Moore, a nailer of Chester
County, paid two dollars a week for their board while their wages
averaged only twelve dollars and ninety cents per month.[15] The men
at the Hampton Furnace in 1839 were also paying two dollars a week for
board.[16] If the iron workers found these rates excessive, they kept that
fact carefully concealed.

Mechanization and standardization had not yet caught up with the
iron industry. The Machine which had transformed and introduced
an oppressive discipline into the textile industry was not in evidence
at the mine pits, the forges, and the furnaces. Those many minute
rules and regulations which the factory operative found distasteful
and degrading, but which formed an essential part of his labor contract,
had no place in the wage bargains concluded between the ironmaster
and his employees. Although, as has been pointed out, the iron workers'
contract dealt with such issues as housing and board, it was primarily
concerned with the question of wages and the quality of the work.
Where the factory hands had an agreement applicable to all, the iron
workers often had an individual contract, written and duly recorded
in the Journals of the furnace or the forge. Undoubtedly the highly
individualistic nature of the relations between the ironmaster and his
workmen was a conditioning factor explaining the complete absence of
protest or evidence of discontent among this group of wage earners.

Despite the particularistic nature of the iron industry in the first half
of the nineteenth century, the wages of the workmen at the different
furnaces and forges scattered throughout Pennsylvania did not vary
too greatly. The greatest variation was to be found among the forge
and furnace managers. They were usually paid on an annual basis
but some of them received monthly salaries. An unusually low sum
was that paid to William Brooke in 1810 for managing the Hampton
Forge. He was given ten dollars a month for his services.[17] At

---

[13] Birdsborough Forge Day Book, Mss., January 1, 1810.
[14] Charming Forge Time Book, Mss., April 1, 1820.
[15] H. Moore Day Book, Mss., December 21, 1822; November 9, 17, 1823. See also
Brandywine Iron Works Day Book, Mss., Feb. 5, 1831.
[16] Hampton Furnace Ledger, Mss., August 27, 1839. See also Mary Ann Forge Time
Book, Mss., April, 1840.
[17] Birdsborough Forge Day Book, Mss., April 13, 1810.

approximately the same time John Smith, manager at the Joanna Furnace, was paid the unusually high sum of $800 a year.[18] Nearer to the average was the salary which Joseph Evans was paid in 1829 for managing a furnace and forge in Union County. "The compensation of the said J. Evans as manager is fixed at four hundred dollars for the present year," stated the agreement between Evans and the proprietors of these iron works. It further stipulated "that for future services in managing the above business J. Evans shall receive $500 and C. Evans three hundred Dollars a year together with their boarding." [19] It is safe to conclude that the furnace managers received between $300 and $600 annually for their services.[20] These forge managers with rare exceptions belonged to and were intimately associated with the managerial and not the wage earning element among the iron workers. They were in many instances owners or co-owners of the iron establishments.

Undoubtedly the most important of the wage earners at the furnaces were the founders. They possessed a higher skill and commanded a higher wage than most of the other workers around the iron works. It was their task when the furnace was in blast to properly regulate the "charge" and the responsibility for the quality of the iron produced was theirs. In addition to making pig iron, they made sand molds and cast the iron into the various shapes ordered by the customer.

The founder's responsibility was great, his hours of work unbelievably long, and occasionally he was burdened with "finding" his own keeper. The wages of these workers were nearly uniform throughout the State. What variation did occur was more among the individual workers than among the various furnaces. The wage bargain in the early decades of the century generally called for a monthly rate, whereas in the later years piece rates were more common. Typical of the agreements between the ironmaster and his founders, and illustrative of the duties of these workmen is the following drawn up between William Darling of the Joanna Furnace and Michael Wolf: [21]

> The said Michael Wolf agrees to blow Joanna Furnace as a
> Founder for the said William Darling and his heirs and

[18] Joanna Furnace Journal, Mss., December 30, 1809; Dec. 21, 1813.

[19] Frazer Collection, Mss. (Uncatalogued), Agreement between Jos. Evans, C. Evans and A. Babbitt, November 25, 1829.

[20] Mount Hope Furnace Day Book, Mss., April 3, 1832. (Grubb Collection, Historical Society of Pennsylvania). See Alfred Gemmell, *The Charcoal Iron Industry in the Perkiomen Valley* (Norristown, Pa., 1949), p. 91; and S. K. Stevens, *Pennsylvania: Titan of Industry* (New York, 1949), I, pp. 68-69.

[21] Joanna Furnace Journal, Mss., January 11, 1832. Agreement between William Darling of Joanna Furnace and Michael Wolf.

assigns during the blast provided he makes iron sufficient to the quantity of stock said Furnace takes, he is to attend to said Furnace at all times night and day to see that Furnace is properly kept and fil'd regularly by the fillers and to attend to all other duties in and about said furnace that is the founders duty to do. For which Services the said Wm. Darling promises and agrees to pay to the said Michael Wolf his heirs and assigns the sum of one dollar and fifty cents for each and every ton of castings made and all other castings except what is made in open sand forge plates and the sum of one dollar and twenty five cents for each and every ton of pig metal and pot gates made.

During the first decades of the nineteenth century the founders at the Joanna Furnace averaged between twenty and twenty-four dollars a month.[22] In the later decades they were paid by the ton. David English in 1833 agreed "to blow Joanna Furnace and find his own keeper" for which he was to receive one dollar and fifty cents a ton for castings and seventy five cents a ton for pig iron.[23] The founders at the Hampton Furnace in 1839 were paid at the rate of one dollar per ton for pig iron,[24] and those at the Mary Ann Furnace in 1850 received one dollar per ton. These figures would suggest that their wages had remained relatively stable throughout the first half of the nineteenth century.[25]

Of all the furnace workers, the wages of the keepers and the fillers showed the slightest variation in the first half of the century. The keepers at the Joanna Furnace were in 1813 paid seventeen dollars per month.[26] Those at the Cornwall Furnace in 1830 received eighteen dollars.[27] At the Hampton Furnace, the keeper in 1838 was paid at the rate of eighteen dollars a month and in the following year received twenty-five dollars. Not only were these unusually high rates but it was specifically stated in the contract of Jacob Eddinger, a keeper, that his wages were to be paid in cash.[28] The wages of the fillers generally ranged from sixteen to eighteen dollars a month. Occasionally they

---

[22] Joanna Furnace Journal, Mss., December 31, 1813. Memorandum of Bargains made with the hands at the furnace.

[23] Ibid., June 1, 1833.

[24] Hampton Furnace Journal, December 24, 1838.

[25] Juniata Forge and Mary Ann Furnace Notebook, June 24 to August 12, 1850.

[26] Joanna Furnace Journal, Mss., April 12, 1809; Dec. 30, 1809; December 31, 1810; December 31, 1811; December 31, 1813.

[27] See Frederic K. Miller, *The Rise of an Iron Community* (Lebanon County Historical Society Publications, XII, 1950-1952), p. 100.

[28] Hampton Furnace Journal, Mss., Dec. 6, 1838; Sept. 23, 1839.

were paid by the turn but not often. At the Joanna Furnace the fillers in the first two decades of the century received eighteen dollars per month, or one dollar and twenty cents a turn when paid on a piece rate basis.[29] During the 1830's, the fillers at the Mount Hope Furnace earned eighteen dollars a month, and when paid on a piece rate basis, one dollar and thirty-seven and a half cents a turn.[30] Those employed at the Hampton Furnace in 1839 had the same basic rates.[31] If they ever found their tasks irksome and weary, if they ever felt that they were inadequately compensated, their protests never saw the light of day.

Another group of workers at the furnaces were the guttermen, who were in charge of the sand molds. Throughout the period under discussion their wages show no wide variation. Those at the Hampton Furnace were an exception. The guttermen employed by the Dale Furnace were paid, in 1800, thirteen dollars and thirty-three cents a month.[32] Thirty years later these same workmen at the Mount Hope Furnace were paid at exactly the same rate.[33] But those at the Hampton Furnace in 1838 and 1839 received seventeen dollars and fifty cents per month which would suggest that they were paid more highly for their services than were the men at the other furnaces.[34]

As essential to the successful operation of a furnace as any of the other workmen were the miners, those men who laboriously grubbed the ore from the earth. The mining operations at this time were almost exclusively surface mining and only rarely was any tunneling done. In addition to raising the ore from the earth, it was prepared for the blast at the mine banks. It was pounded and washed and if the sulphur content was high, it was burned. Wages varied considerably among the individual miners. Some were paid by the ton, while others received a monthly or a daily rate. The monthly earning of the more highly skilled miners throughout the first half of the century averaged about seventeen dollars. Their daily rates varied from fifty to eighty-seven and

---

[29] Joanna Furnace Journal, Mss., Dec. 30, 1809; Dec. 31, 1810; Dec. 21, 1811; Dec. 21, 1813.

[30] Mount Hope Furnace Journal, Mss., October 1832; March 1, 1833; January 10, 1835.

[31] Hampton Furnace Journal, Mss., June 1, 1839.

[32] Dale Furnace Day Book (1799-1801), p. 1, quoted in Gemmell, op. cit., p. 91.

[33] Mount Hope Furnace Journal, October 1, 1832; March 31, 1834.

[34] Hampton Furnace Day Book, Aug. 7, 1838; Feb. 4, 1839; Aug. 1, 1839; and Nov. 14, 1839.

one half cents per day.[85] From the evidence available those men who pounded mine were among the most highly compensated of all the furnace workers. They crushed the larger chunks of ore into bits in preparation for the haul to the furnace. In 1820, according to the investigations of Frederic K. Miller, the mine pounders at the Cornwall Furnace were paid only twelve dollars a month, but by 1830 their wages had more than doubled, and by 1840 they were being paid at the rate of twenty-seven dollars a month. At the Mount Hope Furnace in 1836, they were paid twenty-two dollars a month for this laborious work.[86] Those men who washed mine were, at the beginning of the century, paid on a monthly basis but toward the middle of the century they were working on a piece rate basis. The Joanna Furnace in 1810, gave its mine washers thirteen dollars and thirty-three cents a month. In 1830, they were paid by the load. The contract of Jonathan McEwen is worth quoting as suggestive of the nature of the wage agreements made by these workmen. "Jonathan McEwen," his contract read, "engaged to wash three hundred loads of mine from the red and yellow bank in equal proportion—mine to be clear washed and as good as that he washed last summer for $1.50 per load."[87] The minesetters, those men who prepared the ore for burning, averaged about eleven dollars a month.[88] As with all the other iron workers there is no evidence that the men ever protested, ever complained that their hours were too long or that their wages were too low.

The making of charcoal was an important branch of the iron industry until well into the mid-nineteenth century. Pennsylvania's denuded forests are indicative of the vast stands of timber consumed by this industry. At the Juniata Forge it was estimated that 2,500 cords of wood were consumed annually and this was by no means an exceptionally large amount.[39] The colliers, like so many of the other wage earners at the furnace, often had individual agreements with the ironmasters stipulating in detail the obligations of each party. Let us examine a contract between John Withers and two colliers which may

---

[85] Hopewell Furnace Journal, Oct. 12, 1833; Hampton Furnace Day Book, July 20, 1839.

[86] Mount Hope Furnace Journal, February 10, 1836.

[87] Joanna Furnace Journal, December 21, 1810; February 1, 1833; Memorandum of Mine contracted for at the Warwick Mine holes.

[88] Mount Hope Furnace Journal, April 20, 1833; January 10, 1835; February 10, 1836; Hampton Furnace Day Book, Dec. 9, 1839.

[39] Juniata Forge and Mary Ann Furnace Notebook, p. 8.

be regarded as typical of the bargains concluded between the iron-masters and these laborers.[40]

> Article of agreement made concluded and agreed upon between John Withers of the one part and Joseph and George Matthews, Coliers [sic], of the other part as follows to wit. The said Joseph Matthews and Brothers agreed to coal all the wood on the burnt hill cut this season say between 3 and 500 cord and pay strict attention to the work and make as good coal as they are capable of doing and coal it as fast as to send from 3 to 5 loads of coal per day and commence on Thursday and continue until all is coaled and sent in. The said John Withers agrees to pay the said Joseph Matthews and Brothers the sum of thirty three cents per cord for each and every cord they coal payable when wanted to the said Matthews and Brothers. The said Withers is to give good attendance in delivering the wood in the Harths and also good attendance with a team to haul away the coal.

The colliers in the early decades of the nineteenth century were paid by the month or the load, but the trend in the third and fourth decades was to pay them by the cord. From 1800 to 1820 they averaged between eighteen and twenty-one dollars a month or two dollars and thirty-three cents a load.[41] But from 1820 to 1840 they were generally paid by the cord, and the usual price was thirty cents.[42] The collier was occasionally called upon to find and furnish his own team and when he did so the price he received was increased considerably, as much as twenty-two cents a cord. For any waste or negligence on his part the collier was penalized with a fine. The contract of Daniel Fraye, a collier at the Hopewell Furnace, obligated him "to make as much yield out of the wood as David Hoffman will make out of the same number

---

[40] Frazer Collection, Article of Agreement between John Withers and George Matthews, November 12, 1839. See Haldeman Papers, Agreement between Jacob M. Haldeman and John Koch, July 23, 1831; and between J. Haldeman and Henry Duckhart and John Poor, July 20, 1832. Also see Hopewell Time Book, agreement with Daniel Fraye, February 28, 1824.

[41] Thomas Bull Account Book, Jan. 27, 1824; Hopewell Furnace Journal, Jan. 16, 1803; Nov. 31, 1803; Joanna Furnace Journal, Dec. 30, 1809; Dec. 31, 1810; Dec. 31, 1811; Dec. 18, 1813; Birdsborough Forge Day Book, Jan. 1, 1810; Dec. 31, 1810; Jan. 30, 1811; Dec. 23, 1811; Oct. 14, 1812; Haldeman Papers (Miscellaneous receipts), Jan. 1, 1814; April 24, 1818; Charming Forge Day Book, Aug. 24, 1816; Nov. 14, 1817; Federal Slitting Mill Journal, July 30, 1813.

[42] Dowling Forge Day Book, March 12, 1825; Haldeman Papers (miscellaneous receipts), December 28, 1832; July 1833; Mary Ann Forge Day Book, April 1, 1834; Mount Hope Furnace Journal, Dec. 19, 1835; Hampton Furnace Day Book, Oct. 10, 1838; Oct. 16, 1839; Juniata Forge and Mary Ann Furnace Notebook, June 24, 1850; Miller, op cit., p. 76; Gemmell, op. cit., p. 92.

of cords."[43] While coaling for the Birdsborough Forge, David Hoffman was on one occasion charged six dollars "for his half of the value of 12 cords of wood he burned by neglect when coaling."[44] Similar penalties appear on the records of other furnaces where a collier had been guilty of carelessness and neglect.[45]

To keep a continual and sufficient supply of coals on hand, wood cutters were employed in greater numbers than were any other group of workers at the furnaces and forges. In the winter months when the furnaces were not in blast, founders, fillers, and other men employed by the ironmasters turned out to cut cord wood. The wood cutters averaged thirty-three cents a cord in these first four decades of the nineteenth century. Some of them were occasionally paid forty or forty-five cents a cord. During the years 1821 and 1822 many wood cutters were paid as little as ten cents a cord, but thirty-three cents per cord was the average price. When the cutters supplied the wood from their own land, one dollar was the customary rate.[46]

Among the lowest paid workers at the furnaces were the teamsters. They were the truckers of their day. It was they who kept a continuous flow of supplies to and from the iron works. They hauled the coals and the ore to the furnaces and forges, and they carried the iron to the market. Their wages from 1800 to 1840 ranged between nine dollars and thirteen dollars and thirty-three cents a month. In one or two instances a driver received as much as sixteen dollars a month, but this was extremely rare.[47] Even when trucking was contracted for on a piece-rate basis the rates varied only slightly in this first half of the century. Hauling mine in the first decades was done at the rate of eighty-three cents a load; in the middle thirties, it was

---

[43] Hopewell Furnace Time Book, Feb. 28, 1824.

[44] Birdsborough Forge Day Book, May 1, 1816.

[45] Hampton Furnace Day Book, Sept. 28, 1838.

[46] Federal Slitting Mill Journal, April 3, 1800; Hopewell Furnace Journal, December 20, 1802; Oct. 11, 1803; Joanna Furnace Journal, Dec. 30, 1809; Dec. 31, 1811; Dec. 31, 1813; Birdsborough Forge Day Book, Feb. 25, 1811; Jan. 17, 1814; Haldeman Papers (Miscellaneous receipts), April 1, 1818; Dowling Forge Day Book, April 24, 1820; March 12, 1825; Mount Hope Furnace Journal, Feb. 26, 1822; Mary Ann Forge, May 1820; December 4, 1834; March 12, 1837; Hampton Furnace Day Book, May 31, 1838; July 20, 1838; and August 14, 1839.

[47] Joanna Furnace Journal, Dec. 21, 1810; Dec. 31, 1811; Jan. 27, 1814; Birdsborough Forge Day Book, Feb. 1, 1812; March 21, 31, 1812; Haldeman Papers (Miscellaneous Receipts) March 19, 1813; March 20, 1813; Mount Hope Furnace Journal, Oct. 1, 1832; Mary Ann Forge Day Book, Sept. 20, 1834; Dowell Forge Day Book, May 20, 1829; Hampton Furnace Day Book, Oct. 10, 1838; Hampton Furnace Day Book, Dec. 24, 1838; Aug. 10, 1839; Dec. 17, 1839.

being trucked for seventy-five cents a load.[48] The rates for hauling cordwood revealed an even slighter variation. This charge ranged from twelve and a half cents to fourteen cents a cord.[49] These workers, like all the others who earned their daily bread at the various iron works, were inarticulate and subdued.

An outstanding feature of the iron industry in the decades under discussion was the stability of the nominal wages of the workers. The fluctuations and gyrations which periodically upset the business community were scarcely reflected in the pay rates prevailing at the furnaces and forges. This is not to say that their total earnings were unaffected in times of distress, but their basic pay rates remained substantially the same despite the enormous economic changes which were taking place. This was equally true, not only of the highly paid workmen—the founders, the fillers, the guttermen, etc.—but also of those miscellaneous workers, the common laborers, the carpenters, the blacksmiths and others who were employed about the iron works. The common laborers at the various furnaces and forges in the State earned between eight and ten dollars a month. When paid on a daily basis their wages ranged between forty and seventy-five cents a day.[50] Although the house carpenters were among the more articulate and the more highly compensated group of wage earners in the cities, their brethren at the furnaces and forges ranked just above the common laborers in so far as their wages were concerned. The few fortunate ones hired on a monthly basis earned from thirteen to fifteen dollars a month. But the majority were on a daily rate and received from fifty to seventy-five cents a day.[51]

---

[48] Joanna Furnace Journal, Dec. 31, 1810; Dec. 5, 1811; Mount Hope Furnace Journal, Jan. 1, 1834; Feb. 22, 1834; Dec. 31, 1835.

[49] Hopewell Furnace Journal, July 13, 1802; Joanna Furnace Journal, Dec. 30, 1809; Dec. 24, 1810; Dec. 18, 1813; Hopewell Time Book, Feb. 27, 1823; New Hampton Furnace Journal, Sept. 24, 1836; Haldeman Papers (Miscellaneous Receipts), July 11, 1834.

[50] Hopewell Furnace Journal, Nov. 1, 1802; June 6, 1803; Dec. 1, 1803; Birdsborough Forge Day Book, Nov. 8, 1807; Jan. 16, 1808; March 17, Nov. 1, 1810; Jan. 30 March 4, 1811; Jan. 1, 1813; Feb. 1, 1813; Feb. 1, 1831; Joanna Furnace Journal, Dec. 30, 1809; Charming Forge Journal, April 30, 1807; Charming Forge Time Book, March 1819; Dowell Forge Day Book, April 29, 1828; July 1, 1828; April 24, 1833; May 28, 1833; Spring Forge Day Book, April 28, 1834; Hampton Furnace Day Book, June 18, 1838; June 26, 1838; August 7, 1838; Jan. 2, 1835; Dec. 18, 1839; Alsace Furnace Blotter, March 30, 1839; April 3, 16, 1849.

[51] Birdsborough Forge Day Book, Oct. 30, 1809; April 1, 1810; Dec. 21, 1810; Joanna Furnace Journal, Jan. 27, 1814; Haldeman Papers (Miscellaneous Receipts), Jan. 8, 1830; Mount Hope Furnace Journal, April 20, 1833; March 31, 1834; Mary Ann Forge Journal, May 31, 1834; Aug. 5, 1835.

The workers at the furnaces and forges were, either the most oppressed, the most submerged, or the most contented of all the workers in Pennsylvania. Despite the long hours of work, despite the laborious and strenuous nature of their tasks, despite the fact that they rarely received their wages in hard cash, these iron workers were never moved to protest or to act in concert to improve their status. From all the available evidence they, unlike the city workers, were resigned to their fate and accepted without question their life of hard work and low pay. They appeared unmoved by the democratic forces which were sweeping America in the Jacksonian Era. And the question arises: Why did these rural workers acquiesce and accept with complacency conditions which the urban worker would have found intolerable?

Undoubtedly the highly individualistic and paternalistic nature of the relationship between the ironmaster and his workmen was an influential factor in determining the attitudes and the actions of these laborers toward such issues as hours, wages and conditions of work. The ironmaster's situation was comparable to that of the huge plantation owner of the South. Although his workmen were not slaves, many of them for all practical purposes found themselves in a state of peonage. Among the hundred-odd persons on the payroll at the Hampton Furnace in 1839 over sixty-two found themselves in arrears to the ironmaster's store.[52]

Another factor explaining the lethargy of these iron workers was the absence of that novel and severe discipline to which the factory operatives were subjected by the advent of power-driven machinery. Those minute rules and regulations which burdened the life of the urban workers were not in evidence at the furnaces or forges. While almost every minute of the working day of the factory hands was proscribed, there was in contrast a certain casualness about the time of the furnace workers. An incident which occurred at the Hopewell Furnace is worth quoting in its entirety as illustrative of the lack of a rigid and fixed discipline at the iron works.[53]

> The Castings of Pigs left out Monday Morning September 5, 1825 before day weighed 26-6-14 [a conscientious clerk noted in the *Journal of the Hopewell Furnace*].
> *Note*—The above castings of Pigs was left out owing to Joseph McKewen, George North and Henry Care neglect-

---

[52] Hampton Furnace Journal, November 7, 1839.
[53] Hopewell Furnace Time Book, September 5, 1825.

ing to mold up last Saturday Sept. 3, 1825 as it was their
duty to have moulded up. Thomas Care told them on
Saturday to lade immediately after breakfast and they
refused. He pressed them to do it until 11 o'clock. The
iron at the time was running out of the Furnace.

An explanation for this neglect was to be found in the following brief
statement which the clerk added to this account: "McKewen and
North was out hunting with their guns.[54] There was nothing in the
records to indicate that these men had been discharged for their
deliberate neglect but they were probably penalized, most likely with
a fine, since it was customary around the furnaces to charge the workmen for neglect.[55] Though the pace was set by man and not by the
machines at the iron works, this is not to say that the life of the iron
workers was an easy one. Theirs was a life of hard work and the future
held little promise for easing their labors. Rarely would their meager
earnings enable them to accumulate a sufficient capital to acquire the
vast holdings necessary to become an ironmaster. But until technology
had revolutionized the iron industry and driven an irreparable breach
between master and workman, the iron workers would remain aloof and
isolated from the main stream of the American labor movement.

THE COMMON LABORERS

When Joseph M'Ilwaine, the secretary to the Board of Canal Commissioners, was asked by a committee investigating the conditions of
the poor in Pennsylvania to make a general estimate regarding the
wages of the laborers on the canals he replied:

It is difficult to answer with precision your inquiry as to
the average wages of Canal Laborers. They vary with the
seasons, and are still more dependent upon the proportion
of Laborers to the work required to be done.[56]

This statement was applicable not only to the canal laborers but to
all the other manual workers who were in great demand on the public
works, in the cities and at the mines throughout the State. Their
wages and the general conditions of their work varied considerably
from place to place and from season to season. At Philadelphia their
wages were usually higher than in other parts of the State, and during

[54] Hopewell Furnace Time Book, September 5, 1825.

[55] Birdsborough Forge Day Book, May 1, 1816; Hampton Furnace Day Book, June
2, 1838; June 11, 1838.

[56] *Working Man's Advocate*, May 21, 1831; see Isaac Holmes, *An Account of the
United States of America* (London, 1823), pp. 126, 127.

the summer the common laborers were in greater demand than in the winter.

The men on the turnpike roads who grubbed the tree stumps and spread the gravel were, in this first half of the nineteenth century, the victims of a declining wage. Until the panic of 1819 they were paid at the rate of seventy-five cents a day.[57] In 1819, the *Democratic Press* stated that it had learned "from unquestionable authority that men are now working on our turnpike roads for 12½ cents per day."[58] Even after the crisis had passed the wages of these laborers never again reached their pre-depression levels. In 1821, they were paid fifty cents a day and this rate prevailed until the spring of 1836.[59] The benevolent Mathew Carey writing in 1829 declared that "hundreds are most laboriously employed on turnpikes, working from morning till night at from half a dollar to three quarters per day, exposed to the broiling sun in summer, and all the inclemency of our severe winters." [60] During the boom days of 1836, the wages of the laborers on the turnpikes rose to sixty-two and a half cents a day which would hardly compensate for the tremendous price rise which occurred at this time.[61]

Pennsylvania's grandiose canal projects called for thousands of laborers and their situation was slightly better than that of the workers on the turnpike roads. They like most of the other wage earners in America worked from sun to sun and a ration of whiskey was generally included as a part of their daily wage. "An American labourer," wrote William Cobbett, "is not regulated, as to the time by *cloches* and *watches*. The *sun,* who seldom hides his face, tells him when to begin in the

---

[57] Account Book of Jno. McMaster—Supervisor on the Road between Joseph Springers and Pittsburgh, Oct. 1 to 26, 1803; Account Book—Road Supervisor Henry Crum, March 25, 1811; March 25, 1812; March 25, 1813; Book Containing Statement of the Accounts of the Supervisor of the Roads for the Township of Paxton, April 6, 1818.

[58] The *Democratic Press* as quoted in The *Huntingdon Gazette,* September 9, 1819.

[59] Book Containing Accounts of Supervisor of Roads John Bucher, March 26, 1821; Book of Supervisor of Roads Leonard Crum, March 23, 1822; Book of Supervisor of Roads John Eisenhouer, March 22, 1824; Book of Supervisor of Roads Emmanuel Cassel, March 22, 1825; John Bucher's Book, March 23, 1826; Book of Supervisor of Roads Peter Bergoene, April 1829; Book of Supervisor of Roads John Baldozer, March 22, 1830; Book of Supervisor of Roads Peter Shalle, March 21, 1831; John Eisenhouer's Book, March 22, 1832; Book of Supervisor of Roads Jacob Plank, March 22, 1833; Book of Supervisor of Roads Peter Heikert, April 13, 1835; Book of Supervisor of Roads Abraham Lose, April 11, 1836.

[60] *Hazard's Register of Pennsylvania,* III, January 1829, p. 42.

[61] Book of Supervisor of Roads Abraham Lose, April 11, 1836; Book of Supervisor of Roads Emmanuel Cassel, April 10, 1837.

morning and when to leave off at night." [62] His wages varied considerably from time to time and from place to place, but the general trend was toward a slightly higher pay scale. The men on the works of the Lehigh Coal and Navigation Company in the early 1820's were given sixty-four cents a day or seven dollars and twelve cents a month and a daily ration of whiskey.[63] The laborers employed on the West Branch of the Susquehanna were at this time paid only sixty cents a day.[64] Niles, bemoaning the deterioration of the position of the common laborer, declared "that in 1795 a *common* laborer in Baltimore received 125 cents, and the highest rate of the wages of such is now 75 cents—many of them receive only 62½ cents. " [65] This statement characterized the situation then prevailing in Pennsylvania. In the late 1820's the men employed on the Pennsylvania Canal received only eighty cents a day and this was seldom in cash. The cash earnings of many of these workers were as little as five cents a day.

During the decade of the 1830's, the wages of these laboring men showed a definite upward trend. The Union Canal was, in 1833, paying its employees seventy-five cents a day, and three years later they were earning eighty cents daily.[66] Those employed on the Pennsylvania Canal in 1837 received one dollar a day, and Simon Sallade, one of the contractors, complained "that we have to pay hands $16 a month" and threatened to break his contract.[67] Despite the hard times which prevailed from 1837 to 1840, the canal hands continued to receive one dollar per day.[68] Since their days of employment were intermittent and unemployment was an ever-present and distressing problem, the full story of the canal hands is not revealed by wage statistics alone.

---

[62] William Cobbett, A *Year's Residence* (London, 1822), p. 320.

[63] Lehigh Coal and Navigation Company Journal No. 1, Sept. 30, 1821; March 31, 1822; *Hazard's Register of Pennsylvania*, I, May 1828, p. 312.

[64] Canal Papers (uncatalogued), in the possession of the Public Records Division of the Pennsylvania Historical and Museum Commission. Payroll of George Bennett Commissioner appointed to improve the West Branch of the Susquehanna, August 1, 1823; Sept. 12, 1823.

[65] *Niles' Register*, XXIV, April 12, 1823, p. 86.

[66] Union Canal Papers (Miscellaneous Payroll Receipts), September 1, 1833; May 1836. In the possession of the Berks County Historical Society.

[67] Canal Papers, Letter from Simon Sallade to Richard R. Bryan, June 16, 1837.

[68] Check Roll Beaver Division Pennsylvania Canal, March, April, June, September and November 1838. Uncatalogued Canal papers in the possession of the Public Records Division of the Penna. Historical and Museum Commission. See Testimony against Stonebreaker A Contractor for the Construction of the Juniata Canal, 1838-1839, Thomas Whittaker to G. N. Espy, July 25, 1839.

The day laborers in Philadelphia and those employed on the various railroad projects throughout the State were by far the most articulate of the manual laborers. They not only pushed their wages to higher levels than those received by any of the common laborers but struggled strenuously and sometimes effectively for a shorter work day. The coal heavers on the Schuylkill wharves in 1835 were paid one dollar a day, and in the summer of that year led the fight for the ten hour day in Philadelphia.[69] The following summer the day laborers of Philadelphia and the coal heavers along the Schuylkill wharves demanded one dollar and twenty-five cents a day for their services.[70] Those employed on the Reading and Hamburg Railroad in 1839 asked for an increase in their wages from one dollar to one dollar and twelve and a half cents per day, suggesting that these laborers had, even in the dire days of the depression, been able to maintain their wage standards.[71]

No occupation was more hazardous, none required more back-breaking effort than that of the men who worked in the collieries. "A Shocking Catastrophe"—"A Melancholy Accident"—"It becomes our painful duty to announce"—"We regret to state"—and similar introductory statements appeared periodically reporting the most recent disasters at the coal mines. Fires, cave-ins, poisonous gases, drownings and other mine accidents cut short the uneventful existence of the miner.[72]

Men were in great demand at the mine pits and the newspapers enthusiastically greeted each new arrival of experienced Welch miners. To a group of 358 immigrants who landed in Philadelphia, the *Aurora* advised "those who are in search of employment, to proceed immediately to the Mount Carbon Coal Mines." [73] According to the advertisements

[69] The *Man*, May 5, 1835; *Niles' Register*, IV, June 6, 1835, p. 235; The *National Trades' Union*, June 6, 1835. Microfilm copy in the possession of Columbia University Library. See also Wm. A. Sullivan, "A Decade of Labor Strife," *Pennsylvania History*, January 1950, p. 34.

[70] The *National Laborer*, May 7, 1836; The *Public Ledger*, May 13, 1836; The *Pennsylvanian*, May 16, 1836.

[71] The *Public Ledger*, June 12, 1839; *House Ex. Doc. pt. 5, 50th Congress 1st Session*, p. 1037.

[72] *Doylestown County Patriot*, April 1, 1825; *Poulson's American Daily Advertiser*, April 5, 1825, May 26, 1835; The *Miner's Journal*, Aug. 18, 1827; March 5, 1831; Jan. 12, 1833; *Niles' Register*, XXXII, Aug. 18, 1827, p. 402; The *Working Man's Advocate*, Aug. 18, 1832; The *Bucks County Intelligencer*, Jan. 14, 1835; The *Pennsylvanian*, July 19, 1836.

[73] The *Aurora and Pennsylvania Gazette*, June 25, 1828; The *Miner's Journal*, June 16, 1827; *Poulson's Daily American Advertiser*, June 19, 1827; The *Daily Chronicle*, July 1, 1833; The *Saturday Courier*, July 6, 1833.

which appeared in the *Miner's Journal* not only were the wages high but the hours of work few. "MINERS WANTED—Wage of 20 dollars per Month, Work 8 hours a day" read one of the advertisements which appeared in this paper. Another announced that the miners in the collieries at Pottsville and Mount Carbon were being paid at the rate of one dollar and twenty-five cents a day.[74] From the few scattered records that are still available it would appear that these were highly exaggerated rates. In 1821, the Lehigh Coal and Navigation Company, which was one of the largest and earliest producers in the anthracite district, paid its miners nine dollars and thirty-three cents a month.[75] According to Samuel Wiley, historian of Schuylkill County, the miners in 1842 were receiving five dollars and twenty-five cents per week and these wages were payable in store orders only.[76] Although these records are too fragmentary to formulate any sound conclusions it would appear that the coal miners, especially when one considers the hazardous nature of their occupation, were not only poorly paid but also were confronted with a steadily declining wage.

THE SKILLED ARTISANS

The most aggressive, the most articulate, the most imaginative of all the wage earners in their eternal struggle to secure an equitable share of the wealth which they had helped to create were the skilled artisans —the carpenters and the other workmen associated with the building trades, the shoemakers, the printers, etc. They were the first to organize for collective action, the first to suggest that the traditional work day was inhuman and unjust, and they were the first to flirt fleetingly with the idea of a political organization to right their wrongs. And in the vanguard were to be found the men of the building trades, sensitive and alert to the enormous changes which were taking place in America.

Despite the fact that the carpenters were among the highest paid of all workers in Pennsylvania, it was they who protested most vigorously against the "grievous and slave like system of labor" under which they

---

[74] The *Miner's Journal*, August 11, 1837; *Hazard's Register of Pennsylvania*, IV, June 1829, p. 64.

[75] Lehigh Coal and Navigation Company Journal No. 1, Sept. 30, 1821; H. Fearon, *Sketches of America* (London, 1819), p. 20, stated that the men in the coal excavations at Pittsburgh in 1817 made from four dollars and twenty cents to four dollars and eighty cents a week.

[76] Samuel T. Wiley, *Biographical and Portrait Cyclopedia of Schuylkill County* (Philadelphia, 1893), p. 45.

were compelled to work.[77] Their hours of work, like those of all the other wage earners throughout the country were from "sunrise to sunset" and it was the house carpenters of Philadelphia who initiated the movement for the shorter work day. Not only was the long work day physically taxing but it deprived them of an opportunity for intellectual development or from taking an active part in political affairs, which they asserted denied them their rights as citizens in a democracy.[78]

A premature attempt was made by the Philadelphia house carpenters in 1791 to have their working hours reduced to ten a day,[79] but it was not until the summer of 1835 that they were able to secure the acquiescence of most of their employers in this demand.[80] The house carpenters of Pittsburgh were not as fortunate as their brethren in Philadelphia, for they were in 1837 still striving to induce their bosses to accept the ten hour day, since as they explained, "the Mechanics of other populous cities have established the ten hour system as their rule to work by." "It is no more than just," insisted these men, "that the Carpenters of Pittsburgh should enjoy the same privileges as their fellow laborers elsewhere." [81] Nor did all the master carpenters in Philadelphia comply immediately. As late as 1838 some of the house carpenters in the city found it necessary to strike to secure the shorter work day.[82]

Rising prices without corresponding wage increases added to their burdens and were instrumental in convincing the carpenters that their position was steadily deteriorating. In the early years of the nineteenth century the wage bargains were generally individual agreements between the master carpenters and their journeymen, but by the fourth decade of the century the house carpenters were resorting to collective action to make the wage agreement. During the early years of the War of 1812, the wages of the house carpenters in Philadelphia ranged from one dollar and thirteen cents during the winter months to one dollar and thirty-three cents in the summer months.[83] Shortly after the

---

[77] The *Philadelphia Gazette*, June 14, 1827.

[78] The *Pittsburgh Gazette*, May 31, 1831.

[79] See John R. Commons, *History of Labour in the United States*, I, p. 110.

[80] The *United States Gazette*, June 6, 1835; The *National Trades' Union*, June 20, 1835; *Pennsylvania Annual Report: Industrial Statistics, Part III* (Harrisburg, 1882), p. 263; The *Pennsylvanian*, June 3, 1835.

[81] The *National Laborer*, February 18, 1837.

[82] The *Public Ledger*, October 2, 1838.

[83] John and Moses Lancaster Carpenters Account Book, October 10, 30, November 6, 10, 1813; May 11, 14, 28, 1814; August 9, 20, 1815; in the manuscript division of the Historical Society of Pennsylvania.

conclusion of the War some of the master carpenters were paying as much as one dollar and twenty-five cents to one dollar and seventy-five cents per day to their journeymen.[84] But outside the urban centers the carpenters received about one dollar per day.[85] During the 1830's the journeymen employed by Moses Lancaster, a Philadelphia builder, received from one dollar twelve and a half cents to one dollar and twenty-five cents per day whereas his men in 1816 and 1817 had been paid as much as one dollar and seventy-five cents per day indicating that not only their real but their nominal wages had declined in this period.[86] The available evidence indicates that most carpenters in the city were being paid at these rates.[87] The house carpenters of Philadelphia in 1836, very much agitated over the rising prices and the lowness of their wages, demanded from one dollar and twenty-five cents to one dollar and fifty cents per day as their basic pay rates.[88] In 1839, they were still protesting that while all the "other trades connected with building, receive from $1.50 to $1.75 per day . . . the Journeyman Carpenter . . . receives $1.25 per day."[89]

Wage statistics alone do not tell the whole story. Carpenters frequently had to receive payment in kind instead of in real money, and some of the master carpenters made it a general practice to withhold a large part of the weekly earnings of their journeymen. They were, moreover, perennially faced with the problem of unemployment during the short winter days. The wage agreements which Moses Lancaster made with his men often stipulated that a sizable part of the wages would be paid in groceries or dry goods. Typical of the entries in this builder's receipt book is the following:[90]

> Received May 30, 1829 of M. Lancaster and Co. an order on Bowers Loneleer for Shoes to the amount of $7 which is on account of Carpenter Work done at Amos Akins building in Spruce near 2nd street inside of 2nd story at

[84] John and Moses Lancaster Carpenters Account Book, Nov., 1816; Jan. 1, 1817; July 4, 25, Aug. 9, Sept. 12, Oct. 16, 23, 1818.

[85] John Singles Account Book, March 19, 1815; March 19, 1817; March 19, 1818; James Powell Account Book, Sept. 3, 1816.

[86] Moses Lancaster Receipt Book, July 16, 1834; Jan. 12, 1835; August 15, 1835.

[87] Eastern District Penitentiary Pay Roll, Oct. 25, 1824; Dec. 19, 1835; March 12, 1836; The *Pennsylvanian*, July 9, 1835; *History of Wages in the United States from Colonial Times to 1928* (Washington, 1934), p. 58.

[88] The *Pennsylvanian*, March 21, 1836; The *National Laborer*, March 26, 1836; The *National Trades' Union*, April 9, 1836.

[89] The *Public Ledger*, March 22, 1839.

[90] Moses Lancaster Receipt Book, March 14, 1829; May 30, 1829.

50% of old Price and to be paid one half in Lumber and ½ in cash and the Ballance [sic] in such other trade as may suit both parties.

In 1836, when the carpenters were making a vigorous drive to increase their wages they publicly protested against the policy of payment in kind instead of in money wages, which they charged was a practice of many of the employing carpenters.[91] In addition, these carpenters complained that some of the master workmen paid them only five dollars weekly and retained the balance in their own hands. Not only was this a degrading practice but often occasioned actual hardship on these journeymen who insisted that their full wages were totally inadequate to provide them with the necessities of life. "It must be remembered, that our weekly pay is insufficient for our support, if we received it all as earned," these house carpenters declared.[92]

Of all the journeymen associated with the building trades the bricklayers experienced the sharpest decline in wages. At the beginning of the century they were paid at the rate of two dollars and seventy-five cents per thousand.[93] Moses Lancaster in 1817 had agreed to pay his bricklayers three dollars twelve and a half cents a thousand.[94] His men in 1829 were receiving two dollars and seventy-five cents a thousand while the bricklayers at Lancaster were paid at the rate of one dollar and seventy-five cents per thousand.[95] The Philadelphia bricklayers in 1835 earned only one dollar and seventy-five cents per day and this had fallen to one dollar and fifty cents per day by 1837.[96] Thus it would appear that the bricklayers in Pennsylvania failed to maintain their wage standards, and this fact, when coupled with rising costs, must have meant an actual decline in their living standards.

The wages paid to the masons varied in the different parts of the State. At the furnaces and forges in the interior they scarcely averaged one dollar per day, but their rates in the cities ranged from one dollar

---

[91] The *Pennsylvanian*, March 21, 1836.

[92] The *Public Ledger*, March 22, 1839.

[93] Frazer Collection (Uncatalogued) Agreement between Thomas Kirker, Francis McGurk and Hugh Donnelly, March 15, 1814.

[94] John and Moses Lancaster Account Book, Jan. 22, 1817. Agreement between Moses Lancaster, Carpenter of Northern Liberties of Philadelphia and Pettit A. Smith, bricklayer.

[95] Moses Lancaster Receipt Book, July 14, 1829; Frazer Collection (Miscellaneous Receipts), Richard Water to John Winauer and Michael Algies, February 9, 1821.

[96] Moses Lancaster Receipt Book, June 8, 1835; Eastern District Penitentiary Payroll, Nov. 7, 1835; Van Buren Papers, vol. 26, Letter to Robert Mills Esqr. from William Strickland (Philadelphia), April 6, 1837.

to one dollar and fifty cents per day. Strawn and Myers, contractors, in Bucks County, paid their masons in 1815 from one dollar and twenty-five cents to one dollar and fifty cents per day.[97] Those employed on the construction of the Eastern District Penitentiary received in 1824 from one dollar and twenty-five cents to one dollar and fifty cents per day.[98] The men on this project in 1833 were still paid at the same rate as that which had been paid in 1824.[99] The *Miner's Journal* in the fall of 1826 stated that masons were in great demand at Pottsville and would receive one dollar a day for their services. In 1834, the masons employed on the Union Canal averaged one dollar and twenty-five cents per day, while those employed by Moses Lancaster, the Philadelphia builder, received one dollar and fifty cents per day.[100] In response to a request for information on the prices of labor in Philadelphia in 1837, William Strickland informed his correspondent that the stone masons received one dollar and fifty cents per day.[101] From the foregoing it would appear that, of all the workmen associated with the building trades, the masons were least affected by the adverse wage fluctuations which particularly hit the carpenters and the bricklayers. But, if they experienced no wage reductions in this period, neither did they enjoy any increases in their earnings.

By far the most articulate and the most victimized of all the skilled artisans were the cordwainers. Technological change had little or no effect on the shoemaking industry before 1840, and it remained throughout the first half of the nineteenth century a handicraft. But the broadening of the market had radically affected the relations between the journeymen and their employers. This trade experienced some of the most stubborn struggles between capital and labor. "Order Work" destined for the wholesale market and "Market Work," that is, cheap work sold in the public market, attracted more and more of the capital and the energies of the employing shoemakers.

But the expansion of the market and the production of a cheaper product did not mean better prices and better conditions for the journeymen cordwainers. A Philadelphia shoemaker in the conspiracy

---

[97] Strawn and Myers Masons Account Book, October 1815, in the possession of the Bucks County Historical Society.

[98] Eastern District Penitentiary Payroll, July 16, 1824.

[99] *Ibid.*, October 12, 1833.

[100] Union Canal Company Papers (Uncatalogued), Letter from B. Aycrigg to William Lehman, Esqr., November 5, 1834.

[101] Van Buren Papers, vol. 26, April 6, 1837.

trial against the shoemakers society of that city in 1806 declared that if he was "driven to market work" he "could not make a living" at it.[102] "It was the widening out of these markets with their lower levels of competition and quality," contends one of the ablest students of the American labor movement, "that destroyed the primitive identity of master and journeymen cordwainers and split their community of interest into the modern alignment of employers' association and trade union." [103]

Just prior to, and at the opening of the nineteenth century they waged a continuous and aggressive struggle to secure an advance in their wages. To these Philadelphia cordwainers goes the distinction of having maintained an organization for at least twelve years to assist them in pressing their wage demands. Through a series of strikes they were successful in raising the price of making cossack boots from one dollar and forty cents a pair in 1792 to two dollars and seventy-five cents in 1806. While they had been able through collective action to increase the price which they received for shop and bespoke work, the price on wholesale work was left open to individual bargains.[104] Since they were paid on a piece rate basis it was inevitable that their weekly earnings would vary according to the ability and the ambition of the individual cordwainer. Their weekly earnings in these first decades of the nineteenth century ranged from six to ten dollars. One journeyman shoemaker declared that he "worked from five in the morning till twelve or one at night" and could "only make eight and a half dollars per week." [105]

The Pittsburgh shoemakers, who also had organized, were equally successful in pressing their demands for higher wages. In 1804, they had asked for two dollars and fifty cents for making boots, but whether they were given this price is not known.[106] But in 1812 through a series of turn outs they were able to raise the price of making boots from two dollars and twenty-five cents a pair to three dollars, and by

---

[102] John R. Commons, et al., *Documentary History of American Industrial Society* (Cleveland, 1911), III, pp. 14, 183; Blanche Hazard, *Organization of the Boot and Shoe Industry in Massachusetts before 1875* (Cambridge, 1921), p. 11 ff.

[103] John R. Commons, "American Shoemakers, 1648-1895," p. 231 ff. printed in John R. Commons, *Labor and Administration* (New York, 1913).

[104] Commons, *Documentary History*, III, pp. 104, 107. See Commons, "American Shoemakers," p. 239.

[105] Commons, *Documentary History*, III, pp. 83, 123.

[106] Erasmus Wilson, *Standard History of Pittsburgh*, p. 200.

1815 they were paid at the rate of three dollars and twenty-five cents per pair.[107]

But catastrophic changes were taking place in the shoe industry which were to be instrumental in undermining the strong position which the journeymen cordwainers had maintained in these early years of the nineteenth century. The merchant capitalist, with control of vast amounts of capital and the widespread markets of the South and West, appeared and was a threat not only to the journeymen but also to their employers. During the depression of 1819, the cordwainers suffered from unemployment as did all the other tradesmen. The *Aurora* in the fall of 1819 reported that at least five hundred journeymen shoemakers whose average wages were about six dollars per week, were unemployed.[108] The records of William Ramsey, a shoemaker of Chester County, reveal the steady decline in his wages. In 1822, he was paid at the rate of two dollars and eighty-seven and a half cents a pair for Monroe boots; the following year he received two dollars and seventy-five cents, and in 1824, he was given only two dollars and twelve and a half cents a pair for making these same boots.[109] According to Mc-Clane's Report, the men employed in the shoe industry in Western Pennsylvania in 1832 averaged between eight and ten dollars a month in the country and eighteen dollars a month in the towns. They worked twelve hours a day throughout the whole year.[110] Some of the master shoemakers reported profits as high as twenty-five and thirty percent, and one stated that his profits were fifty percent.[111]

In the early 1830's, the journeymen shoemakers of Philadelphia had organized into the "United Beneficial Society of Journeymen Cordwainers." In an address to the "Journeymen Cordwainers of the City and County of Philadelphia" this organization disclosed the difficulties which had overtaken the men employed in this trade. Their wages had fallen sharply. First-rate journeymen who formerly had received two dollars and seventy-five cents for a pair of boots were now paid only one dollar twelve and a half cents. Their weekly earnings had declined to between four and six dollars per week, and even to make such wages they had to work in many instances fourteen hours a day. The other

---

[107] Commons, *Documentary History*, IV, pp. 28, 33, 54.

[108] The *Aurora and General Advertiser*, Oct. 6, 1819.

[109] William Ramsey—Shoemakers Account Book, April 11, 1822; May 1823 and December 27, 1824.

[110] *McClane's Report*, II, pp. 590, 591, 592, 593, 594, 596-598.

[111] *Ibid.*, pp. 512, 590, 593, 595.

wage earners in the city, the shoemakers declared, were able to make
eight to twelve dollars a week while working only ten hours daily.
"How can it be," they asked, "that without any positive reduction of
our wages, we are unable to earn more than two thirds as much as we
were a short time ago?" [112]

> The answer [they reply] is plain and simple—by making
> cheap work, triple the quantity has to be made to obtain
> a living; this produces, at dull seasons, a surplus of work
> in the market; and these large manufacturers taking ad-
> vantage of the times have compelled their journeymen to
> make the work so far superior to the manner in which
> it was originally made for the wages given, that it is now
> brought into competition with first-rate work. This again
> lessens the quantity of first rate work made, and the
> journeymen, formerly working for employers who gave
> them $2.75 for each pair of Boots made, are forced to seek
> employment of the very men who had ruined their busi-
> ness. Thus it is that journeymen who formerly worked
> on nothing but first rate work, are brought into direct
> competition with those of inferior abilities in point of
> workmanship.

The merchant capitalist had driven the skilled journeymen, who
made high quality boots, into competition with the workmen of less
skill, and during times of distress the journeymen found themselves
producing high quality products at rates formerly given for boots of
low quality. The journeymen shoemakers felt that these merchant
capitalists were largely responsible for their predicament. [113]

> "The cunning men of the East" have come to our city,
> [complained the cordwainers] and having capital them-
> selves, or joining with those who had, have embarked in
> our business, and realized large fortunes, by reducing
> wages, making large quantities of work, and selling at
> reduced price, while those who had served their time to
> the trade, and had an anxious desire to foster and cherish
> its interests, had had to abandon the business or enter
> into the system of manufacturing largely in order to save
> themselves from bankruptcy.

Nor had their situation been measurably improved by 1836. The
journeymen declared that working ten to twelve hours a day, they
could average no more than five dollars and sixty-four cents a week. [114]

---

[112] The *Pennsylvanian*, April 4, 1835; see J. R. Commons, "American Shoemakers,"
pp. 241, 242.

[113] *Ibid.*

[114] The *Pennsylvanian*, April 18, 1836.

In addition, they found themselves forced into competition with even cheaper sources of labor. Prison labor was being used extensively by the large-scale producers and the journeymen cordwainers charged that this was not only financially harmful but was demoralizing and degrading to have these felons encroach on their trade.[115] The distinctions between capital and labor were becoming more sharply defined in this trade than any other, with the probable exception of the factory operative, and they in no sense belonged to the category of the skilled artisan.[116]

A conviction permeated almost all the working classes that their situation was growing steadily worse. The skilled and the unskilled alike protested, and when their protests occasioned no remedial action, strikes became the order of the day. Spokesmen for labor and self-appointed champions of labor pointed out two courses of action which might relieve them of their burdens. There were those who urged the workingmen to seek a solution to their most pressing problems through direct political action. And there were those who urged the workingmen to organize into trade unions. It was the latter who had found the most effective weapon for labor in its struggle against oppression.

[115] The *Pennsylvanian*, September 5, October 1, 1835; The *National Laborer*, April 2, 1836.

[116] See Commons, "American Shoemakers," p. 252 ff.

IV

GROWTH OF TRADE UNIONS

THE WAGE EARNERS of Pennsylvania during these early decades of the nineteenth century found their situation degrading and steadily growing worse. It was inevitable that they would resort to organized and concerted action to remedy their weakened position. A number of factors appeared which ultimately compelled them to organize and to utilize collective bargaining techniques to maintain and to improve their status. Of prime importance was the growth of a wage earning class without whose existence organized labor would probably never have had an excuse for being. The appearance of the merchant capitalist with his control of large amounts of capital and vast markets sharpened the distinctions between capital and labor and drove the workers to defensive action against what they termed, the aggressions and "inroads of a *Mushroom Nobility*."[1]

The development of this idea of antagonistic interests between the workers and their employers was of slow but persistent growth. Early in the nineteenth century at the trial of the Philadelphia cordwainers this discord which was to characterize the relations between capital and labor was very much in evidence. Subsequent decades saw it spread to most of the other trades. By the middle 1830's it had permeated almost all group of workers including the factory operatives and the day laborers. This growing awareness on the part of the wage earners that their interests as a class were separate and distinct from the other classes in society found expression in the numerous labor organizations which sprang up throughout the State and in the increasing strife, and charge and counter-charge which marred the relations between the workers and their employers. In fact, the *National Laborer,* the organ of the National Trades' Union, found it necessary to refute the charges that the object of the Trades' Union and trade unions was to incite class war and despoil the wealthy of their property. This Union paper indignantly brushed aside as "nonsensical" the accusation that it was the desire of the trade unions to engender class conflict. And as for the conten-

---

[1] The *Pennsylvanian*, March 4, 1836.

tion that they had designs on the property of the wealthy, the *National Laborer* declared:[2]

> The Trades' Union and its members have more at stake than these possessors of ill-gotten spoil. They are the most anxious that property should be protected, for they have suffered most from its violations; and they differ from aristocracy on this point in but one particular, which is this —the members of the Trades' Union wish to see the property of *every* citizen protected, while the aristocracy wish all *they* possess to be guarded in every way, and the property of the productive laborer exposed to their depradation.

The *Public Ledger* found all this talk about classes disquieting and prejudicial to the best interests of the country. "There was a time, and not far distant," bemoaned the *Ledger*, "when we heard nothing from American presses, about classes and *distinctions* of *rank. Then,* all occupations were considered *equally honorably* [sic], and distinctions between *individuals* were founded, not in trades and *professions,* but in character and conduct."[3] The most incisive evidence disclosing this feeling of class solidarity among the wage earners was revealed in the testimony of Charles V. Hagner, a former mill owner. The anti-capitalist sentiments of the factory operatives, he was inclined to believe, were congenial. "They [the factory children] early acquire the views and feelings of some of the older hands and seem to me in some instances to inherit an antipathy to their employers, which 'grows with their growth and strengthens with their strength.' "[4]

One compelling factor driving the workers into trade unions and enhancing the growth of a class-conscious labor movement was the threat to their living standards, especially of the skilled artisans, almost coincident with the appearance of the merchant capitalist. The skilled artisans found their bargaining position seriously impaired by the profound charges which were taking place in America's industrial development, and they were the first to organize for collective action. No longer were they intimately concerned in the profits of buying and selling, and hastening the development of a trade union movement was

---

[2] The *National Laborer,* March 26, July 9, 1836.

[3] The *Public Ledger,* October 11, 1837.

[4] *Pennsylvania Senate Journal,* II, 1837-1838, p. 326. Testimony of Charles V. Hagner before the Senate Committee investigating factory conditions in Pennsylvania.

this separation of the workers from the customers by an intervening wage bargain.[5]

As the bargaining position of the wage earners grew progressively weaker, their pleas for union grew stronger. "These institutions [trade societies]," explained the journeymen cordwainers, "became necessary to protect the mechanic in his wages. . . ." [6] Trade Societies and Trades' Unions, they contended, were absolutely essential to protect the wage earner against oppression. At the Convention of the Trades' Union in 1835, it was stated, "that the formation and permanency of Trade Societies and Trades' Unions, presents the only security against the entire degradation of the whole mass of working men in the United States to the level of mere beasts of burden, similar to the situation to which insatiable avarice has reduced the labouring classes in Europe. . . ." Furthermore the convention decided that these societies were the most effective means for "protecting [the working classes] from the encreasing encroachments of capital on the rights of labour."[7] But it was the *Philadelphia Trades' Union* which had grasped the fundamental and impelling motive which induced men to join these trade organizations. "The consciousness that they are members of an institution that can, and will, protect them from the avaricious encroachments of unfeeling employers," this journal divined as the motivating force which induced many wage earners to unite together into trade unions.[8] According to the *Lancaster Journal*, it was the desire for protection from grasping employers which drew many workers into these organizations. The journeymen mechanics, this paper declared, have organized "avowedly to protect themselves and their families against the cupidity of the employers, who not content with taking every advantage of the working men to reduce their wages, carried on a system of encroaching upon their time to such a degree, that they were literally reduced to a state of slavery." [9] Undoubtedly the conviction on the part of a large number of workers that they were being oppressed and

---

[5] John R. Commons, *History of Labour in the United States* (New York, 1911), I, p. 29; see Sidney and Beatrice Webb, *History of Trade Unionism*, (London, 1911), p. 35.

[6] The *Pennsylvanian*, March 4, 1836.

[7] The *National Trades' Union*, October 10, 1835. Columbia University Library has microfilm copy of transcripts which are in the possession of the Wisconsin State Historical Society.

[8] From the *Philadelphia Trades' Union* as quoted in the *National Trades' Union*, December 6, 1834.

[9] The *Lancaster Journal*, June 12, 1835.

that their oppressions were increasing in number was an important factor in accounting for the rise of a trade union movement at this time.

Another force of incalculable importance for the growth of the labor movement was the desire on the part of many of the laborers to implement the ideals and aspirations expressed in the Declaration of Independence. The workers were inclined to contrast the noble sentiments expressed in that memorable document with their deplorable situation. Although the Declaration of Independence states *"that all men are created free and equal,"* the United Beneficial Society of Journeymen Cordwainers in an address to all the working shoemakers in the city asked: "How can we be free while we have no control over the price of the only commodity we have to dispose of—our labor. How can we be equal when we are slaves of heartless monopolists?" Freedom and equality, the journeymen cordwainers were told, could only be achieved through the establishment of trade societies.[10]

If the forces which led the wage earners of Pennsylvania to organize were compelling and varied, those which deterred them from taking such action were equally strong and diverse. The opposition of the press and the clergy, and the general apathy of large segments of the working class, made the task of the champions of labor formidable indeed. In addition, the organized opposition of the employers, the hostility of the courts, and the general antipathy of the public toward trade unions discouraged all but the most courageous from joining the labor movement.

The most persistent charge levelled against these newly-formed trade unions by the opponents of labor was that they were inspired and dominated by foreigners. Approvingly the *Saturday Evening Post* reprinted the following description of trade unions which had appeared in the *New York Commercial Advertiser:*[11]

> These Unions it is said, are based upon the same principles as the pernicious Trades Unions in England, and in almost every case, we are informed, they are managed and controlled by foreigners.

The master carpenters of Philadelphia contended that "combinations of this description are indebted for their origin to the discontented and disorganizers in a monarchial government; they are not of American birth."[12] Joseph Ripka, the owner of a large textile manufacturing

[10] The *Pennsylvanian,* April 4, 1835.
[11] The *Saturday Evening Post,* March 12, 1836.
[12] The *Pennsylvanian,* March 17, 1837.

establishment, found himself in complete agreement with the master carpenters. According to him, the only evil existing in the operation of the factory system in Pennsylvania was the principle of Trades' Union which he asserted had "been imported to this country by English and Irish men within a few years and which had a tendency to destroy the good feeling which has, heretofore, existed between the employer and the workmen in this country."[13] These oft-repeated charges finally forced a spokesman for the Trades' Union to present a carefully documented refutation of the charge of foreign domination.[14]

There were those who feared that the trade unions, like Pandora's box, would open the country to a host of unknown evils. Some suggested that they were instrumental in stifling investment and curtailing business expansion.[15] Others charged that they were cruel and tyrannous. They stripped the workingman of his liberties and compelled him "to march like conscript militia through the streets, under the command of some foreigner," contended still others.[16] And there were those who saw trade unions as instruments for promulgating atheism "and for overturning the civil and religious institutions of the country." "It is strange," remarked the *Pennsylvanian*, in commenting on a denunciatory article on trade unions which appeared in *Poulson's Daily American Advertiser*, "what fears these old, real tory prints have of the people, and how alarmed they are at every tendency towards their association."[17] Some viewed the trade unions as institutions for engendering immorality and encouraging inebriety.[18]

Probably far more effective in staying the growth of the labor movement and in deterring many of the wage earners from entering wholeheartedly into the activities of the trade unions at this time was the unwillingness on the part of many of them to accept their status as permanently fixed. Opportunities real and imagined, the perennial hope of advancement which drew so many of them to America, were everpresent factors which led many wage earners to question the efficacy and the advantage of trade unions. A correspondent of the *Miner's Journal* estimated that "one half or certainly one third at least of all the master mechanics and manufacturers in the United States, many of

---

[13] *Pennsylvania Senate Journal*, II, 1837-1838, p. 357.
[14] The *National Laborer*, April 9, 1836; see The *Pennsylvanian*, April 5, 1836.
[15] The *Germantown Telegraph*, March 16, 1836.
[16] *Poulson's Daily American Advertiser*, April 10, 1835.
[17] The *Pennsylvanian*, July 17, 1834.
[18] *Ibid.*, March 1, 1836.

whom are now worth 20, 30 or 50,000 dollars, were originally journey-men." And he concluded "this is among the most auspicious feature in the character of American Society."[19] Another journal made the astounding assertion that it found "a greater proportion of mechanics growing rich and amassing fortunes than of merchants, factors, lawyers, and physicians."[20] And again and again the question was raised: "Why should the working man be jealous of the capitalist? Does he forget that in this free country, it is just as much in his power to become a capitalist, as it was for those, who now stand in that situation . . .?"[21] Nor were these the sentiments only of those hostile to the labor movement.

> The mechanics will find [declared the *Mechanic's Free Press*] that many of their own classes are their worst enemies. Some of the young mechanics are actuated by the idea of setting up their business, and living on the profits arising out of the labour of others, and this will make them try to defeat every measure calculated to better the hard condition of that class generally.[22]

In the spring of 1836, when the charges of oppression were voiced loudly and frequently by many wage earners of Philadelphia, a writer under the pseudonym of 'Franklin' addressed himself to the mechanics of that city. "Who are these employers," he asked, "who are the authors of these oppressions. Look around and you will see that every man of them was but a short time since, a Journeyman like yourselves."[23] There was a large element of truth in this assertion. The journeymen carpenters, in the course of a strike to raise their wages, found it necessary to allay the fears of both the public and some of their own numbers by proclaiming that "it is not our purpose to war with our employers. We are of the opinion that our interests are nearly allied. . . ."[24] Undoubtedly this conviction on the part of the wage earners that they too would eventually become employers was an important element in explaining their apathy towards the efforts of the trade unions. The hostility of the employers and the other enemies of labor was readily understood, but it was a trying experience for those who

---

[19] The *Miner's Journal*, July 22, 1826.

[20] The *Philadelphia Mercury*, December 29, 1827.

[21] The *Free Trade Advocate*, II, November 14, 1829, p. 317.

[22] The *Mechanic's Free Press*, June 6, 1829.

[23] The *Pennsylvanian*, March 14, 1836.

[24] The *Public Ledger*, March 22, 1839.

spent their energies in a continuous struggle in furthering the cause
of the working men, to find their best efforts wasted because of the
unwillingness of many wage earners to bestir themselves in their own
behalf. "Awake from this lethargy and arise in your own defence," the
journeymen house carpenters of Philadelphia were advised during their
early struggle for the ten hour work day.[25] "Many of the evils complained of by the mechanics of this country," the journeymen cordwainers were told, "are owing to the neglect and apathy evinced by
many of them on this all-important subject [trade societies]—a subject
which should at all times occupy their most serious attention. . . ."[26]
It remained for the *National Trades Union*, the journal of the organized
workmen in the United States, to point out in no uncertain terms where
a great weakness in the labor movement lay.[27]

> We say, it is not the hostility of our open enemies that is
> most likely to destroy us. That we always expected would
> follow, of course; we had no right to look for anything
> else; but it is the heedlessness, the lethargy, the total
> insensibility to the open and covert means of destruction
> which are preparing—nay, which are now in actual opera-
> tion—that will harm us most. Not only are the professed
> friends of Trades' Unions sitting in comparative idleness,
> and making no concerted resistance, while their enemies
> are endeavoring to sap the walls of our Citadel; but they
> seem to have lost sight, that continual *efforts* are requisite,
> even if we are left unopposed by enemies, to make our
> Unions what they were intended to be—the means of
> permanently improving the moral and physical condi-
> tion of the producing classes.

It appears remarkable indeed that the wage earners of Pennsylvania
were able to organize into trade societies and maintain these organizations for any length of time. The lethargy of the workers coupled with
the active opposition of the employers armed with tremendous economic
power and the formidable weapons of the blacklist and the lockout
made theirs an unrewarding task.

LABOR ORGANIZATION: 1800-1828

Today organized labor in America is an instrument of enormous
economic power and political significance. It numbers its adherents
by the millions, and its treasuries are bulging with funds. Yet the roots

[25] The *Mechanic's Free Press*, June 14, 1828.
[26] The *Pennsylvanian*, April 4, 1835.
[27] The *National Trades' Union*, November 28, 1835.

of these powerful labor unions can be tracked back to the primitive societies of the cordwainers and printers of Pennsylvania who fought some of the earliest battles of American labor. The cordwainers of Philadelphia were the first of the American wage earners to establish a permanent organization for the purpose of maintaining or advancing their wages. To these men fell the task of formulating the objectives and devising the means by which they could most effectively advance their own interests. Almost instinctively when the pressures became too great they banded together into trade societies whose primary aim was to obtain unity of action among the workmen in that trade.

These trade unions in the first three decades of the nineteenth century were small local organizations whose membership hardly numbered one hundred, and whose jurisdiction extended only to the men of the particular trade in the immediate locality. According to one estimate, the Federal Society of Journeymen Cordwainers of Philadelphia which was established in 1794, had five years later "upwards of one hundred" members.[28] There is no evidence to suggest that its membership had increased appreciably before the 1830's. The Pittsburgh cordwainers had organized into a trade union sometime in 1809, but no information is available as to the number who were attracted to it. From the notices which appeared in the Chester County newspapers it was apparent that the cordwainers in that area were organized, but there is no information as to the size of that body.[29]

The only other group of wage earners to maintain an organization between strikes in the opening decades of the nineteenth century were the printers of Philadelphia. In 1802, the printers of that city had

---

[28] Commons, *Documentary History*, III, p. 75.

[29] The following notice appeared in the *Downingtown American Republican*, December 29, 1812.

TO CORDWAINERS

All persons who think proper, are requested to attend a meeting of a society now forming for fixing uniformity in prices—the meetings to be held at the house of Abraham Kindig, in Brandywine township, Chester County, at 1 o'clock, on the first day of January next, by order of the society.

Signed—Benjamin Worrell, Thomas Pylis.

On August 31, 1813 this notice was printed in the *American Republican*.

TAKE NOTICE

The Society of Cordwainers and others of the Craft, are requested to attend an adjourned meeting at the house of Jacob Hauer, in Brandywine township, on the 11th of September next, at 2 o'clock, P.M.

Signed—James Cardell, Sec'ry.

organized the Philadelphia Typographical Society.[30]   At its inception the membership numbered fifty-five.   In 1810, there were 119 members in good standing but by the end of that year its ranks had been reduced to fifty-five.[31]   Its membership fluctuated in subsequent years, but it never again reached the high point which it had attained in 1809.

To insure the effectiveness of these organizations, their constitutions generally specified that the members not only had to pay an initiation fee and monthly dues, but they had to take an oath swearing to uphold the principles of the organization.   The initiation fee of the Philadelphia Cordwainers' Society was eleven pence.[32]   Monthly dues were collected and fines were imposed on those who violated the rules of this union.   Regular attendance was required at the meetings, and according to one who had been a member of the Society, a fine of twenty-five cents was imposed for each absence.[33]   Four consecutive absences usually resulted in expulsion.   For those who committed the more serious offense of working below the list prepared by the Union, or scabbing, the penalty was far more severe.   Expulsion was automatic and a scab would not be reinstated until he had paid a heavy fine.[34]

The practices of the Pittsburgh cordwainers were similar to those of the Philadelphia organization. An initiation fee of fifty cents was required and the monthly dues were twenty-five cents.[35]   An oath was required of all the members which clearly indicated the means by which it hoped to accomplish its aims.   These journeymen shoemakers were required to swear that they would not "work for any employer who did not give the wages and beside any journeymen who did not get the wages."[36]   This union had a progressive system of fines for penalizing absentee members.   Those not present at the first meeting were charged twelve and a half cents.   If absent from the second, the fine was doubled; and for the third offense they were expelled from the

[30] Ethelbert Stewart, *Documentary History of the Early Organizations of Printers* (Indianapolis, 1907), p. 89. See George E. Barnett, "The Printers: A Study in American Trade Unionism," in the *American Economic Association Quarterly*, Third Series, vol. 10, No. 3, p. 4.

[31] Stewart, *op. cit.*, pp. 31, 38; Barnett, *op. cit.*, pp. 9, 10.

[32] Commons, *Documentary History*, III, p. 92.

[33] Commons, *Documentary History*, III, p. 84.

[34] *Ibid.*, III, pp. 94, 95.

[35] *Ibid.*, IV, p. 35.

[36] *Ibid.*, p. 26.

union unless they paid three dollars.[37]   But apparently the Pittsburgh cordwainers had no effective means for punishing scabs, for, as one member who had determined to leave the organization stated, its "laws were so ameliorated that any member might work without belonging to the society."[38]

If the fees were any criteria, the printers' society was a far more exclusive organization than that of the cordwainers.   In 1802, when the society was first organized, the initiation fee was one dollar.   By 1807, it had been raised to four dollars and three years later it was set at five dollars.[39]   The monthly dues at the inception of this society were twenty-five cents.[40]   The penalty for working below the union scale of prices was expulsion and the same punishment was meted out to those who undertook to instruct in the art of printing any person who had attained the age of eighteen.[41]   A five dollar fine was imposed on those individuals who procured positions for non-members in preference to members of the society out of employment.

Since the primary purpose of these early organizations of wage earners was to maintain or advance wages, it was necessary for them to develop or to utilize those trade practices which would most effectively enable them to accomplish these ends.   Collective bargaining, shortly after the formation of the trade unions, became the accepted mode for formulating the wage contract.   At first the men would agree on a wage scale and then would pledge themselves not to work for any employers who paid less or with any journeymen who worked for less.[42] The first attempt at collective bargaining in the modern sense of the word was made in 1799 when the journeymen shoemakers of Philadelphia called for a conference with their employers to negotiate the differences which beset their trade.   The men were locked out for having refused to accept a reduction of their wages.[43]   Although David Saposs in the *History of Labour in the United States* dogmatically asserts that "it [collective bargaining] was not due, as it generally imagined, to the enormous economic power exercised by the employer, or because

---

[37] *Ibid.*, p. 31.

[38] *Ibid.*

[39] Stewart, *op. cit.*, Appendix A, No. 1, p. 91; pp. 13, 28. See Barnett, *op. cit.*, p. ii.

[40] Stewart, *op. cit.*, Appendix A, No. 1, p. 91.

[41] *Ibid.*, pp. 13, 15.

[42] Commons, *Documentary History*, IV, pp. 25, 26, 30, 43.

[43] *Ibid.*, III, pp. 113-114. See Commons, *History of Labour*, I, p. 122.

of superior bargaining ability," [44] the facts would suggest otherwise. The employers had the initiative in this struggle. It was they who ordered the reduction in wages which brought on the strike, and according to the testimony of one of them, "the society of masters, in 1798 or 1799, entered into a kind of resolve not to employ any body men, in order to break them up altogether, root and branch. . . ." It would seem to place too much credence on coincidence alone to explain the resort to collective bargaining by the journeymen cordwainers at this time, and it would seem far more probable that the reason for their action was to match the combined strength of the employing shoemakers. The lawyer for the Pittsburgh cordwainers justified their organization because "it enables them to meet the employers on a footing of equality." [45]

The printers at first, like the cordwainers, utilized a primitive form of collective bargaining, that is, sending committees to the individual employers with the union's price list to formulate the wage bargain. In 1807, a committee was appointed by the Philadelphia Typographical Society "to inquire into the present state of the art, and whether any and what abuses are practiced, and what regulations it may be expedient on the part of the society to adopt, to check and do away with all such abuses and irregular practices hostile to the interests and well-being of its members. . . ." In its report, the committee concluded that "in order to maintain that harmony which as yet happily exists between the society and the master printers, it would be expedient to hold a conference with them on the subject, and make such regulations in the prices as the nature of the times may require. . . ." [46] They had made a clear-cut plea for collective bargaining as the best mode for establishing the working conditions in that trade.

Then as now, the employers were reluctant to accede immediately to the demands of the journeymen and a strike was often the result. [47] Effective collective bargaining without a trade union is unthinkable. For this reason these early trade societies attempted to maintain a union if not a closed shop, and if necessary were willing to make extensive use of the boycott to accomplish this end. Those thrown out of work for supporting the articles of the trade union were generally entitled to some type of financial support. Although the Philadelphia

---

[44] Commons, *History of Labour*, I, p. 121; *Documentary History*, III, p. 127.

[45] Commons, *Documentary History*, IV, p. 68.

[46] Stewart, *op. cit.*, p. 14.

[47] This aspect of the study is discussed more fully in a subsequent chapter.

Cordwainers' Society made no specific provision for strike benefits, it allowed fifty cents a week for each member of a family in distress.[48] The Pittsburgh cordwainers had "no fixed allowance for poor members on a turn-out," but when members were distressed for market money they "were allowed to take three or four dollars out of the box." [49] The printers on the other hand gave out strike benefits in the form of a loan and the society assumed collective responsibility only after it was ascertained that the individual could not repay the money given him.[50] None of these early societies, with the exception of the New York cordwainers, felt the need for a permanent strike fund.[51]

While the primary aim of these early protective associations of labor was, as has been stated, to maintain or advance wages, some of them combined sick and death benefits with their purely trade purposes. Although the Philadelphia shoemakers had no provision in their constitution for this purpose, their society did occasionally help members in distress.[52] A member of Pittsburgh Cordwainers' Society stated that their union was a beneficial organization. "It is a benevolent society," this union man declared. "If a member is sick, he has three dollars a week." [53]

From the very beginning the Philadelphia Typographical Society was a benevolent as well as a trade organization. Its constitution stipulated that once its funds had exceeded one hundred dollars, "the board of directors may award such sums to sickly and distressed members, their widows and children, as to them may seem meet and proper; provided, that such sum shall not exceed $3 per week." Ten dollars was allowed for the funeral expenses of deceased members.[54] After 1810, although this organization still retained its trade regulating functions, its beneficial activities were its main attraction.[55]

---

[48] Commons, *Documentary History*, III, p. 83, 91.

[49] *Ibid.*, IV, p. 34.

[50] Stewart, *op. cit.*, Appendix A, No. 1, pp. 91-92; Commons, *History of Labour*, I, p. 123.

[51] See Commons, *History of Labour*, I, p. 124.

[52] Commons, *Documentary History*, III, p. 120.

[53] *Ibid.*, IV, p. 34.

[54] Stewart, *op. cit.*, pp. 91, 92.

[55] See Barnett, *op. cit.*, p. 10. At an anniversary meeting of the Philadelphia Typographical Society, it was said by one of the speakers that "Time has proved the great utility of Benevolent institutions, and among the numerous associations of this kind, we may congratulate ourselves as not being the least efficient in this grand design and intention of such bodies." Quoted in The *Aurora and General Advertiser*, Nov. 13, 1819.

None of the other trades in these early years of the nineteenth century matched the efforts of the cordwainers and printers to improve their wages. Their struggles were spasmodic and their organizations were ephemeral. Even the printers and the cordwainers had not as yet been able to cope with the large problems associated with the labor movement. Their organizations were only local in scope and only a few fleeting gestures were made toward securing cooperation on a broader basis. The printers corresponded occasionally with Typographical Societies in other cities on trade matters but as yet had not felt the need for a permanent organization to regulate and coordinate their activities.[56] Although it is known that the cordwainers' societies were aware of the existence of each other, there is no evidence to suggest that they corresponded with one another. At a meeting of the Pittsburgh cordwainers in June 1814, it was resolved "to write to the societies in Baltimore and Philadelphia, and to agree with them not to receive any members of their societies, unless they produced certificates of belonging to their societies, and then if he came to the place without one, they would not work with him." [57] The house carpenters of the West End of Chester County in this same year took the initiative in a drive for uniform prices for the wage earners of that trade in Chester and Lancaster counties. A call was made for [58]

> every member of [the] craft in the following townships, in Chester and Lancaster Counties, be requested to meet the 5th of March next, at 2 o'clock, P.M. in the manner following, to choose delegates, viz: Upper and Lower Oxford, East and West Fallowfield . . . Little Britain . . . Colerain, and Bart. . . .

It was further suggested that

> one delegate be chosen, at each of the aforementioned places, to meet on Friday following, being the 11th of March next, at Capt. James Hayes' tavern at 10 o'clock, A.M. to regulate and establish the prices aforesaid.

The reasons for the collapse of these early trade unions are not readily discernible. Although the early conspiracy trials of the cordwainers might have dampened the ardor of some working shoemakers for union, they were not instrumental in destroying this sentiment al-

[56] Commons, *History of Labour*, I, p. 127.

[57] Commons, *Documentary History*, IV, p. 31.

[58] The *American Republican*, February 15, 1814.

together.[59] One authority stated that it was the depression of 1819 which "forced the journeymen societies either to disband or to subordinate their economic activities." The cordwainers' organizations were specifically singled out as "victims of the industrial crisis." [60] Ethelbert Stewart attributed the decline of the printers' societies to the "free membership" clause in their constitutions.[61] But Barnett advanced the most plausible explanation for the decline of these early typographical unions. "The real reason for the relinquishment by the societies of their trade aims . . . was the lack of support from the journeymen printers as a whole," contended Barnett.[62] Undoubtedly, all these factors combined speeded the downfall or the conversion of these early trade societies into beneficial organizations.

---

[59] For a penetrating discussion of the first conspiracy trial of the journeymen cordwainers of Philadelphia see Walter Nelles, "The First American Labor Case," *Yale Law Journal* (1931), vol. XLI, pp. 165-200. See also G. G. Groat, *Attitude of American Courts in Labor Cases* (New York, 1911), p. 57 ff.

[60] Commons, *History of Labour*, I, p. 135.

[61] Stewart, *op. cit.*, pp. 8, 9.

[62] Barnett, *op. cit.*, p. 9.

V

LABOR ORGANIZATION DURING THE AGE OF JACKSON

THE RETURN of prosperity in the decade of the 1820's saw a resurgence of trade union activity, and the real beginnings of a labor movement in the United States. The period is characterized not only by the tremendous increase in labor strife and unrest but also by the appearance of stable organizations in numerous trades, such as, the carpenters, the tailors, the hatters, the bricklayers, the house painters, the stone cutters, the cabinet makers, the cordwainers and others. Moreover many of these trade unions participated in the founding of the city central which marked the beginning of the labor movement not only in Pennsylvania but in the United States.[1] All trade union activity prior to this time had been conducted by separate trade societies and as John R. Commons so aptly stated, "an isolated society might create a disturbance—not until it united with others could it create a labor movement."[2]

Spurred on by the democratic forces which were making themselves felt throughout the country at this time, the wage earners of Pennsylvania, keenly aware of their importance both as a political and an economic force and convinced that their oppressions were great and constantly increasing, played an active and leading part in urging the working men to present a common front in their struggle to right these wrongs.

In 1827, the drive of the building trades' workmen in Philadelphia for the ten-hour day resulted in the formation of the Mechanics' Union of Trade Associations, the first coordinated movement of different trades in the United States.[3] For the first time these workers evinced an awareness of the universal nature of their problems, and a realization that these could only be solved through their united efforts. "It has often been necessary for those who feel aggrieved, to associate, for the purpose of affording to each other mutual protection from oppres-

---

[1] See George E. McNeill, The *Labor Movement, the Problem of Today* (New York, 1887), pp. 71, 72; Richard T. Ely, *The Labor Movement in America* (London, 1890), p. 3; Commons, *History of Labour*, I, pp. 156, 169, 185.

[2] Commons, *Documentary History*, V, p. 21.

[3] The *Pennsylvanian*, April 5, 1836.

sion," asserted these pioneers of the labor movement, and in further justification of their action declared:[4]

> We, the journeymen Mechanics of the City and County of Philadelphia, conscious that our condition in society is lower than justice demands it should be, and feeling our inability, individually, to ward off from ourselves and families those numerous evils which result from an unequal and excessive accumulation of wealth and power into the hands of a few, are desirous of forming an Association, which shall avert as much as possible those evils which poverty and incessant toil have already inflicted, and which threaten ultimately to overwhelm and destroy us.

They made a vigorous protest against the economic and social inequalities which constantly plagued the workingmen, and revealed that they were motivated in their actions by the most noble of purposes.[5]

> The real object, therefore, of this association [these trade unionists declared] is to avert, if possible, the desolating evils which must inevitably arise from a depreciation of the intrinsic value of human labour; to raise the mechanical and productive classes to that condition of true independence and equality which their practical skill and ingenuity, their immense utility to the nation and their growing intelligence are beginning imperiously to demand; to promote, equally, the happiness, prosperity and welfare of the whole community—to aid in conferring a due and full proportion of that invaluable promoter of happiness, leisure, upon all its useful members; and to assist, in conjunction with such other institutions of this nature as shall hereafter be formed throughout the union, in establishing a just balance of power, both mental, moral, political and scientific, between all the various classes and individuals which constitute society at large.

Their ambitions were lofty, they probably soared too high. These trade unionists had neither the experience nor a well-established organization to assist them in carrying out this grand design. The Mechanics' Union of Trade Associations in 1828 was composed of fifteen trade societies with an undetermined number of members. It obviously lacked a well-formulated program and disciplined membership, for, despite the fact that its constitution specifically forbade all political action, this organization dissipated its energies in forward-

---

[4] The *Mechanic's Free Press*, October 25, 1828, Preamble of the Mechanics' Union of Trade Associations, as reprinted in Commons, *Documentary History*, V, p. 84.

[5] *Ibid.*

ing the interests of the "Working Men's Party." William English, an ambitious and an untrustworthy trade union leader, recalled that "from that moment, as it [the Working Men's Party] advanced the Union retrograded and though at one time it embraced 15 societies, at the end of the year the number was reduced to four, and the Union adjourned *sine die*." Moreover there is no evidence to indicate that this organization ever supported a strike.[6]

While this first attempt of the wage earners of Pennsylvania to present a unified program of action failed, the separate trades maintained their organization and carried on a struggle for higher wages and shorter hours. The journeymen cordwainers apparently were organized throughout the State. In Philadelphia they were active, but suffering from organizational difficulties. Cognizant that the struggles of all wage earners were the same, the cordwainers met in the late winter of 1828 to devise some means of assisting the cotton spinners who were on strike.[7] During this same year notices appeared in the *Mechanic's Free Press* announcing meetings of the United Trade Society of Ladies Cordwainers.[8] But two years later the Philadelphia shoemakers were informed that "a meeting of the Journeymen Ladies Cordwainers will be held . . . for the purpose of forming a Trade Society," suggesting the possibility that the previous union had floundered with the Mechanic's Union of Trade Associations.[9] "It is hoped the Journeymen will generally attend, as union of action is necessary for the purpose of resisting oppression practised by the few, who enjoy every comfort at the expense of the many," counseled the organizers of this meeting.[10]

The constitution of this newly formed United Trade Society of Ladies Cordwainers did not make for a strong and effective labor organization. The most serious deficiency was the provisions respecting the finances of the union. No dues were to be collected from the members unless the funds of the organization were under thirty dollars. These funds were to be expended "for the purpose of defraying the necessary expenses, and for burying the deceased members" but no mention was made of money for the support of strike action. In addition, their constitution required a majority of two-thirds for the

---

[6] The *Man*, September 6, 1834.

[7] *Mechanic's Free Press*, December 20, 1828.

[8] *Ibid.*, April 19, 1828.

[9] *Ibid.*, February 20, 1830.

[10] *Ibid.*

regulation of wages.[11] A conspiracy trial for the journeymen shoemakers of Franklin County revealed that not only were these artisans organized, but that this Society corresponded with "similar societies in Pittsburgh, and other places, and that such societies existed in most of the towns." [12]

Organization was widespread among the building trades' workmen who led the movement for the ten-hour workday. The carpenters of Philadelphia and Pittsburgh were actively engaged in this struggle for the economic and social betterment of the working classes.[13] At Philadelphia, the bricklayers appealed to their employers to bargain collectively with them. This, they believed, was the most efficient means of resolving the differences between the two parties. It was resolved at a meeting of the journeymen bricklayers "that a committee of thirteen be appointed to solicit a call of a meeting of Master Bricklayers of Philadelphia in order that they may appoint a committee from their meeting to confer with one from this for the purpose of arranging matters to the satisfaction of both parties." [14] Along with the carpenters and bricklayers, the painters and glaziers had organized to resist any encroachments on their wage standards.[15]

The journeymen tailors of Philadelphia had been for many years organized into a trade society. So effective was their protective association that they found themselves in 1827 indicted and charged with "a conspiracy to raise their wages above the usual rate. . . ." [16] Whether the verdict of guilty which was found against the journeymen tailors was instrumental in smashing their union is not known, but we learn that two years later these wage earners are advised to "form into an association" since it is "the best means to prevent the monopoly of wealth by profits." [17]

---

[11] The *Mechanic's Free Press*, March 6, 1830.

[12] The *Pittsburgh Gazette*, January 12, 1830.

[13] The *Aurora and Franklin Gazette*, June 14, 1827; The *Mechanic's Free Press*, April 12, 1828; The *Norristown Herald*, Dec. 24, 1828; The *Allegheny Democrat and Farmers' and Mechanics' Advertiser*, March 24, 1829; The *Pittsburgh Gazette*, May 31, 1831; The *Statesman*, March 25, 1829.

[14] The *Democratic Press*, June 20, 1827.

[15] *Poulson's Daily American Advertiser*, Sept. 22, 1824; The *Democratic Press*, June 16, 1827.

[16] The *American Sentinel*, September 25, 1827.

[17] The *Mechanic's Free Press*, April 25, 1829, March 27, April 3, 1830. Edwin Witte, "Early American Labor Cases," *Yale Law Journal* (1926), vol. 35, p. 825 ff. These early cases Professor Witte says "did not turn upon the legality of the unions per se, but on the methods which they employed to gain their ends. But if combinations of workingmen to raise their wages were regarded as unlawful conspiracies, the effect was the same as if the unions themselves were regarded as unlawful."

A host of other trades were organized into trade societies at this time. The journeymen weavers had formed a union, and insisted that the principles on which it was founded would prove "advantageous to both the employer and the employed." [18] The journeymen cabinet makers were organized and so were the saddlers, harness makers and trimmers. [19] The journeymen tobacconists were organized, and the brushmakers, the millwrights and steam engine builders were urged to attend a meeting "to consider and adopt a regular system through the Trade." [20]

This was the germinating period of the early American trade union movement and the decades of the 1830's were to see its fruition. The events in the latter years of the previous decade were suggestive of the changes which were to take place. Increased strife, the intensification of the class struggle, and the brief essay of the wage earners of Philadelphia to form a central union of all trades was indicative of the growth which the labor movement had undergone. Even the disastrous flirtation with politics revealed an enlargement in the ideas of the workers. But more important were the changes which were taking place within the old labor organizations. Formerly the tendency had been for labor to band together into fraternal organizations to protect their members against sickness and distress. Now the tendency was for these benevolent institutions to transform themselves into trade regulating bodies, and although many of them still retained their benefit purposes, these were subordinated to the trade functions of these organizations. The Philadelphia Typographical Society, which in 1810 had been incorporated as a benevolent institution, was in 1833 supplanted by the Philadelphia Typographical Association whose "primary and paramount intention" was "the determination and support of adequate wages for journeymen printers." [21] A similar transformation converted the Pennsylvania Society of Journeymen Cabinet-Makers into a trade regulating organization. [22]

The appearance of the factory operatives as an articulate and organized force was a measure of the growth of the labor movement in Pennsylvania. They gave to the trade union movement two of its

[18] The *Mechanic's Free Press*, April 3, 1830.

[19] *Ibid.*, January 25, May 2, 1829.

[20] *Ibid.*, February 14, 1829; March 27, 1830.

[21] See Barnett, *op. cit.;* also see The *National Trades' Union*, September 6, 1834; The *National Laborer*, Nov. 19, 1836.

[22] Commons, *History of Labour*, I, pp. 336-337.

most energetic and forceful leaders, John Ferral and William Gilmore.[23] The latter was still active in 1839 trying to keep alive the sentiment for union when most of the other leaders were silent and the movement was suffering from the debilitating effects of the great depression.[24]

The impetus for the great trade union movement of the 1830's appears to have come from these oppressed factory workers. An attempted twenty per cent reduction of their wages in the summer of 1833 convinced them of the vulnerability of their position and they resolved that a "permanent union be established amongst them." [25] Inexperienced in organizational activity and ignorant of trade union rules, they addressed an appeal to the different trade unions throughout the United States requesting information concerning their regulations.[26] This appeal resulted in the formation of the ambitious but short-lived "Trades Union of Pennsylvania." In an address to the working people of Manayunk these operatives explained what motivated them in this action.[27]

> We have long suffered the evils of being divided in our
> sentiments, but the universal oppression that we now all
> feel, have roused us to a sense of our oppressed condition,
> and we are determined to be oppressed no longer.

This organization was founded in September 1833, and went out of existence in December of that year. It was composed of delegates from Blockley, Gulf-Mills, Brandywine, Pikecreek, Roseville, Haddington, Haverford, Norristown and Manayunk, all manufacturing towns. It was formed "for the purpose of mutual support in endeavouring to ameliorate the condition of the working classes in general" and it was hoped that the members while in pursuit of these objects would "carefully avoid all political questions whatever." [28] At its last meeting in December 1833, a committee of three was "appointed to wait upon the Mechanic's Union of the city and county of Philadelphia . . . to suggest to them the propriety of uniting with us for the general weal of the *Farmers, Mechanics* and other *Working-Men* of Pennsylvania." [29] This is the last we hear of this premature effort of the factory hands to

---

[23] The *Pennsylvanian*, August 28, December 24, 1833.

[24] The *Public Ledger*, January 26, 1839.

[25] The *Pennsylvanian*, Aug. 22, 1833; Commons, *Documentary History*, V, p. 325.

[26] The *Pennsylvanian*, August 28, 1833.

[27] *Ibid.*

[28] *Ibid.*, December 24, 1833.

[29] The *Pennsylvanian*, Dec. 24, 1833; The *Germantown Telegraph*, November 27, 1835.

found a consolidated trade union movement, and some of the member unions and the leaders of this movement were absorbed into the Mechanic's Union of Philadelphia City and County.

The realization of the need for union was making itself felt among many of the organized trades in Philadelphia. "That state of feebleness . . . that in the first case suggests a union of members of a trade into Societies," the mechanics and working men of Philadelphia were told, "suggests also, in the second, a union of the Trade Societies which should be carried into effect throughout the United States." [30] The subject was broached in October 1833, and in November representatives from the tailors', the bookbinders' and the cordwainers' societies met for the "purpose of considering the propriety of forming a general trades union . . . on a similar basis to those already in existence in New York and Baltimore." It was further resolved at this meeting "that the several Trade Societies now in existence, be respectfully requested to appoint three delegates to meet this convention at its meeting; and those trades not having societies be solicited to form themselves as soon as practicable, and appoint delegates to meet as above." [31] These three societies at this time comprised "less than four hundred members." [32]

This inauspicious start signalled the launching of the most successful trade union movement of Pennsylvania wage earners in the first half of the nineteenth century. Not only did the Trades' Union of the City and County of Philadelphia grow in strength and numbers, but the component members of this Society experienced a corresponding increase in adherents. The *Philadelphia Trades' Union*, the organ of this newly formed Society, stated that "since it has been discovered that its success was certain, almost every trade belonging to it has received a more rapid increase of members than formerly, and the mechanics of several trades who could not confide in societies depending upon their individual resources, have united and joined it." [33] It was not until the spring of 1834 that this organization went into active operation. At its first meeting in March of that year after a constitution had been

---

[30] The *Pennsylvanian*, January 9, 1834, as reprinted in Commons, *Documentary History*, V, p. 339.

[31] *Hazard's Register of Pennsylvania*, XII, Nov. 1833, p. 351; The *Pennsylvanian*, March 31, 1836.

[32] The *Pennsylvanian*, March 31, 1836.

[33] From The *Philadelphia Trades' Union* as quoted in The *Man*, Mar. 10, 1834.

adopted, seventeen separate trade unions were represented.[34] These delegates spoke for approximately 1500 to 2500 members. In the summer of the following year, the Trades' Union was composed of twenty-three societies which had a combined membership of seven thousand.[35] Two years later "upwards of Fifty Societies, comprising more than Ten Thousand Members" made up the Trades' Union of the City and County of Philadelphia.[36]

For a moment it seemed that a new era for labor had dawned. Trade unions grew in strength and aggressiveness, and societies appeared for the first time among the common laborers, the female workers, the "segar" makers and a host of other trades. The desire for higher wages and shorter hours embraced most of the wage earners and it was not long before they realized that the most efficacious means of fulfilling their desires was to organize into trade societies.

The most persistent and in some ways the most successful champions of the idea of union were the journeymen cordwainers. "If we do not attempt to remedy our condition, ourselves, no one will do it for us," the working shoemakers of Philadelphia were warned. "So long as we continue separate and disunited we can accomplish nothing," but "IN UNION THERE IS STRENGTH," the cordwainers were reminded.[37] Apparently the advice was heeded for the United Beneficial Society of Journeymen Cordwainers (Men's Branch) which in the spring of 1835 had only two hundred members was reported in the fall of 1836 to have a membership of eight hundred.[38] They were especially active in promoting the cause of the Trades' Union. At a meeting of these artisans it was resolved that "Trades' Unions are the sheet anchor of our

[34] The *Pennsylvanian*, March 13, 1834. The following trade unions sent delegates: United Beneficial Society of Journeymen Cordwainers (Men's branch); Philadelphia Benevolent and Trade Society of Tailors; Bookbinders Trade Society; United Benevolent Trade Society of Journeymen Cordwainers (Ladies Branch); Journeymen Carpenters' Benevolent Association; Journeymen Brushmakers' Society; Association of Journeymen Shell Comb makers; Blockley and Haverford Association; Journeymen Hatters' Association; Tobacconists' Trade Society; Typographical Association; Association of Moulders; Association of Journeymen Stone Cutters; Journeymen Umbrella Makers' Society; Association of Leather Dressers, No. 1; Association of Leather Dressers, No. 2; and Journeymen Saddle and Harness Makers' Society. See The *Man*, March 17, 1834; and The *National Trades' Union*, Sept. 6, 1834.

[35] The *Pennsylvanian*, June 4, 1835.

[36] *Ibid.*, March 31, 1836; The *National Laborer*, April 2, 1836.

[37] The *Pennsylvanian*, April 4, 1835.

[38] The *Pennsylvanian*, April 4, 1835; The *National Laborer*, Oct. 29, 1835.

hopes, that they deserve, and shall receive, our care and support; and that we earnestly recommend all trades that have not yet formed societies, to do so immediately, and become members of Trades' Unions —believing, as we do, that through their instrumentality every trade will be able, in a short time to redress their wrongs, and redeem the character of mechanics." [39]

The movement caught like wildfire. Not only were the workers of the skilled professions drawn into it but the unskilled and the female workers, the most oppressed of all the wage earners, resorted to organized activity as the only effective means to combat the aggressions of their employers. The weavers in 1833 united "under the designation of the Handloom Weavers' Association of the City and County of Philadelphia." [40] They too felt that the Trades' Union was the only effective means for advancing the cause of the working men. These handloom weavers deemed it their "duty to join in a bond of union with our fellow workingmen, that we may by our united effort stay the power of capital in its unhallowed attempts to enslave the useful classes of our community." [41] The seamstresses organized in that same year, and the first federation of women workers in America, the Female Improvement Society of the City and County of Philadelphia, was founded in 1835. Seamstresses, tailoresses, binders, milliners, folders, mantua makers and stock makers were represented in it. Lists of prices were drawn up for the respective trades and their employers conceded without a strike.[42] In November 1836, it was reported that the female workers in Jameson's Power Loom Mill at Norristown, who had not been organized previously, "have since formed one in connection with the Trades' Union" which would suggest that that organization was doing more than just sympathizing with the plight of these workers.[43]

Since the primary purpose of these trade societies was to assist the wage earners in either pressing their wage and hour demands or in resisting all attempts by their employers to reduce their earnings, it was inevitable that the main function of the Trades' Union would be to

---

[39] The *United States Gazette*, April 25, 1835.

[40] The *Pennsylvanian*, May 15, 1835.

[41] *Ibid.*

[42] "Labor Troubles in Pennsylvania," in *Pennsylvanian Bureau of Industrial Statistics*, III, p. 265.

[43] The *National Laborer*, Nov. 5, 1836. See John B. Andrews and W. Bliss, *History of Women in Trade Unions*, Senate Document, No. 645, 61st Congress, 2d Session (Washington, 1911), p. 45.

give material assistance to the wage earners when conflict arose in their pursuit of these ends. Article XVI of the constitution of the Trades' Union of the City and County of Philadelphia subtitled "Aggression, Hours and Wages" made specific provision for this purpose.[44]

> Any society, [section 1 of this article stipulated] wishing to repel aggression, or desirous of Striking for Hours or Wages, shall give written notice of the same, through their proper officers, to the President of the Union, who shall immediately direct the Secretary to call a Special Meeting, if no stated meeting should occur before said Special Meeting could be called, when the vote of two-thirds of the Societies present shall be requisite to the granting of pecuniary aid to any such represented society.

It further provided that

> no society shall be entitled to pecuniary aid from the Union until it has been represented in the same for the space of six months, and complied with all other constitutional requisitions.

Without adequate funds this article would have been meaningless. It was therefore required of every society represented in the Trades' Union to pay into its treasury six and a quarter cents for each member on admission, each society was to pay two months dues in advance.[45] As one ardent advocate of the Trades' Union expressed it, "for this trifling assessment, each man is protected from the rapacity of the greedy employer, and sure of the support and the protection of nearly every mechanic in Philadelphia." [46] To substantiate his argument, this same individual declared that "within the last six months more than one half of the Societies in the Union have struck, and no instance is known where a Society has struck, under the sanction of the Union, and failed in that strike." [47] Its monthly receipts at this time ranged from four to five hundred dollars.

The year 1836 opened auspiciously for the trade union movement of Pennsylvania. Special funds poured into the treasury of the Trades' Union to supplement its regular revenues to support those members on strike. The largest single contribution came from the journeymen

[44] Constitution of the Philadelphia Trades' Union is to be found on the cover of The *National Laborer.*
[45] *Constitution of the Philadelphia Trades' Union,* Art. XIV.
[46] The *Pennsylvanian,* February 9, 1836.
[47] *Ibid.*

cordwainers working on men's shoes. At a special meeting in March of that year they resolved that [48]

> with a view to lend a helping hand in these days of trial, each member of this Society contribute immediately the sum fifty cents (making nearly $400) and that a further contribution of 12½ cents per week, for four weeks, be collected from each member, and that after that time 12 cents per month for each member of this Society.

The marble laborers too had decided "to pay for each member twelve and a half cents per week into the funds of the Union." And the shell comb makers decided to pay ten cents per week for each member.[49] The hatters not only withdrew their members on strike "from the support of the Union" but reported that "each and every member had agreed to pay weekly into the funds, twelve and one half cents." [50]

Despite these apparent signs of health and vigor, the Trades' Union of Philadelphia had to combat the destructive effects of internal dissension and the stout resistance of the employer groups who felt that they were being victimized by this organization. Its success was marked by overorganization and the appearance of jurisdictional disputes between allied trades. In June, the horseshoers applied for admission into the Trades' Union, but the journeymen blacksmith's society objected. The Trades' Union appointed a committee "to ascertain if a reconciliation could be affected between the two societies. . . ." A month later the committee reported that it could not agree. A minority and a majority report was made, "both lengthy, and giving rise to considerable debate." The horseshoers finally withdrew their application.[51] A dispute arose at this same time between the Hand Loom Weavers, Nos. 1 and 2, and it was recommended that a committee of five from each society be appointed "for the purpose of arranging their difficulties amicably in such manner as will eventually subserve the interests of both." [52] Late in July the committee appointed, "presented a very favorable report" but that is all that is known of the differences between these two organizations.[53] The most prolonged jurisdictional dispute was between the Leather Dressers Societies Nos. 1 and 2. In May 1836, a report

[48] The *Pennsylvanian*, February 9, 1836.
[49] *Ibid.*
[50] *Ibid.*, March 15, 1836. See Commons, *History of Labour*, I, p. 376.
[51] The *National Laborer*, June 11, July 2, 23, 1836. See Commons, *History of Labour*, I, pp. 376, 377.
[52] The *National Laborer*, July 2, 1836.
[53] *Ibid.*, July 23, 1836.

which "recommended co-operation between the two Societies" was accepted, but in the late fall of that year it was evident that the differences between the two unions had not been composed.[54]

The employers, aroused by the successes of the Trades' Union, felt compelled to counter with organizations of their own. The master workmen in the following trades joined together in employers' associations to counteract the efforts of their employers: the Master Bookbinders, the Master Carpenters, the Master Cordwainers, and the Master Tailors. "One course alone remained for the employers—they have adopted it," explained the master bookbinders in justification for their action. The master carpenters of Philadelphia were even more explicit. We "find ourselves compelled in self-defence to form an Association for the purpose of putting down the combination called the Trades' Union."[55]

While the Trades' Union was struggling to ward off these threats, its most effective weapon, the strike, was being attacked by friend and foe alike. "I conceive strikes, in any shape or manner, to be the blunder in which you have fallen," contended a correspondent of the National Laborer.[56] A group of trade union leaders warned that the effect of strike action was to prejudice the public mind "to such a degree, that it is almost impossible to be undeceived. To depend solely on them for success in our undertakings, would be the height of impolicy."[57] While the trade union members and their sympathizers began to question the efficacy of strikes, the employers never doubted the disastrous consequences of them and had always condemned the use of the strike.

Neither disappointment with or opposition to the Trades' Union movement could stifle it completely. The Pittsburgh trade unions banded together and, at the beginning of 1837, the National Laborer reported that the "Pittsburgh Trades' Union is in a flourishing condition." Nine trades were represented in this organization; the coopers, two societies of cordwainers, tailors, carpenters, cabinet-makers, iron moulders, painters and black and white smiths.[58] And although the Miner's Journal in the spring of that year gloatingly reported a large meeting of working men in Philadelphia as being "the last gasp of the Trades' Union—which was gotten up by a few designing foreign radicals,

---

[54] Ibid., May 28, November 26, 1836.
[55] The Pennsylvanian, March 7, 1836.
[56] The National Laborer, November 12, 1836.
[57] Ibid., April 30, 1836.
[58] The National Laborer, January 21, 1837.

to plunder the honest, industrious and unsuspecting mechanic," this organization continued to function despite this premature obituary.[59] The last notice of the Philadelphia Trades' Union as far as this writer could determine was on April 8, 1839. In it the unions were reminded that a "stated meeting of the Trades' Union will be held on Tuesday." [60]

Not only was the widespread disappointment in the effectiveness of the Trades' Union reflected in the decline in its activity and its influence on the economic life of Philadelphia, but it was also evidenced in the switch from trade union activity to cooperation. The organization of cooperatives by wage earners to control the means of production was not a novel practice. The Philadelphia carpenters in 1791 as a result of an unsuccessful strike offered to "undertake buildings, or give designs, of *any work* in the line of our occupation, for any one who may think advisable to give us employment, at 25% below the current rate established by the Master Carpenters, and that we will give any reasonable security for the faithful execution of the work so entrusted to us to perform."[61] The cordwainers of Philadelphia, the victims of an adverse decision in a conspiracy trial, chose to become employers themselves rather than bow to the dictates of their prosecutors.[62]

But it was during the prosperous years in the middle 1830's that the movement had an attraction for a wide variety of trades. In 1833, the journeymen cabinet makers opened a wareroom, and by 1836 they had one of the largest furniture stores in the city.[63] The cordwainers working on ladies' shoes opened a cooperative "manufactory of their own." They took this action because "it [would] obviate the necessity of long and vexatious *strikes,* which your committee (with the utmost deference to the opinions of others) beg leave to represent as the most ineffectual means of advancing the interests of the workman when compared with the facilities which joint and conjoint stock would afford."[64] A proposal was brought forward at the national convention of cordwainers in New York in 1836 that "the best means to effect this object [creating a unity of feeling and concert of action among the

---

[59] The *Miner's Journal,* May 27, 1837.
[60] The *Public Ledger,* April 8, 1839. Commons states that the last notice was on August 14, 1838. Commons, *History of Labour,* I, p. 378.
[61] An address of the Journeymen Carpenters reprinted in *Poulson's American Daily Advertiser,* May 11, 1791, cited in Commons, *History of Labour,* I, p. 127.
[62] The *Aurora and General Advertiser,* April 28, 1806; Commons, *History of Labour,* I, p. 129.
[63] The *Pennsylvanian,* October 3, 1833; The *Public Ledger,* June 11, 1836.
[64] The *National Laborer,* April 30, 1836.

journeymen cordwainers of the United States] . . . to be by cooperation and association."[65] In November of that year, the shoemakers dissatisfied with the progress of their joint stock enterprise "resolved to reorganize it on a different plan, and instead of a *stock company*, to make it a Co-operative Union."[66] Even John Ferral, one of the most militant of the trade unionists, was to be found in the ranks of those "urging the immediate formation of Co-operative Societies."[67]

So widespread had the movement for cooperation become that the *National Laborer* took cognizance of it in its columns. This paper urged that "every trade society in Philadelphia adopt a resolution requiring of its members a weekly or monthly contribution to enable them to enter into business for themselves, and at the same time continue their dues to the Union, to be applied to the same end."[68] It was even suggested that the Union relinquish its trade regulating functions and "let the dues of the Union be continued, and reserved exclusively for the purpose of loaning to Trade Societies entering into Co-operation." The members of the Trades' Union were told that cooperation paved the way to freedom. "Persevere in Co-operation and you will not long endure the vulgar dominion of ignorance and profligacy."[69]

Another manifestation of the maturing of the labor movement in Pennsylvania and the United States was the formation of the National Trades' Union. Although the inspiration for the organization came from the General Trades' Union of New York, the Pennsylvania trade societies gave wholehearted support to the movement. Two leaders, William English and John Ferral, conspicuous in the trade union movement of the State, were to be found devoting much of their energies in behalf of the National Trades' Union. In the spring of 1834, the New York Society proposed "a National Union of the Trades," and the idea received warm support from the Philadelphia Trades' Union. "A National Union we think will be productive of the happiest results," the Philadelphia Union declared.[70]

When the convention convened in New York in August of 1834, Ely Moore of that city was called to the chair, and William English of

---

[65] *Ibid.*, March 26, 1836.

[66] *Ibid.*, May 14, September 17, November 26, 1836.

[67] *Ibid.*, November 26, 1836.

[68] The *National Laborer*, November 26, 1836.

[69] The *National Laborer*, Feb. 11, 1837; see Commons, *History of Labour*, I, pp. 466-468.

[70] From the *Philadelphia Trades' Union* as cited in The *Man*, May 12, 1834.

Philadelphia was appointed secretary.[71] The constitution as adopted
by these delegates revealed the provincialism of the labor movement.
The association was to "be styled the National Trades' Union of the
United States" and "this Union shall be composed of delegates from
the several Trades' Unions in the United States."[72] It was to be an
organization of local Trades' Unions each with its societies rather
than a union "of national 'trade' Unions each with its locals."[73] The
object of this organization "shall be to recommend such measures to
the various unions represented herein as may tend to advance the moral
and intellectual condition and pecuniary interests of the laboring
classes; promote the establishment of Trades' Unions in every section
of the United States."[74]

In the discussion of the numerous problems before the convention
and in the work of the committees, both John Ferral and William
English took an active and leading part. The former was chairman of
the committee which had the task of drafting resolutions expressing
the views of the National Trades' Union on the social, civil, and
intellectual condition of the laboring classes."[75] The original recom-
mendation creating this committee provided that it present the views
of the convention "on the social, civil, and political conditions of the
labouring classes," but this resulted in a vigorous controversy over the
word "politics." Michael Labarthe, representing the Association of
Journeymen Hatters of Philadelphia, "was in favor of striking out the
word political." William English, too was of the opinion that the
formation of a third party "would be . . . inimical to the interests of
the Unions." He recounted the disastrous effects of the "Working
Men's Party" and concluded that "the same cause . . . would produce
the same effects."[76] John Ferral, although "fully satisfied that the
working classes would never effectually remedy the evils under which
they were suffering until they carried their grievances to the polls, and
[made] them known by a judicious selection of law makers," agreed,
that if "the word political in the resolution was calculated to retard
the formation of . . . Union," to strike it out.[77] And it was he who

---

[71] The *Man*, August 26, 1834.
[72] The *Man*, September 2, 1834 as reprinted in Commons, *Documentary History*,
VI, pp. 224-225.
[73] Commons, *Documentary History*, V, p. 32.
[74] *Ibid.*
[75] *Ibid.*, pp. 204, 205.
[76] The *Man*, September 6, 1834.
[77] *Ibid.*

offered the conciliatory amendment substituting the word "intellectual" for "political" which ended the controversy.

The National Trades' Union at this time was little more than a debating society. The subject of education was discussed, and it was recognized that the condition of the female workers was of concern to it. But this organization was impotent to do more than make recommendations. Its officers had no authority over the constituent members and although a finance committee was created, no provision was made for the creation of a permanent fund to carry on the work of the Union.[78]

The National Trades' Union met again in the fall of the following year, and John Ferral of Philadelphia was elected president.[79] The subject of hours and wages figured prominently in the discussions of this convention. But the National Trades' Union remained primarily a society for agitation. No material changes were made in the constitution which would have strengthened it and given to its officers some authority over the member societies. To further the cause of the Trades' Unions throughout the United States it was recommended that a "Board of Commissioners for the Protection of Labour whose duty it shall be to take measures to form Trade Societies and Trades' Unions in all the cities and towns of the United States," be established. Since the National Union had no funds, the financing of the activities of the Board was to be undertaken by the various Trades' Unions.[80]

Philadelphia was the site of the convention of the National Trades' Union in 1836. John Ferral was active in these proceedings as he had been in the past. William English was present but not as a delegate. A special motion was put before the convention to allow him to sit in on the proceedings.[81] The questions of hours and wages; the problems of the factory workers; and the insidious competition of prison labor occupied much of the time of the convention. But the real measure of

---

[78] *Ibid.;* Commons, *Documentary History*, VI, p. 226.

[79] William English was not present at this convention and his absence might be explained by the fact that he was in all probability an employing shoemaker at this time. The *Pennsylvanian* on April 23, carried the following advertisement:

BOOTS, SHOES, AND PUMPS

William English begs leave to inform his friends and the public, that he has taken the store No. 31 North Fourth Street, (first door above Arch, east side) and intends carrying on the above business, in all its various branches.

[80] The *National Trades' Union*, October 10, 1835.

[81] The *National Laborer*, September 3, 1836.

progress and the maturity of the labor movement was reflected in the new constitution.

The most significant accomplishment of the '36 meeting was the adoption of a provision establishing a "national fund" by a levy of two cents per month from each of the members of the "different Unions and Trade Societies composing the National Union."[82] The dues were to be paid annually and any society which failed to pay forfeited its membership in the National Union. No longer was the Union a mere debating society. It was stipulated that "all acts or resolutions adopted by this Union, shall be equally binding on the different Unions and Societies who may ratify this Constitution." In addition the officers were given the "power to convene . . . [the Union] when considered necessary."[83] Since the Union remained throughout a federation of Trades' Unions, the disintegration of those societies was accompanied by the decline and disappearance of this organization.

The convention of 1836 was the last whose proceedings were published. The National Trades' Union met again in 1837 but its attendance had fallen considerably. Joseph Miller, the Secretary, let it be known that "the Workingmen and Citizens generally" were invited to attend its sittings.[84] And this is all that is known of this meeting.

Equally indicative of the tremendous advances being made by labor at this time were the premature efforts of some of the trade societies to organize national associations to coordinate the activities of the particular trade. Expanding markets accompanied by improved means of transportation brought wage earners of larger areas into competition with one another and impressed upon them the necessity of a national union. In this movement as in all the others, the wage earners of Pennsylvania played a leading and an aggressive role.

The first to attempt a national trade union were the cordwainers. Their trade was probably more than any other in the hands of the merchant capitalist, and it was they who first felt the withering effects of the competition of cheaper sources of labor on their wages. The cordwainers of Philadelphia in the summer of 1835 complained that the employing shoemakers were "preparing materials (in this city) in order to send them into the towns of the Eastern states (where living and labor were cheaper, and workmanship not so good) to get the same made into shoes, then to be brought here and sold for Philadelphia

---

[82] *Ibid.*

[83] The *National Laborer*, November 5, 1836.

[84] The *Public Ledger*, May 4, 1837.

manufacture . . .", in order to evade the demands of the journeymen.[85] They grumbled about the importation of French shoes and declared that this was a factor causing their impoverishment.[86] Other sources of cheap labor, apprentices and prison labor, threatened the wage standards and the bargaining position of the working shoemakers. The Pittsburgh cordwainers were among the first to prescribe certain types of work on which apprentice labor could not be employed, and they were among the first to encourage the formulation of a general set of rules applicable to all journeymen cordwainers. It was they who proposed that the Philadelphia and Baltimore societies adopt the "Union card" as a method of distinguishing fair from foul journeymen.[87]

But the first concrete steps toward the formation of a national organization of cordwainers were taken in the fall of 1835 after the convention of the National Trades' Union. The Philadelphia shoemakers had resolved not to receive any "Journeymen, as members of our Society who come from places where Societies with whom we have a correspondence are situated, unless they produce a certificate from such a Society." The New York cordwainers concurred in this action. And on the last day of the convention, delegates from the various cordwainers' unions met and agreed "to endeavor to form a general Union of the Cordwainers throughout the United States.[88]

In March of the following year, the first national convention of this trade was held in New York. John Caney, of Philadelphia, presided as chairman. Pennsylvania was well represented at this first national assembly of cordwainers. In addition to representatives from the two Philadelphia unions, there were delegates from the Easton, the Columbia and the Lancaster cordwainers' societies. They were all extremely active in the deliberations of the convention and in the various committees which had been set up. William English was appointed to the committee to draft rules of order for governing the convention, and was also on the committee "to draft a plan of co-operation among the various Societies of Cordwainers of the United States, with a view of sustaining each other in all strikes within their respective limits."[89]

---

[85] The *Pennsylvanian*, June 20, 1835.
[86] *Ibid.*, April 18, 1836.
[87] Commons, *Documentary History*, IV, p. 3.
[88] The *National Trades' Union*, October 10, 1835, printed in Commons, *Documentary History*, VI, pp. 314, 315. See also Commons, *History of Labour*, I, p. 449.
[89] The *National Trades' Union*, Mar. 26, 1836, reprinted in Commons, *Documentary History*, VI, p. 217.

It was he who offered the resolution which was to be the most important achievement of the convention. He proposed that a special committee be established to formulate "a standard bill of wages for the societies represented in this Convention."[90] After reading the proceedings of this first national convention of journeymen cordwainers one must conclude that it was very much dominated by the Philadelphia delegation.

Other trades soon followed the path of the cordwainers. The Journeymen House Carpenters Association of the City and County of Philadelphia took the initiative in proposing a national convention of the workingmen in that trade. Delegates from Pittsburgh and Philadelphia were in attendance in addition to representatives from Albany, Baltimore and Washington. Like the cordwainers they urged that "there should be a corresponding uniformity of prices throughout the different towns, villages, and cities in the United States." Apart from this plea for a standard wage, and a plea for the ten-hour day, little was accomplished at this convention. They decided to meet again in the spring of 1837 in Baltimore but whether this convention was held is not known.[91]

At the same time that the carpenters met, the handloom weavers assembled at Philadelphia. They too felt that it was necessary "to fix the standard of prices to be paid for the various fabrics of Hand Loom Weaving throughout the United States."[92] But the deliberations of these wage earners have been lost and nothing is known of the actions proposed at this convention.

The printers, too, made a short-lived attempt to establish a National Typographical Association. They sought an organization which would better protect their trade from the encroachments of the merchant capitalist and from the widespread use of apprentice and semi-skilled labor. The inspiration for the movement came from the Franklin Society of Cincinnati.[93] Washington was the locale of its first convention. Delegates from Philadelphia and Harrisburg were present, but the representative from the printers' society of Philadelphia was barred from the proceedings because he was on the "rat list." His local

---

[90] *Ibid.*

[91] The *National Laborer*, Nov. 19, 1836. See Commons, *History of Labour*, I, pp. 452, 455.

[92] The *National Laborer*, February 13, 1836.

[93] *National Trades' Union, October* 17, 1835, reprinted in Commons, *Documentary History*, VI, p. 343; Stewart, *op. cit.*, pp. 55, 56.

expelled him immediately when it learned of this.[94]   A second convention of the National Typographical Society was held in New York in the fall of 1837.   Both the Philadelphia and Harrisburg Typographical Societies were represented at this meeting.   It is impossible to gauge the extent or the importance of their activities at this meeting, but some very important measures were taken to strengthen the national union.   Article X of their constitution stipulated that each society was to contribute twenty percent of its annual receipts "to defray all expenses incurred by the association. . . . ."[95]   To prevent the employment of men who had not been properly bred to the trade, provision was made for a "Union Card."[96]   No convention was held in 1838, and although plans were made for one to be held in Pittsburgh in 1839, it is very doubtful that it ever took place.[97]

Thus by 1840 the Pennsylvania wage earners in their endeavor to protect their status and improve their bargaining position had traversed a full cycle.   In the beginning local trade societies, except for isolated strikes, constituted the only organized efforts of labor.   Later these trade societies united into Trades' Unions, which in the 1830's were the chief medium of labor activity.   It was also during the decade of the 1830's that an attempt was made to build national organizations, but with the Panic of 1837 these efforts came to naught.   And by 1840, at the close of this study, only local trade societies remained to protect the wage earners against any encroachments on their living standards.

---

[94] Stewart, *op. cit.*, p. 58.

[95] *Ibid.*, p. 62.   See *Public Ledger,* July 21, 1837.

[96] Stewart, *op. cit.*, p. 62.

[97] *Ibid.*, p. 63.

VI

THE SKILLED ARTISANS AND INDUSTRIAL STRIFE

IN LABOR'S STRUGGLE for economic and social equality often its most effective and always its most dramatic weapon is the strike. The strike is an old instrument, as old as history itself, for ameliorating working conditions and effecting a wage-bargain. In Colonial America, strikes and concerted action by combinations of workmen for enhancing their status were rare, almost unheard of. Scarcity of labor, the comparatively high wages, and colonial law combined to deter them from uniting for common action.[1] But after the War for Independence labor strife and unrest became increasingly more evident, and the Pennsylvania wage earners were among the first in America to seize upon the strike as a means for improving their lot.[2]

Why were the workers compelled to resort to such drastic means to accomplish their ends? Obviously, old methods and practices no longer sufficed. Expanding markets required more efficient productive techniques and the introduction of them produced profound changes in the attitudes and bargaining position of employer and employee. Export work, designed to fill the requirements of the western and southern markets, seriously jeopardized the position of the skilled artisans specializing in high quality work. Individual bargaining appeared incompatible with an expanding economy, and the wage earners felt that equity was not to be attained by such a practice. They turned to collective action for a solution and a strike was often the result.

In Pennsylvania, in the period under consideration, there were one hundred and thirty-eight strikes for varying reasons.[3] This enumera-

---

[1] See Richard B. Morris, *Government and Labor in Early America* (New York, 1946), pp. 44, 137.

[2] One of the foremost students of the American Labor Movement states that the first strike of wage earners in America occurred in Philadelphia in 1786. The printers in that city struck for a minimum wage of six dollars per week. See John R. Commons, *History of Labor in the United States* (New York, 1918), I, p. 25. A more recent student of the labor movement has pointed out that there was an earlier strike among the journeymen tailors of New York in 1768. See Morris, *op. cit.*, p. 196.

[3] See Appendix B listing all the strikes which this writer could uncover in the course of his investigation.

tion does not include the many riots among the canal workers which often resulted in the stoppage of work, considerable damage to property and injury to workers and civilians alike.

The majority of the strikes in the first quarter of the nineteenth century grew out of the demands of the workers for higher wages. Resistance to the aggressive designs of the employers in reducing wages accounted for only one or two of them.[4] Except for the efforts of the Philadelphia hatters in 1825 to standardize the wages in that industry, and the resolutions of the millwrights and mill workers championing the ten-hour day, higher wages was the main issue in all the strikes during the first twenty-five years of the nineteenth century.[5]

Of all the wage earners of Pennsylvania, the cordwainers were the most persistent and aggressive in the struggle for higher wages. They were the first to attract public notice and the first to be charged with criminal conspiracy for their organized activity. These articulate, intelligent shoemakers of Philadelphia have the honor of establishing the first trade union in the United States.

This trade union, the Federal Society of Journeymen Cordwainers, conducted in 1799, an obstinate strike of nine or ten weeks against the master shoemakers.[6] This dispute is of particular interest, for it possessed many characteristics of a modern labor disturbance. The problem of directing and financing the strike was one of major importance. How to maintain unbroken the ranks of the strikers, and to discipline the scabs was an urgent and persistent issue. And last, but not least, was the necessity of successfully resisting the efforts of the master workmen to break the strike.

From its inception in 1794 to the turn out of 1799 the Federal Society of Journeymen Cordwainers had wrung two or three successive increases from the employing shoemakers of Philadelphia. Alarmed by the aggressions and the victories of their journeymen, the master shoemakers organized in 1799 and ordered a reduction in wages. It was this action which caused the strike in that year.[7] "It was not a turn-

---

[4] See The *Allegheny Democrat*, January 18, 1825.

[5] The millwrights and mill workers of Philadelphia met one day in a tavern and passed resolutions favoring the ten-hour day. This was in the year 1822. Whether any further action was taken by them is not known. Cited in John B. McMaster, *History of the United States* (New York, 1900), V, p. 84.

[6] John R. Commons, *Documentary History of American Industrial Society* (Cleveland, 1910), III, p. 113.

[7] *Ibid.*

out on the part of the journeymen, but of the masters who were about to reduce the wages the journeymen then received," insisted James Geoghan, the President of the Society.   One of the master workmen corroborated this.   "That turn-out," revealed this master shoemaker, "was occasioned by the attempt of the masters to reduce the prices of the journeymen's wages."[8] About one hundred cordwainers were involved in this dispute.[9]

For ten long weeks these Philadelphia shoemakers resisted all efforts to reduce their wages, but they were finally compelled to accept a cut. Declining prices and economic distress undoubtedly influenced them in their decision since the united efforts of the master shoemakers to break the strike were of little success.   The master shoemakers had organized in 1798 or 1799 with the express purpose of destroying the journeymen cordwainers' society.   One employer divulged that the masters' organization was determined to blacklist all society men and destroy the journeymen's association.[10]   Handbills were circulated among the striking workers promising them protection from the trade union if they would return to their benches.   This effort proved futile. Only one or two men responded to this call; the others remained loyal to the strike.[11]

Industrial peace prevailed in all parts of Pennsylvania in the opening years of the 19th century.   An occasional shop was scabbed, but even these disputes were rare.   Unfortunately a far more serious disturbance plagued the American business man and wage earner alike. A depression, one of the worst that American business had experienced thus far, took place between the years 1801 and 1803.   Business failures were common; unemployment was rife.[12]   At its best it proved an unstable basis for industrial peace.

Resumption of war in Europe in 1803 meant increased business prosperity for America.   With the upsurge in business activity, conflict between labor and management broke out anew.   In the fall of that

---

[8] Commons, *Documentary History*, III, p. 127.

[9] *Ibid.*, p. 75.

[10] *Ibid.*, pp. 99, 127.

[11] *Ibid.*

[12] See Arthur H. Cole and W. B. Smith, *Fluctuations in American Business 1790-1860* (Cambridge, 1935), p. 17.

year the "Journeymen Curriers in all parts of the Union" were advised that[13]

> Your brethren of Philadelphia . . . have turned out unanimously for higher wages. They therefore think that as they ask no more than the prices established in New York, that their brethren of the trade will take no notice of any advertizements [sic] of the employers here to allure them to the city; more especially as the master curriers have entered into resolutions to lower prices that have been current for twenty years past.

In the succeeding years the cordwainers continued to press for higher wages. During the fall of 1804, the Philadelphia shoemakers induced their employers to raise the price of making boots from two dollars and fifty cents to two dollars and seventy-five cents per pair.[14] This was a dubious victory, for the master cordwainers in December of that year reduced the wages of the journeymen to their former level. Reports from the frontier revealed that the Pittsburgh cordwainers were restive and dissatisfied with their schedule of wages.[15]

The year 1805 was a crucial one for the laborers of Pennsylvania. In the fall, the Journeymen Cordwainers' Association of Philadelphia demanded an advance ranging from twenty-five to seventy-five cents on

---

[13] The *Aurora and General Advertiser*, Nov. 9, 1803. See Philip S. Foner, *History of the Labor Movement in the United States* (New York, 1947), p. 77.

[14] Commons, *Documentary History*, III, p. 123.

[15] On December 19, 1804, the following strike notice appeared in a Pittsburgh newspaper:

> This notice is intended to inform the travelling journeymen shoemakers of Pennsylvania, or of any other State, that the journeymen of this town made a turnout for higher wages. Two or three of their employers had a meeting, and having a number of apprentices thought proper to advise the other shoemakers to raise the boarding from $1.50 to $2.25 per week. We think it our duty to give this notice to all journeymen shoemakers that they may be guarded against imposition. The following are the prices which we turned out for, viz.: Fine shoes, 75 cents; coarse shoes, 75 cents; women's slippers, 75 cents; bootees, $2.00; long boots, $2.50; coffacs [sic]), $2.50.
>
> N. B. We would not advise any journeymen to come here unless they want a seat at cobbling.

Cited in Erasmus Wilson, *Standard History of Pittsburgh* (Chicago, 1898), p. 200. Myer A. Sanders: Labor Ch. VII, p. 123 in George E. Kelly: *Allegheny County, Pittsburgh. The Allegheny County Sesqui Centennial Committee*, states that the Pittsburgh shoemakers walked out in their first strike for higher wages in the year 1799 but does not cite the source.

their work.[16] The master shoemakers countered with a resolve "not to give any more wages than we have for some times past. . . ."[17] The strike was on. For six weeks the journeymen persisted in their efforts and then the employers struck back with a devastating blow. They turned to the courts and to the principles of common law, and there found an effective instrument for resisting the encroachments of their journeymen.

Several striking shoemakers were lodged in the Philadelphia jail and were charged with conspiring to raise their wages.[18] The Democratic press in the city was aroused. "Is there any power that can lawfully and constitutionally determine the price of a man's labor to be less than what he chuses [sic] to accept voluntarily . . . ," queried the *Aurora*. "If there is, the constitution is a farce, and the bill of rights is only a satire upon human credulity."[19]

The journeymen, fully aware of their predicament and cognizant of the importance of winning the approval of the public for their struggle, published an "Address of the Working Shoemakers of the City of Philadelphia to the public" explaining their position. "Under circumstances unexampled in a free country," deplored the striking shoemakers, "we are induced to lay a statement of our case before our fellow citizens."[20] That their constitutional rights were being violated; that it was a notorious fact that for the past fifteen years the working shoemakers had assembled together and regulated their wages; that in a long drawn-out struggle the employers were at a decided advantage; that the master shoemakers refused to bargain in good faith; that all they asked for was parity with the New York worker; all this and more was directed toward the edification of the public. What would the future be, asked the striking shoemakers, "if the Associations of men to regulate the price of their own labor, is to be converted into a crime, and libelled with the same reproachful terms as a design against the freedom of the nation . . . ?" "The prospect is a very sad one for Pennsylvania," they glumly predicted.[21]

---

[16] Commons, *Documentary History*, III, p. 106. The old scale of prices and those now asked were as follows:
Fancy tops were $4.25 proposed to be raised to $5.00.
Back straps were $3.75 proposed to be raised to $4.00
Long boots were $2.75 proposed to be raised to $3.00.
Cossacks were $2.50 proposed to be raised to $3.00.
[17] *Ibid.*, p. 122.
[18] The *Aurora and General Advertiser*, November 27, 1805.
[19] *Ibid.*   [20] *Ibid.*   [21] *Ibid.*

Although the charge was conspiracy, "the legal controversy, both out of court and in," Walter Nelles has pointed out in a very penetrating analysis of this trial, "was part of the major political controversy of the time—then still usually expressed as between 'aristocracy' and 'republicanism' (which meant Jeffersonian democracy)."[22] Jared Ingersoll, foremost champion of English common law in America, prosecuted the case; and Caesar Rodney, an ardent supporter of Jeffersonian democracy, was counsel for the striking shoemakers.

Victory was with the employing shoemakers. They had an almost invincible ally in the courts and "justice". Jared Ingersoll argued effectively for the prosecution that the cordwainers' society and similar combinations of workmen were against public policy and therefore criminal.[23] The prosecution contended that unlimited expansion of business was beneficial to the community. But the Journeymen's Society, said Ingersoll, would ruin industries and bring desolation to our cities.[24]

Rodney contemptuously dismissed the charge that the trade unions would drive business from Philadelphia. He bitterly assailed English common law and demonstrated its inapplicability to the American scene. His main contention was that the prosecution of the cordwainers was subversive of American freedom. Surely, argued the young Republican, the Society of Journeymen Cordwainers "had as much right to create itself, as the associations to promote commerce, agriculture, the arts, or any other object."[25]

The arrest of the strikers and the charge of conspiracy had accomplished its purpose. Long before the trial had begun the strike was broken. Despite the spirited plea of the eloquent Caesar Rodney, despite the courageous efforts of the striking shoemakers, the court decided against them and it would be another thirty years before the cordwainers would again be in the vanguard of the labor movement in Philadelphia.

---

[22] See Walter Nelles, "The First American Labor Case," *Yale Law Journal*, vol. 41, December 1931, p. 174.

[23] See Edward P. Cheyney, "Decisions of Courts in Conspiracy and Boycott Cases," *Political Science Quarterly*, IV, June 1889, pp. 264, 265.

[24] See Commons. *Documentary History*, III, p. 236 ff. See also Nelles, *op. cit.*, p. 174.

[25] Commons, *Documentary History*, III, p. 175. See Nelles, *op. cit.*, p. 174; and Philip S. Foner, *History of the Labor Movement in the United States* (New York, 1947), p. 80.

But all was not lost. Pennsylvania labor was to profit from the experiences of these early shoemakers. These pioneers in the labor movement had introduced the trade union, the shop committee, collective bargaining, picketing, and a crude form of strike benefits. They had conducted their strikes with a minimum of violence and with considerable success. Not without significance was the fact that by means of a strike they had exacted a series of increases from the master shoemakers. In 1794, the price for making a pair of boots was twelve shilling and nine pence; in 1805, the price had advanced to eighteen shilling and nine pence.[26]

In the years to follow, in the years of the Embargo and Non-Intercourse Act, labor strife was practically non-existent in Pennsylvania. Economic dislocation and industrial readjustment, the resultants of President Jefferson's peace policy, brought peace if not harmony in labor-management relations. To what extent the decision in the recent cordwainers' trial in Philadelphia acted as a deterrent to labor unrest is unknown, but in all probability it was not a decisive factor.

This facade of industrial peace was marred by the feeble efforts of the Philadelphia Typographical Workers to raise their wages in the fall of 1810.[27] Unlike their more aggressive brethren in New York, who in the previous year had wrested an increase from their employers, the endeavors of the Philadelphia printers were ineffectual.[28] The strike proved a disastrous adventure for the Society of Printers in the City. Its treasury evaporated and its membership halved.[29] Timid leadership and a split in the ranks debilitated and undoubtedly were important factors which defeated the Philadelphia printers in their essay for a wage increase.[30]

---

[26] Commons, *Documentary History*, III, p. 118.

[27] Ethelbert Stewart, A *Documentary History of Early Organizations of Printers* (Indianapolis, 1907), p. 28. See also George A. Stevens, *New York Typographical Union No. 6* (Albany, 1913), p. 65.

[28] Stevens, *op. cit.*, pp. 53, 54.

[29] When the year opened there were 119 members in good standing; at the close of the year there remained 55 members, or "only one more than in 1802 . . . the first year of [the society's] existence." Stewart, *op. cit.*, p. 28.

[30] Against the wishes of the President of the Philadelphia Typographical Society, John Childs, and after much anxiety and hesitation, the membership expressed its willingness to exchange scab lists with the New York printers. Contrast also the spineless statement of Philadelphia printers regarding the New York printers' strike of 1809 with the spirited promise of cooperation from the New York Society in reference to the strike of the Philadelphia printers in 1810. See Stevens, *op. cit.*, pp. 51, 53, 65. During the year 78 members resigned or were expelled. Stewart, *Documentary History*, p. 28.

During the war years the scene of labor discontent shifted to the interior and to the west. The stolid farmers in the Susquehanna Valley were aggrieved by reports that the weavers and carpenters were "holding meetings for the purpose of raising the prices of their work. . . ."[31] This action "will fall rather heavily on the Farmers, who must expect soon to get but a poor price for their produce," gloomily predicted one farmer of Lancaster County. A town meeting was suggested to determine what remedial action could be taken. And a boycott was advocated as being the most efficacious. Would it not be wiser "to cease having any more work done, than what they can't absolutely do without, . . . [and] to withhold their work from those who join in combination to force them to pay high prices," suggested another farmer. Of the outcome of this brief flurry between the mechanics on the one hand and the farmers and the tradespeople of Lancaster County on the other nothing is known.[32]

At Pittsburgh, the Journeymen Cordwainers' Society modelled after the Philadelphia organization, fought doggedly for six years to secure wage increases for its members.[33] As early as 1809 they had threatened to turn out for a twelve and a half cent increase on shoes but compliance by their employers made a strike unnecessary.[34] All increases were not to be had so readily. In the year 1812 and again in 1814, the working shoemakers of Pittsburgh turned out for higher wages, but not without resistance from the master cordwainers. The same old problems—collective bargaining, the union shop, scab workmen, benefit funds for strikers and employer resistance—which had perplexed the Philadelphia shoemakers, reappeared to plague them. Shops were scabbed to maintain the effectiveness of the union; vigilant committees were organized to preserve the solidarity of the strike, and for the hard-pressed worker there were union funds to carry him through the period of distress.[35]

At the same time the employing shoemakers revealed that the lessons of the early cordwainers' strike in Philadelphia had not been lost to them. The Master Cordwainers' Association was speedily converted into an organization to meet the exigencies of the strike. Various pres-

---

[31] The *Lancaster Journal*, April 15, 1813.
[32] The *Lancaster Journal*, April 15, 1813.
[33] Commons, *Documentary History*, IV, pp. 16-87. See Pittsburgh Cordwainers, 1815, Commonwealth v. Morrow.
[34] *Ibid.*, p. 26.
[35] *Ibid.*

sures, not the least of them being economic, were directed against those employers who refused to stand firm in resisting the demands of the journeymen.[36] One master cordwainer disclosed "that [he] could not have the house where [he] lived if he gave the prices [the journeymen struck for]," and explained that "this was the reason why [he] discharged the journeymen." Another was threatened with a boycott because he had complied with the demands of the striking shoemakers. A Pittsburgh rentier, William Eichbaum, disclosed that various master shoemakers had offered him double the rent which he received from the two employing shoemakers who had acceded to the demands of the strikers.[37]

Nor had they forgotten how effectively the courts had subdued the striking shoemakers of Philadelphia. When the Pittsburgh cordwainers struck in the winter of 1814 for higher wages, they were haled into court and rather than await the outcome, they compromised the dispute and paid the costs.[38] In the turnout of 1815, they once again were charged with conspiring to raise their wages. Walter Forward, one of the most prominent attorneys in Pittsburgh, acted as their counsel, but to no avail. The jury "found all the defendants guilty . . . and the court fined them . . . one dollar each, and the costs of the prosecution.[39]

Despite the serious imposition placed on them by the court's decision, the working shoemakers had been notably successful in pressing their demands. They had succeeded in raising the price of making cossacks from $1.75 a pair in 1811 to $3.25 a pair in 1815, and through their united efforts they had restricted apprentice work and thus eliminated a source of competition.[40] Shortage of skilled workmen was a decisive factor which had enabled them to wring concessions from their employers. One employer acknowledged that this was his reason for complying with the journeymen's demands. "Some of the journeymen were tramping out of town," he stated, "and . . . if I did not give the wages I would not have a stock of work to go down the river."[41] This

---

[36] Walter Glenn, a master cordwainer, revealed that the "employers often met in [their] own defence, when journeymen turned out. . . ." Commons, *Documentary History,* IV, p. 47.

[37] Commons, *Documentary History,* IV, p. 55.

[38] *Ibid.*

[39] *Ibid.,* p. 87.

[40] *Ibid.,* IV, p. 36.

[41] *Ibid.,* p. 53.

scarcity of skilled journeymen, combined with the inability of the master shoemakers to present a united front, were important factors in explaining the success of the journeymen.

The dizzy prosperity of the war years was ephemeral. A crisis—a phenomenon which was to become a recurring feature of American economic and social history—staggered the business community.[42] Labor as well as business suffered from this severe depression.

Workers without work—employers without employees—this was hardly the time for labor-management difficulties. But the journeymen shoemakers and the intrepid ship carpenters of Philadelphia were not to be daunted by a depression. Some time in the latter part of 1820, the journeymen cordwainers (Ladies' Branch) apparently had compelled their employers to raise the prices on their work. Whether this was accomplished through a strike or not is unknown. In retaliation the master shoemakers had combined for the express purpose of reducing the wages of the cordwainers to their former level. But the journeymen brought charges of conspiracy against their employers, the first instance of its kind. In his decision Chief Justice Gibson of the Pennsylvania Supreme Court held that "where the act is lawful for an individual it can be the subject for a conspiracy, when done in concert only where there is a direct intention that injury shall result from it, or where the object is to benefit the conspirators to the prejudice of the public or the oppression of individuals, and where such prejudice and oppression is the natural and necessary consequence."[43] It was lawful then for the masters who had been forced by their employees to combine to restore the wages to their "natural level". Beyond this they could not go.

In the winter of the following year, the ship carpenters at the Philadelphia Navy Yard walked off their jobs. They refused to work at

---

[42] See The *Aurora and General Advertiser*, Oct. 19, 1818. See also The *Pittsburgh Gazette*, June 29, 1819; The *Berks and Schuylkill Journal*, Nov. 20, 1819; *Niles' Register*, XVII, for August and September and October 1819 for graphic descriptions of the effects of the depression on the working classes. See also Samuel Rezneck, "The Depression of 1819-1822, A Social History," The *American Historical Review*, Oct. 1933, vol. XL, pp. 662-689. See also letter from Benjamin Page to John Hammond, Pittsburgh 3d January, 1825, Bakewell Page Collection, for the impact of the depression on the manufacturing people in western Pennsylvania.

[43] See Frederick C. Brightly, *Reports of Cases decided by the Judges of the Supreme Court of Pennsylvania in the Court of Nisi Prius at Philadelphia* (York, Pa., 1898), pp. 40, 41. Commonwealth ex. rel. Chew v. Carlisle, February 5, 1821. See also Commons, *History of Labour*, I, p. 163.

reduced wages and all efforts to have them return to the yard met
with little success. The president of the Navy Board used his good
offices to end the dispute, but met with no greater success than did the
Commandant of the Yard.[44]

A revival of business activity in 1822 indicated that the worst of the
depression was over. In the latter years of this period new issues which
were to characterize the labor movement throughout the Jackson era
appeared. The agitation for higher wages, although never forgotten,
would for a brief moment be subordinated to the struggle for the ten-
hour day. The gigantic army of unskilled workers, which would give
inspiration and dynamic leadership to the labor movement, showed
signs of shrugging off its lethargy.

While the unskilled wage earners vainly sought to reduce the burdens under which they labored, the skilled workingmen, for a fleeting
moment, successfully carried their demands for higher wages and
shorter hours. In the early years of the Jackson Era their efforts met
with defeat, but by 1835 both the labor movement and the American
economy had undergone a momentous change. The skilled artisans had
organized a Trades' Union to press their demands, and American business, prosperous and expanding, found it increasingly difficult to put
off the wage earners' requests for shorter hours and higher wages.

The workmen associated with the building trades led in the drive
to wrest these concessions from their employers. In the summer of
1827, upwards of 500 journeymen carpenters in Philadelphia unanimously resolved, "that ten hours industriously employed . . . [is] sufficient for a day's labor."[45] Five days later the master workmen retali-
ated. Over one hundred and twenty of them pledged themselves "not
to employ any journeymen who will not give his time and labor as
usual."[46] When the master carpenters lamented that if they met with
the demands of their employees, they would be denied "a fifth part of
the usual time of working," the journeymen suggested that their real
fear was an awareness that "if this alteration takes place, it will de-
prive them [the masters] of the power they have hitherto had of em-

---

[44] Letter from W. Bainbridge, Commandant of the Philadelphia Navy Yard to Com-
modore Rodger, President of the Navy Board, Washington, D. C., December 17,
1821. Letters from Commandant of Philadelphia Navy Yard 1815-1821.

[45] The *Philadelphia Gazette,* June 14, 1827. See also The *Democratic Press,* June 14,
1827.

[46] The *Aurora and Franklin Gazette,* June 14, 1827. See also The *Saturday Evening
Post,* June 23, 1827.

ploying a man during the summer, in the long days, and either discharging him in the winter, or reducing his wages, as it will make a journeyman of nearly as much value in the winter as in the summer."[47]

On June 18 the carpenters struck. A bargaining committee of twelve was named to negotiate with the representatives of the master carpenters.[48] But the master workmen were in no mood for collective bargaining. Instead, they invited three to four hundred journeymen to come to Philadelphia where hands were scarce and wages high.[49] Indignantly, the Philadelphia carpenters charged that this advertisement was "a most gross imposition upon the credulity of our working brethren," since there were sufficient hands in the city.[50] Although their efforts were premature, this strike of the house carpenters of Philadelphia resulted in the formation of the first union of all organized labor in any city: The Mechanic's Union of Trade Associations.[51]

Later that year the dismissal of six journeymen tailors for demanding higher piece rates brought on a strike in that trade. Not until the six were reinstated would the other journeymen return to their benches. "It is a new scene for workmen to compel us to employ men we no longer want," complained one of the master tailors.[52] The shop of Robb and Winebrenner, the struck tailors, was effectively picketed and their work was boycotted by the journeymen tailors in other shops.[53] Charges of violence were tossed about by both parties to the dispute. When the strikers proved adamant, the master tailors turned to the courts and an indictment charging the journeymen tailors with a conspiracy to raise their wages was drawn up against them.[54] As in the past, the verdict was guilty.[55]

Sporadic strikes by the various trades—the carpenters, the bricklayers, the shoemakers, the hatters, the glass cutters, the marble workers and the leather dressers—were indicators of the unrest which pre-

---

[47] The *Democratic Press*, June 20, 1827. See Commons, *Documentary History*, V, pp. 82, 83.
[48] *Freeman's Journal*, June 15, 1827.
[49] The *Democratic Press*, June 18, 1827.
[50] *Ibid.*, June 20, 1827.
[51] See Commons, *History of Labour*, I, pp. 189-190.
[52] *Niles' Register*, XXXIII, October 6, 1827, p. 91. See also Commons, *Documentary History*, IV, p. 116.
[53] *Ibid.*
[54] The *Norristown Herald*, September 19, 1827; The *American Sentinel*, September 25, 1827.
[55] *Ibid.*

vailed among the wage earners of Pennsylvania in the years preceding the general strike of 1835. Abortive drives for the ten-hour day were made by the bricklayers and carpenters of Philadelphia in the summer of 1828. Some of the master carpenters offered as much as "12½ cents and even 25 cents more per day" to entice the men back to their jobs under the old rules. "Can you not see that it is owing to the unsettled state of affairs that they make you the offer, and [you can] rest assured," the striking carpenters were admonished, "if they once more get you under as they formerly had, you will be more oppressed than ever, in both wages and labour, and justly you will deserve it."[56]

Late in the winter of that year, the Pittsburgh carpenters revealed their intentions to demand a twenty-five percent increase on their old prices.[57] The following spring they made a futile effort to impress their demands on the master carpenters. The strike was feebly organized and lacking in leadership. At a strike meeting a self-defeating resolution was adopted. It was resolved: "That the Journeymen Carpenters bind themselves, individually, not to violate those prices by taking work below them, unless the employers shall first transgress, in that case they will feel themselves at liberty to adopt the present mode of taking whatever they can get for it."[58] That same summer the shoemakers of Franklin County struck to establish a bill of prices for all the journeymen cordwainers, but the courts speedily quashed their efforts.[59]

An advertisement appearing in the *Pittsburgh Gazette* on May 20, 1831—"Wanted Immediately, Two Hundred Journeymen Carpenters" —signalized the outbreak of new disturbances between the master workmen and their employees.[60] The carpenters had struck for the ten-hour day.[61] Prior to this they had been working "not during set hours" but under such arrangements as had been "mutually agreed upon by master and workmen." The master carpenters now insisted that their employees work from sunrise to sunset.[62]

---

[56] *Mechanic's Free Press*, June 17, July 19, 1828.

[57] The *Norristown Herald*, December 24, 1828.

[58] The *Statesman*, March 25, 1829. See also The *Allegheny Democrat and Farmers' and Mechanics' Advertiser*, March 24, 1829.

[59] Mathew Carey, *Select Excerpts*, I, p. 273, Nov. 17, 1829. See also *Niles' Register*, XXXVII, Jan. 2, 1830, p. 293.

[60] The *Working Man's Advocate*, May 28, 1831.

[61] The *Pittsburgh Mercury*, May 25, 1831. See also The *Miner's Journal*, June 4, 1831.

[62] The *Baltimore American and Commercial Advertiser*, June 7, 1831.

As soon as the strike was underway the master workmen shrewdly presented their case to the citizens of Pittsburgh. They pointed out the dangers inherent in this turn out to the prosperity and the well-being of the community. The striker's slogans, "Equal rights and privileges," one spokesman for the employing carpenters charged, "aim at the subversion of society, and give strength to that disorganizing clamor, which has been stated in some of the dark corners of our land. . . ." If the ten-hour system were enacted, the master carpenters declared, it would ". . . impede the progress of wealth." It violated an old established custom in the trade, and furthermore, the master carpenters inferred that the ten-hour system would have pernicious effects on the journeymen. "Will it not necessarily be accomplished with temptations, prodigality, and dissipation?" the master workmen added.[63] In addition, they contended that the journeymen were being misled by ambitious leaders "who have wit enough to be wicked" and were leading the workingmen to their own ruin.[64]

The striking workers responded immediately and indignantly. "Why do they appeal to 'intelligent Journeymen'," they asked, "after having ranked us (without exception) among the lowest and most degraded orders of society. . . ." Contemptuously they rejected the charges that they were the blind tools of malicious leaders. "We, like other men, have minds of our own, and have not asked the direction nor followed the dictates of others we have not dictated for our former employers, but for ourselves," angrily asserted the carpenters. And as for "aiming at the subversion of the good order of society" they declared, "we love rule and good order as well as they, and will in our several places and relations, do as much to support them." The journeymen felt that a little time for their own improvement, "say enough, at least, to read the public news," would not be of any injury to the community. As for the doctrine of custom and usage, the strikers pointed out, "the slaveholder might justify himself in the right to hold his fellow man in bondage."[65]

Once again the master workmen hopefully appealed to the courts for aid. The strikers were indicted. It was alleged that the journeymen carpenters had combined with several hundred others; that they had resorted to threats and force to win their demands; that they had massed in front of the shops to induce the other carpenters to quit work.

---

[63] The *Pittsburgh Gazette*, May 31, 1831.

[64] *Ibid.*

[65] The *Pittsburgh Gazette*, May 31, 1831.

The jury was out for a short time and returned with the astonishing verdict of not guilty.[66] Labor had dented the armor of the capitalists. The court victory did not settle the strike issue. The carpenters still continued to labor under the old system, from sunrise to sunset. A few master workmen had conceded to their wishes, but the remainder were firm in their stand against the ten-hour system. Though the strike was lost, their spirit was not broken. In September, they disclosed their intention of reintroducing the ten-hour question in the following spring.[67] During the strike of the past summer the master carpenters had asserted that they could not meet with the strikers' demands because of the short notice which attended the walk out. Yet in the spring of 1832, and although the employers had been notified weeks in advance, they still treated the requests of the journeymen with contempt.[68] Unable to break the resistance of the master workmen, they decided to contract work themselves.[69]

At Philadelphia, the journeymen cabinet makers were confronted with equally obdurate masters. In the autumn of 1833, the Cabinet Makers Union, unable to obtain adequate wages, and proscribed by their employers, opened a wareroom to sell their products.[70] Their difficulties had just begun. An open letter published by them in the spring of 1834 revealed the overwhelming odds against which they struggled. The opening of the wareroom was followed by the immediate discharge of about two hundred journeymen cabinet makers. These men, the cabinet makers charged were "thrown suddenly upon the slender resources of our infant Institution for the purpose of crushing us more effectually."[71]

When the leather dressers and finishers turned out in the winter of 1834, they introduced a grievance which had been foreign to the American labor movement. They were striking against the introduction of machinery for the finishing of leather, an eloquent testimonial to the progress which was being made in American industry. The Trades' Union with liberal appropriations stood solidly behind the leather workers in their strike. The Union paper, The National Trades' Union, added its voice in opposition to the introduction of labor-saving machinery. "Notwithstanding the boasted benefits of labor-saving machinery," this

[66] The Allegheny Democrat, August 9, 1831.
[67] The Pittsburgh Gazette, September 30, 1831.
[68] The Pittsburgh Gazette, March 20, 1832.
[69] Ibid.
[70] The Pennsylvanian, October 3 and December 24, 1833.
[71] Ibid., May 11, 1834.

paper contended, "the operatives in almost every business into which it has been introduced, have severely suffered by it." Pessimistically it added, "we believe that it never will be really beneficial, until it aids the productive power of the operative, without diminishing, if it does not increase, his means of subsistence."[72]

Labor strife was becoming an accurate barometer of business conditions. From Boston to Baltimore the wage earners were growing restive. In the spring of 1835, the harried cordwainers of Philadelphia sought an explanation for the difficulties which beset their trade. "A few years ago," observed the shoemakers, "the slowest of our profession could earn at least seven or eight dollars per week, and that, by no greater exertion than it now requires to make four or five."[73] At Boston, the mechanics had declared their intention to strike for a ten-hour day, and in a circular addressed "to all Branches of Mechanical Labour in the City, and Commonwealth and elsewhere," rationalized their action.[74]

While the cordwainers of Philadelphia pondered their plight, the coal heavers on the Schuylkill acted. They struck for the ten-hour day and their action stirred the smoldering desires of most of the wage earners in the City. Shortly afterwards the Boston Circular reached Philadelphia and the National Trades' Union broadcast it far and wide. "Its effect was electric," exclaimed John Ferral; "[it] became the absorbing topic of conversation."[75] It decided the issue for the workingmen there. Never before had the artisans of Pennsylvania been so aroused over any issue as they were in the summer of 1835 over the demand for the ten-hour day. It means more than just a reduction in the hours of work; the ten-hour day also implied the same wages as had been given formerly for the longer workday.[76]

In the critical days at the beginning of June when it appeared that the Schuylkill laborers could no longer carry on against the combined

---

[72] The *National Trades' Union*, November 29, 1834.

[73] The *Pennsylvanian*, April 4, 1835.

[74] See Commons, *History of Labour*, I, p. 388.

[75] The *Man*, June 29, 1835. Letter from John Ferral, President of the National Trades' Union, to Seth Luther of Boston. Cited in Commons, *Documentary History*, VI, p. 40.

[76] The *Pittsburgh Gazette*, June 3, 1831. This was clearly indicated in the attitude of the Pittsburgh carpenters when they insisted that in ten hours they could perform the same amount of labor as in the longer work day and demanded the same pay. See also Richard B. Morris, "Andrew Jackson was no F. D. R.," *Labor and the Nation*, May-June 1949, p. 138.

will of the merchants, the journeymen cordwainers (Ladies' Branch) turned out for higher wages.[77] The shoemakers—700 of them—led a procession down to the Schuylkill wharves to express their sympathy and solidarity with the day laborers. ". . . We are all day laborers," recalled the shoemakers, and in keeping with their promise of support and cooperation they resolved, "that we will not buy coal of any company that does not accede to their [the coal heavers] reasonable demands before Saturday next; knowing ten hours per day to be enough for any man to labor."[78] The carpenters joined the ranks of the strikers and their banners bore the inscription, "From 6 to 6".[79] Mass meetings were held at Independence Square and the State House yard by the various trades affirming the justice of their stand on the ten-hour day.[80]

Not many days later the bricklayers, the plasterers, the masons and the hod carriers added their voices in the cry for the ten-hour day.[81] Black and white smiths, sheet iron workers, plumbers and leather dressers soon joined the procession.[82] The cordwainers who had been out on strike for higher wages now declared that they too would abstain from work until the ten-hour day had been achieved. On June 10, the *Saturday Evening Post* listed twenty trades on strike for hours and wages.[83]

The ranks of the strikers continued to grow. ". . . Each day added thousands to our ranks," John Ferral exultantly declared.[84] Daily processions blocked the streets of Philadelphia and the working men grew confident of the outcome of their struggle.[85] A march to the public works by the carpenters, cordwainers, and laborers brought a halt to the work going on there. The exuberant pen of the President of the National Trades' Union recorded the event:[86]

> We marched to the public works, and the workmen there
> joined in with us; when the procession passed, employ-

---

[77] The *Pennsylvanian*, June 3, 1835. See Commons, *Documentary History*, VI, p. 40.
[78] The *Pennsylvanian*, June 4, 1835.
[79] The *United States Gazette*, June 3, 1835.
[80] *Ibid.*
[81] The *National Laborer*, June 6, 1835. See also The *Pennsylvanian*, June 6, 1835 and The *Saturday Evening Post*, June 10, 1835.
[82] The *Pennsylvanian*, June 6, 1835.
[83] Journeymen Cordwainers, carters, seamen, weavers and manufacturers, leather dressers, carpenters, tobacconists, tailoresses, seamstresses, stockmakers, saddlers, plumbers, binders, and folders, block and pumpmakers, bricklayers, cabinet makers, bakers, wood-sawyers, hod carriers and coal heavers.
[84] Commons, *Documentary History*, VI, p. 41.
[85] The *Saturday Evening Post*, June 10, 1835.
[86] Commons, *Documentary History*, VI, p. 42.

ment ceased, business was at a stand still, shirt sleeves
were rolled up, aprons on, working tools in hand were the
orders of the day. Had the cannon of an invading army
belched forth its challenge on our soil, the freemen of
Philadelphia could not have shown greater ardor for the
contest; the blood-sucking aristocracy, they stood alone
aghast; terror stricken, they thought the day of retribu-
tion was come, but no vengeance was sought or inflicted
by the people for the wrongs they had suffered from their
enemies.

Even the press was beginning to acknowledge the justice of their
cause. The conservative Niles wrote: "Ten hours of labor is as much
as a man ought to perform, especially if exposed to the sun."[87] A Jackson paper declared: "Politically it is of immense importance that a
change should be effected. . . . Our institutions place all power in the
hands of the very men, who are now, in a great measure, debarred from
mental improvement, and shut out from that cultivation which alone
can render them capable of wielding their tremendous strength to the
advantage of our common country."[88] Even the hostile *New York
Journal of Commerce* agreed that ten hours a day was sufficient for any
person performing work requiring much physical exertion.[89]

The mass meetings and the public protests had accomplished their
purpose. The public responded sympathetically to the desires of the
wage earners of the city. Fearful of antagonizing the public, the house
carpenters disavowed the procession and the parades through the streets
of Philadelphia. Such activity, they surmised, had a tendency to cause
undue excitement and would secure for them only the "disapprobation
of that portion of the public who are otherwise favorable to our proceedings." At the same time the carpenters petitioned the City Councils to recognize ten hours as a day's work for those employed by and
paid from city funds.[90] This request was followed by a monster petition
"signed by many thousand citizens" demanding the ten-hour day.[91]

With amazing speed the City Councils acted. Despite the fact that
the city government was controlled by Whigs, it was unanimously resolved, "that the hours of labor, of the Workingmen employed under

---

[87] *Niles' Register,* June 13, 1835, XLVIII, p. 249.

[88] The *Pennsylvanian,* June 3, 1835.

[89] From the *New York Journal of Commerce,* June 8, 1835, as cited in Commons,
History of Labour, I, p. 392.

[90] The *United States Gazette,* June 5, 1835.

[91] The *Pennsylvanian,* June 6, 1835.

the Authorities of the City Corporation, shall be from SIX to SIX during the summer season; allowing one hour for breakfast, and one hour for dinner."[92]

At Southwark, a suburb of Philadelphia, the board of commissioners not only reduced the number of hours of labor but also raised the wages of the men in its employ from eighty-seven and a half cents to one dollar per day.[93]

Victory was near. Time would compel the private employers to concede the ten-hour day. On June 6, the master bricklayers agreed to adopt the shorter work day: the master carpenters had already yielded to their journeymen's requests.[94] Before the month was out the master cordwainers had complied with the wage demands of their employees.[95]

One newspaper censured the Common Council of Philadelphia and charged it with the burden of responsibility for the success of the workingmen. "It having been the first to knock under, prepared the way for all the rest," lamented this paper.[96] But the president of the National Trades' Union more accurately appraised the result: "The mechanics of Philadelphia stood firm and true; they conquered, because they were united and resolute in their actions."[97]

Spurred on by the success of the ten-hour movement in Philadelphia, the unrest spread to the lesser trades and to other parts of the State. At Philadelphia, the stone cutters contended for the union shop; the seamen demanded eighteen dollars a month and small stores; the oak coopers inveighed against prison labor; and the bakers strove for the elimination of Sunday work.[98] The mechanics at Germantown won their demands without a strike,[99] and at Norristown, the master cordwainers were compelled to give higher wages to their journeymen.[100] The journeymen tailors of Reading met with no resistance in their requests for a uniform schedule of prices,[101] and at Pittsburgh, the journeymen shoemakers strove for a ten percent advance on their pres-

---

[92] The *Pennsylvanian*, June 6, 1835. See also The *United States Gazette*, June 6, 1835.
[93] The *Pennsylvanian*, June 8, 1835.
[94] The *United States Gazette*, June 3, 1835.
[95] The *Pennsylvanian*, June 22, 1835.
[96] The *Berks and Schuylkill Journal*, June 22, 1835.
[97] Commons, *Documentary History*, VI, p. 41.
[98] Poulson's *American Daily Advertiser*, June 24, 1835.
[99] The *Germantown Telegraph*, June 24, 1835.
[100] The *Pennsylvanian*, June 22, 1835.
[101] The *Democratic Press*, November 24, 1835.

ent wages.[102] The future looked good to the wage earners of Pennsylvania.

But instead of peace, the year 1836 was to be a year of unparalleled industrial strife. Rising prices, without corresponding wage increases made hollow the victories of the previous year, and the strike was labor's only effective weapon for winning the desired increases. "The plan now usually adopted by tradesmen and artisans to procure an advance on their labor is perhaps, the *only* means which could be used to insure them, not only a fair compensation for their labor, but by which they can resist the oppression of severe and tyrannical employers," the *Harrisburgh Chronicle* surmised.[103]

The year opened inauspiciously as far as labor and management harmony was concerned. In January, the journeymen shoemakers (Ladies' Branch) at Reading had wrung an advance from all the employers except one.[104] Ominous reports emanating from Philadelphia foreshadowed a crisis in the book industry there. In the middle of January, the Trades' Union received a notice from the Journeymen Bookbinders' Association of that city that they were struggling to stave off a thirty percent reduction in their present wages.[105]

Their employers, smarting from a successful effort by the Journeymen's Society to establish uniform rates in the industry the previous October, bided their time.[106] With "extensive contracts to fulfill," they grudgingly accepted the bookbinders' terms as a lesser evil until they had "time to confer together." At the close of the year an Employers' Association was formed and with dispatch a reduction in the rates paid to their journeymen was decreed.[107] Anticipating the reaction of their employees, a blacklist containing the names of seventy journeymen was distributed among the master bookbinders of New York and other cities.[108] Fearful that the journeymen might organize a cooperative, the employers hastened to ally themselves with the book sellers and publishers of Philadelphia. "Where are the *National Gazette*, the *Journal of Commerce*, the *American*, and the *Commercial*, and others that they

---

[102] The *National Trades' Union*, September 26, 1835.
[103] The *Harrisburgh Chronicle*, November 20, 1836.
[104] *Ibid.*
[105] The *Pennsylvanian*, January 15, 1836.
[106] *Ibid.*, January 4, 1836.
[107] *Ibid.*
[108] *Ibid.*

do not, as usual, raise their voices against combination?" sardonically inquired the Union paper.[109]

The bookbinders denounced the avaricious conduct of their employers. They saw their struggle as a far more serious conflict than a dispute over the question of wages. To them it was a class war. "The war of capital against labor, which is now waged by a majority of the Employing Bookbinders in this city, against the rights and pecuniary interests of the Journeymen," the strikers warned, "is a warfare of serious import to every good citizen, but more especially does it effect the vital interests of productive laborers. . . ."[110] Optimistic employers' reports of conditions in the book industry were challenged by the journeymen. When the employers published a list of workmen who earned as much as fifteen dollars per week, the strikers countered with a charge that this was a very select group, and declared that the average bookbinder earned about seven dollars per weeek. A reduction at this time insisted the journeymen, was designed to smash the Trades' Union.[111]

To sustain the bookbinders in their strike, financial aid poured into Philadelphia from all directions. The Trades' Union contributed thousands of dollars. Societies in New York, Baltimore and Washington dipped into their treasuries to give to the striking bookbinders. At least twenty-one of the various organized trades in Philadelphia gave unstintingly to insure the success of the journeymen bookbinders' stand.[112]

Early in March the master bookbinders relented. The employers announced that they did not wish "to enforce *their* list of Prices as prepared by the Master Bookbinders Society, but have always been and still are ready to meet them [the Journeymen] by a Conferring Committee or otherwise, for the amicable adjustment of the matter at issue between them." A bargaining committee was appointed to meet with the spokesmen of the Employers' Association. One month later in an "address of the Journeymen Bookbinders of the City and County of Philadelphia" it was proclaimed: "The long contest in which we were involved . . . is now come to an end, in a manner highly beneficial to us."[113]

[109] The *National Laborer*, April 30, 1836.

[110] The *Pennsylvanian*, February 5, 1836.

[111] *Ibid.*

[112] The *Pennsylvanian*, Feb. 5, March 11, 12, 1836. See also The *National Laborer*, April 30, 1836, and The *National Trades' Union*, February 6, 1936.

[113] The *Pennsylvanian*, March 7, 8, 1836. See The *National Laborer*, April 9, 30, 1836.

While the bookbinders' strike was in the process of being settled, the journeymen cordwainers (Ladies' Branch) and the female shoe binders and corders struck for an advance in their prices. The journeymen asked for a five-and-a-quarter-cent increase on each pair of shoes; the women for only a slight advance.

The master shoemakers acted expeditiously. They organized and took their case to the people. At a meeting of the master workmen it was uncompromisingly asserted that "the wages paid to the Journeymen previous to the present turnout, was a sufficient compensation for their labor, and as the present list of wages . . . is an unjust demand . . . the Employers will not accede to it under any consideration." Furthermore they accused the journeymen of striking frequently and "without the slightest notice" which made it impossible for them to have "any confidence in carrying on their business." In addition, they charged that the working shoemakers through threats and force had compelled satisfied employees to quit their jobs.[114]

Angrily and explicitly, the journeymen replied to the charges levelled against them. They calculated that the proposed raise would increase their wages by sixty cents per week which would bring their weekly average to $5.64. "The most superficial observor," they explained, will perceive that this increase in his weekly income can in no wise meet the enormous advance in the prices of provisions, house rent and other necessaries." Bitterly they attacked the employers for attributing every price rise to the actions of the journeymen. "Whenever we have asked our employers for an advance of wages, they have universally demanded of the public an average advance of about three times as much as they have given us. . . ." They pointed out that at the conclusion of the strike of 1835 while their advance averaged five cents, the employers raised the price of shoes eighteen and three-quarters cents. "And they have ever attempted to justify this exertion by telling their customers that they were compelled to act thus, in consequence of the exorbitant demands of the Journeymen," grumbled the strikers.[115]

The journeymen cordwainers scoffed at the charge of "frequent turn outs" and defied their employers "to prove the occurrence of more than two TURN-OUTS within the last TEN YEARS!!!" As for the present difficulties, they insisted, "that the Employers were aware that the

---

[114] The *Pennsylvanian*, March 29, 1836. See The *Public Ledger*, May 16, 1836.
[115] *Ibid.*

Journeymen had the present STRIKE in contemplation two months previous to its occurrence." But the striking shoemakers asked, "do the Employers give their Journeymen a day's notice when they discharge them?" "We declare they do not." To the charge of coercion, they replied with an accusation that it was the employers and not they who were guilty. "We are able to prove," triumphantly declared the journeymen, "that you have sent committees to different employers who have complied with our demand, which . . . have strenuously urged said employers to break their contracts with the journeymen, and threatened to break them up by underselling them in case they refused to comply with their [the employers'] requests."[116]

In a last desperate move to expose the specious arguments of the master cordwainers, the striking shoemakers challenged them "to lay before a committee of disinterested citizens, a part of which [is] to be chosen by yourselves. [sic] Your books, containing the amount of money each journeyman has weekly earned; and to said committee we will prove the correctness of every statement respecting our trade made by us in the daily papers."[117] The challenge went unanswered.

For three months or more the journeymen cordwainers put up a determined resistance against all efforts to break their strike. The National Trades' Union and some of the local Trade Societies contributed funds to maintain them during the turn out. But the employers were equally adamant in their resolve not to acquiesce in their journeymen's demands. They combined with the shoe merchants, the leather merchants and the dry goods dealers and agreed not to trade with any employer who had complied with the requests of the striking shoemakers. Although the strike continued into the middle of June, already in May there was evidence that the journeymen had acknowledged that theirs was a lost cause. Preparation was being made to open an "establishment of [their] own, by which [they would] become [their] own employers." In June, a shop was opened and through cooperation they hoped to find a solution to their economic problems.[118]

The journeymen house carpenters struck for higher wages almost simultaneously with the cordwainers. In the autumn of 1835, the master carpenters had been informed that "on the 20th of March next" the

[116] The *Pennsylvanian*, March 29, 1836. See The *Public Ledger*, May 16, 1836.
[117] The *Pennsylvanian*, March 29, 1836.
[118] The *National Laborer*, April 12, June 11, 1836. See The *Public Ledger*, May 16, 1836 and Commons, *History of Labour*, I, p. 399.

journeymen would demand one dollar and fifty cents per day during the summers and one dollar and twenty-five cents per day during the winters. Although wages was the only issue in the strike, the journeymen listed a long train of abuses under which they labored. The master carpenters customarily withheld one-third of their wages. They palmed off shoddy merchandise on them in payment for their labor. And finally, they denounced the practice of employing men only during the long days of the summer, discharging them as soon as the days become short.[119]

The master carpenters did not flinch before the accusations of their journeymen. Instead they vented their wrath on the Trades' Union and bluntly declared that they had formed an Association "for the purpose of putting down the combination called the Trades' Union." They complained that "it was arbitrary in its measures, mischievous in its effects, subversive of the confidence and good feelings that formerly existed" between the employers and their workmen. They readily acknowledged the justice of the strikers' demands, but insisted on the right of maintaining an open shop. "We are willing, owing to the advanced price of living, to increase the wages to good workmen, [but] we deem it inexpedient to name any sum, prefering [sic] that every man be at liberty to make his own bargain."[120] In this age of aggressive capitalism, the master carpenters were to be ranked among its staunchest defenders.

Early in April the City Commissioners complied with the demands of the journeymen house carpenters.[121] Whether the private employers ever consented is not known.

Higher wages was the cry among the journeymen throughout the State in the spring of 1836. At Philadelphia, the brass and stirrup finishers, the leather dressers, the horn comb makers, the chairmakers and a motley of other trades were out on strike at one time or another.[122] The carpenters and cordwainers at Lancaster joined with their Philadelphia brethren in demanding higher wages.[123]

With the return of summer the ten-hour issue reappeared. Although most of the strikes which occurred during the summer of 1836 were for

---

[119] The *Pennsylvanian*, March 21, 1836.

[120] The *Pennsylvanian*, March 17, 1836.

[121] The *National Laborer*, April 2, 1836.

[122] The *Pennsylvanian*, March 5, 1836. See also The *National Laborer*, April 23 and May 21, 1836.

[123] The *Lancaster Journal*, April 15, 1836.

wages, the most notable one, that of the ship carpenters and caulkers of the Philadelphia Navy Yard, was for the shorter work day. The Federal Government now remained the only important employer in the Philadelphia area who had not conceded the ten-hour day.[124]

When the Navy Yard workers struck, the Commandant, in an attempt to crush the move, offered higher wages than those given to the workmen in the other ship yards. A fear spread through the wage earners in the City that it was the design of the Commandant to subvert the ten-hour system.[125] Protest meetings were held and the President was petitioned by the Philadelphia workers for the establishment of the shorter work day in the Navy Yard.

The Secretary of Navy, Mahlon Dickerson, succumbing to various pressures, not the least of them being the forthcoming Presidential election, on August 31 directed the president of the Navy Board that the "same regulations . . . as are generally observed at the private ship yards" be instituted at the Philadelphia Navy Yard.[126] Although the action was belated and bestowed begrudgingly, it was welcomed by all the wage earners of Philadelphia.

Later that same year the biscuit bakers, after contemplating their plight, quit work. They were the victims of technology and cheap labor. Steam engines were introduced into the biscuit making industry, and negro hands were hired to supplant the few hands necessary to operate the new machines.[127]

In the subsequent years, the workingmen of Pennsylvania continued to protest but their cries were feeble and went unheeded. At Pittsburgh, the carpenters vainly sought the ten-hour day, and the glass cutters struggled against a reduction in their wages. The Harrisburg printers strove for higher wages, and at Philadelphia the carpenters pursued the same fantasy.[128]

---

[124] The *National Laborer*, Aug. 30, 1836. See R. B. Morris, "Andrew Jackson was no F. D. R.," *Labor and the Nation*, May-June 1949. Professor Morris in this revealing article sheds new light on the liberalism of the Jacksonians.

[125] The *National Laborer*, August 13, 20, 1836.

[126] Morris, *op. cit.*, p. 39.

[127] The *National Laborer*, October 1, 1836.

[128] The *National Laborer*, February 4, 1837. See also The *Public Ledger*, February 10 and March 22, 1839.

VII

LABOR STRIFE AMONG THE UNSKILLED WAGE EARNERS[1]

THE POLITICAL DEMOCRACY which ushered in the Jackson Era had its repercussions in the labor movement. The skilled and the unskilled, the men and women workers, all on one occasion or another expressed their disapproval of existing conditions. Shorter hours and Sunday work, higher wages and the union shop caused many bitter conflicts between capital and labor. Provocative efforts by the entrepreneurs to lower wages, the speed up, and the introduction of new machinery often initiated a spirited resistance by the wage earners. But the disputes over hours and wages overshadowed all others in the "Age of Jackson."

Probably nowhere can a better expression of this insurgent democracy be found, than in the struggles of the factory operatives and the manual laborers to raise their status in society. In the fall of 1828, the cotton spinners of Philadelphia and its suburbs struck against a proposed reduction of twenty-five percent in their wages.[2] They complained of the "avarice of their employers, who are attempting to reduce the prices of labour, although they already accumulate in the form of profits *more* than is obtained by the journeymen as wages."[3] While the spinner could make only "from $7.50 to $8.50 per week . . . by working the full period of twelve hours," the strikers contended that, "in doing this he actually earned for the millowners, from $40 to $50 dollars per week."[4] As the strike progressed, feeling between the strikers and those who persisted in working grew taut. At Norristown, a few children sneered at a scab and were taken to court and charged with assault.[5] Three striking spinners at Manayunk were bound over by the Philadelphia County Court to keep the peace because it was alleged that they had threatened strike breakers.[6] Despite a standout of over three months and

---

[1] Paper read before the annual meeting of the Pennsylvania Historical Association which convened at Dickinson College, Carlisle, Penna., October 1949. Printed in *Pennsylvania History*, 17, January 1950, pp. 23-38.
[2] The *Mechanic's Free Press*, November 15, 1828 and April 17, 1830.
[3] *Ibid.*, December 20, 1828.
[4] As cited in Commons, *History of Labour*, I, p. 418.
[5] *Mechanic's Free Press*, Nov. 15, 1828.
[6] *Hazard's Register of Pennsylvania*, III, Jan. 17, 1829, p. 39.

financial aid from the journeymen carpenters and cordwainers, the spinners were compelled to accept a reduction of ten percent on their present wages.[7] This marked the beginning of the aggressions by the employers, and within two years successive reductions totaling thirty percent had been imposed upon the factory operatives.[8]

The factory owners in the summer of 1833 once again decreed a reduction of about twenty percent in the wages of the factory hands.[9] Both factions in this dispute exhibited a keen awareness of the necessity of crystallizing public opinion in their favor. The strikers turned to the press to plead their cause before the people. They exposed the degrading and iniquitous system of labor which compelled them to work from thirteen to fourteen hours per day for weekly wages which averaged four dollars and thirty-three cents.[10] With sentiments, which today would stigmatize them as Marxists, the factory workers charged "that as the poor are sinking, the rich are rising." "Are we so debased," they asked, "as to be afraid to assert our rights, the rights of freemen, to break the shackles of oppression?"[11] Although an old biblical maxim stated that "he that will not work, neither let him eat," the operatives were keenly aware that, "in the present state of society, it happens that many contrive to eat at the expense of those who work."[12]

Under the pseudonym "Observer," there appeared in the *Germantown Telegraph* articles in defense of the mill owners. The operatives were convinced, however, that the anonymous writer was a paid propagandist drawn from the ranks of the factory hands.[13] This apologist for the owners wrote platitudes on the equality of the rich and the poor and hailed the virtues of the individual contract. He asserted that the employers exercise "no kind of control" over the employees. "He [the worker] is perfectly at liberty to reject or accept [any] offer, and if he can get higher wages elsewhere, he will, and is right in so doing," insisted this spokesman for the factory owners.[14]

Answering this argument of the "Observer," a worker reminded him of the enormous economic power which the owners possessed and of the

---

[7] *Mechanic's Free Press*, Dec. 20, 1828, April 17, 1830.

[8] *Ibid.*

[9] The *Germantown Telegraph*, August 7, 1833; *Daily Chronicle*, August 8, 1833.

[10] The *Germantown Telegraph*, August 28, 1833.

[11] The *Germantown Telegraph*, August 28, 1833.

[12] *Ibid.*

[13] *Ibid.*, October 30, 1833.

[14] *Ibid.*, September 4, 1833.

"blacklist." "If he [the worker] is honest enough to proclaim his wrongs, and assert his rights," this factory operative pointed out, "he is excluded by the proscription from getting employment in any other of these slave shops, and being unable from want of physical strength . . . to follow out-door labor, he becomes a burden to his friends, his spirit is broken, and he sinks into the grave another victim of our equal laws."[15]

Whether the immediate object of the strike was obtained is not known. Though the factory workers might have failed in resisting a reduction in their wages, the turnout was not a complete failure. It had provided inspiration for the trades' union movement of Philadelphia and had introduced to the workers John Ferral, a handloom weaver, who became one of the foremost labor leaders in the United States during the Jackson Era.

Prophetically the factory workers during the strike of 1833 had expressed the fear "that the attempted reduction in our wages is but a forerunner of greater evils, and greater oppressions."[16] To their dismay, the mill owners of Manayunk and Blockley, early in March 1834, ordered another reduction of twenty-five percent on their present wages.[17] A strike of the operatives was the inevitable result, and it occurred during the bank war and the hard times of 1834.[18] The workers appointed a relief committee—three men and two women—to solicit aid for the widows and orphans of those "who have been unable to save anything from their miserable earnings and are now destitute of the means of subsistence."[19] A picket line was organized and the strikers showed a remarkable solidarity in the crisis. One owner made an effort to coax the workers back with a fifteen percent reduction, but the strikers were firm.[20]

Determined to break the strike, the employers hired strikebreakers and secured police protection for the scabs.[21] At a public meeting held May 9, 1834, the factory workers indignantly declared, "that we, the free citizens of this republic, deprecate with well-merited contempt, the

---

[15] *Ibid.*, September 18, 1833.

[16] The *Pennsylvanian*, August 28, 1833.

[17] The *Germantown Telegraph*, March 19, 1834; The *Man*, April 15, 1834.

[18] The *Man*, April 15, 1834.

[19] The *Pennsylvanian*, May 9, 1834; The *Man*, April 15, 1834.

[20] The *Pennsylvanian*, April 22, 1834; see John B. Andrews and W. D. P. Bliss, *History of Women in Trade Unions*, Senate Document, No. 645, 61st Congress, 2d Session (Washington, 1911).

[21] The *Man*, April 29, 1834.

attempted bullying of the working people, into a reduction of their wages."²² Not even the clergy were immune to this struggle and their voices were raised in behalf of the owners. The operatives had only pity for these misguided clergymen, "from whom better might be expected," and who used their influence, "to force some [workers] to go to work at the reduced prices."²³ But the strike was broken, and the strikers were urged "to use every exertion on their part, immediately to procure such work elsewhere as will suit each one of them individually."²⁴ Some of the hands returned to work at an advance of five percent but the remainder, it was understood, "are likely to procure work elsewhere."²⁵

In the following year the factory owners persisted in their efforts to reduce the wages of their employees. At Norristown, in the spring of 1835, one employer proposed to discharge all his old hands and secure new ones from another state. This was to be accomplished "by such a reduction in the prices of wages, as would be tantamount to an actual discharge of those at the present in his employ."²⁶ "What rendered the act particularly censurable as well as uncharitable," remarked the *Germantown Telegraph*, "was the fact, that those now in his employ, were principally constituted of persons who were brought up to the business in that establishment."²⁷ This same proprietor defrauded his workers by paying them in worn-out, defective pieces of coin, whereby he made a profit of ten to fifteen percent. The citizens of Norristown almost unanimously condemned this high-handed operator and an aroused citizenry compelled him to continue with his old hands at the old prices.²⁸

Alarmed by these continued assaults on their wage standards, the hand-loom weavers of the City and County of Philadelphia met in May. At this meeting it was resolved that, "The Trades' Union Societies are the only means by which the laborers can evade the crushing grasp of unfeeling employers."²⁹ John Ferral, one of the organizers of the meeting, anticipating the Marxists by many years, declared, "'War

²² The *Pennsylvanian*, May 9, 1834.
²³ The *Pennsylvanian*, May 9, 1834.
²⁴ The *Man*, May 29, 1834.
²⁵ The *Germantown Telegraph*, April 15, 1835.
²⁶ *Ibid.*
²⁷ *Ibid.*
²⁸ The *Germantown Telegraph*, May 15, 1835.
²⁹ The *Man*, May 8, 1835; The *Pennsylvanian*, May 15, 1835.

to the Knife' is the only security for the laborer in his contest with capital."[30] The weavers agreed then and there to "unite under the designation of 'The Handloom Weavers' Association of the City and County of Philadelphia."[31]

While most of the wage earners in 1835 were aggressively pushing forward their demands for a ten-hour day, the textile workers were still struggling against wage reductions. It is true that, in June, the factory hands at Manayunk did manage to secure an "agreement with the proprietors . . . that their day's service shall close at a somewhat earlier hour."[32] But this brief reference is the only indication that these unskilled workers were in a position to demand a shorter workday. In the summer, the tailoresses, seamstresses, binders, folders, and stock workers of Philadelphia turned out for an advance in wages and met with indifferent success.[33] Late in the fall of that year, the weavers once again were compelled to resist an attempted reduction of their wages.[34] Several hundred strikers paraded through the streets of Philadelphia with music playing and banners flying. The National Trades' Union, whose president was John Ferral, promised financial aid, and the Trades' Union of Newark pledged "individually and collectively to make the most strenuous efforts to assist them in throwing off a yoke which no Republican ought to submit to."[35]

The year 1836 was a year of labor unrest, not only in Pennsylvania but throughout the United States. Skyrocketing prices, which accompanied the business prosperity of the previous year, seriously menaced the living standards of the wage earners. Although most of the trades were successfully contending for higher wages the textile workers continued to be on the defensive resisting the aggressions of their employers. At Fairmount the handloom weavers vainly fought to resist wage reductions totaling twenty-five percent.[36] Throughout the fall, intermittent strikes broke out among these workers generally because of

---

[30] The *Pennsylvanian*, May 15, 1835.

[31] *Ibid.*

[32] The *Pennsylvanian*, June 4, 1835; The *Germantown Telegraph*, June 24, 1835.

[33] The *Saturday Evening Post*, June 10 and 27, 1835; The *Republican Standard and Downingtown Journal*, June 30, 1835.

[34] *National Trades' Union*, October 31, 1835. See *Niles' Register*, XLIX, October 10, 1835, p. 84. Niles says that the turn out was for higher wages.

[35] *National Trades' Union*, Oct. 31, 1835.

[36] The *National Laborer*, September 10, November 12, 26, 1836. It was reported that the handloom weavers had established a cooperative association.

the unwillingness of the mill owners to bargain in good faith.[37] At Norristown, the female operatives were out on strike because of an effort by the employers not only to reduce the price of their labor but also to introduce the speedup.[38]

At Pittsburgh, it was the ten-hour issue which agitated the factory hands. The Pittsburgh press in October, reported that "a number of workmen have been discharged by their employers" for assembling to advocate the shorter workday.[39] "Sixty hours in a week or ten hours each day is sufficient for any one to work more especially for the young and tender," contended the operatives. They pointed out that "in England, where a Monarch reigns, and the Nobility its Law-Makers, children are protected by a special law of the Realm."[40] "It is not for the *men* we wish the time of labour reduced," explained the strikers; "we plead for the *poor children, male and female*." They found it difficult to reconcile the altruistic actions of many of their employers "who [gave] hundreds of dollars to 'missionary societies' and other 'benevolent purposes'" while at the same time they kept "poor little children in servile bondage, from 13½ to 14 hours."[41]

Erroneously they likened their status to that of a slave or even worse. In an address to the citizens of the city, the factory workers declared, "we consider the white children that are employed in the Cotton Factories of this city, equal, if not in a worse situation than the black slaves of the South."[42] The charge was reiterated by the editor

---

[37] The *National Laborer,* September 19 and 26, 1836. The Fairmount Trade Association reported that an "agreement was entered into and settled by Mr. S. McBride meeting with a committee from the hands appointed for that purpose at a general meeting. . . . On the morning of the 22nd inst. the mill went into operation, the hands cheerfully joined their work satisfied that although they had lost a little time they had succeeded in maintaining their prices, and were, if possible, more firmly united than before the strike took place; but what was their surprise to hear that those men who had given notice to quit the factory previous to the strike if the prices were not raised, but intended to continue if they were, that they were all paid off and discharged immediately, which has actually been done."

[38] The *National Laborer,* Oct. 15, 22, 1836. The factory operatives complained that the employer having reduced their prices far below those paid in other places, resorted to a sneaking mode of increasing the quantity of their labor. They were paid a certain price for what is called a "cut" and the respectable employer, without intimation, added to it two or three yards, thus compelling them to perform additional labor without any additional compensation.

[39] The *Allegheny Democrat and Working-Man's Advocate,* October 21, 1836.

[40] *Ibid.,* October 7, 1836.

[41] *Ibid.,* October 21, 1836.

[42] The *Allegheny Democrat and Working Man's Advocate,* October 7, 1836.

of the *Allegheny Democrat.* "It is an absolute fact," averred this editor, "that the females in the Cotton Factories in this city, and its vicinity, are treated and abused worse than the female black slaves of the South."[43]

Although unsuccessful in securing the shorter work day, the efforts of the Pittsburgh factory workers were not fruitless. The public was aroused and shortly afterwards a movement was initiated which culminated in an investigation of factory conditions in Pennsylvania by a committee of the State Legislature.[44]

In the years to follow, in the years of the great panic, there were only a few recorded instances of strikes by the textile workers, and as always, these disputes grew out of the efforts of the mill owners to reduce the wages of their employees. During the summer of 1839, the handloom weavers of Philadelphia struck against a proposed reduction of their wages. They complained that their weekly earnings now averaged only $4.86, and if the proposed reduction went into effect it would reduce their weekly wages by $1.08, leaving them only $3.76 to cover the costs of house rent, fuel, light, loom and tackling repairs.[45]

During the Jackson Era, the factory workers fought a losing battle to maintain their living standards. Although economically weak, feebly organized and their ranks composed largely of women and children, they had a notable record of resistance, and although they lost, their struggles were not in vain. These lowly factory hands had given inspiration to the trade union movement of Pennsylvania, and to the trade union movement of the United States they had given an outstanding leader, John Ferral.

This spirit of unrest which had moved the factory hands to a vigorous defense of their rights permeated the large mass of inarticulate workers —the day laborers, the canal hands, the carters, the wood sawyers and others—and often culminated in serious riots. The use of the police and the militia to break these strikes was widespread. The causes for these outbursts varied, but the question of wages figured prominently in most of the disputes.

It was reported in the fall of 1828, that the canal workers near Harrisburg had rioted. The New York Mammoth Company, which had

---

[43] The *Allegheny Democrat and Working Man's Advocate,* December 9, 1836.

[44] *Ibid.,* Dec. 23, 1836, Feb. 3, 1837. See *Pennsylvania Senate Journal,* II, 1837-38. See also J. Lynn Barnard, *Factory Legislation in Pennsylvania: Its History and Administration* (Philadelphia, 1907), p. 7.

[45] The *Public Ledger,* August 30, 1839.

undertaken the construction of this section of the canal, had stopped payment of wages and was in arrears as much as $400 to some workmen.[46] One year and a half later, riots again broke out among the canal hands near Harrisburg.

During the severe winter of 1828-1829, canal hands, numbering two to three hundred, were unemployed and had become "indebted to storekeepers and others for their subsistence."[47] A freshet in the Susquehanna had ruptured the dam at Clark's Ferry and the men, taking advantage of the crisis, demanded that their wages be increased from eighty cents to one dollar per day before any repairs would be made. The contractors refused to comply with their request. Apparently the strikers had anticipated this, for sympathetic hands from other sections of the Susquehanna and from the Juniata section appeared, and a general turn out of all hands on that section was ordered.[48] "All this appears to have been done with perfect coolness," a Harrisburg paper reported, and expressed the fear, "that an understanding to the same effect exists along the whole line of [the] canal, as canalers from various other contracts were on the ground, encouraging the rioters."[49]

The local police, the militia, and the clergy were called upon to put down the strikers. From Dauphin County the sheriff with cavalry and with the assistance of the Halifax infantry, armed with bayonets and muskets, rushed to the scene of the strike. As the military approached, "the labourers armed themselves with clubs, and threatened to repel any attack." A Catholic priest, Reverend Fr. Curran, used "his personal influence over the rioters" to "induce them to submit to civil authority," and received the commendation of the press for his intercession in this disturbance.[50] This threat of force combined with the exhortations of the clergyman appears to have broken the strike, since nothing further was reported about it.

The impetus which the common laborers gave to the struggles for the shorter work day was, without a doubt, their greatest contribution to the labor movement in Pennsylvania. In May 1835, about three hundred coal heavers on the Schuylkill wharves struck for the ten-hour day. A complete stoppage of work was effected. Seventy-five vessels

---

[46] *Poulson's American Daily Advertiser,* September 25, 1827.

[47] The *Baltimore American and Commercial Advertiser,* April 9, 1829.

[48] The *Pennsylvania Reporter,* April 7, 1829.

[49] *Ibid.*

[50] The *Pennsylvania Reporter,* April 7, 1829; *Baltimore American and Republican Commercial Advertiser,* April 9, 1829; *Crawford Mesenger,* April 11, 1829; *Norristown Herald,* April 8, 1829.

were reported in the river waiting to take on freight, but "the hands in the boats dare not attempt to load, lest their vessels should be scuttled."[51] Niles estimated that the loss to the community was $2,000 per day.[52] Late in May, the employers met and resolved not to accede to the demands of the day laborers, and offered one dollar a day for those who would "work from sunrise to sunset."[53] They also agreed: "That unless the terms offered be accepted by the laborers, and they return to duty, at the respective yards, by tomorrow ... all hands heretofore employed by us shall be discharged, and not again employed by [any] of us."[54] One or two men responded to the call and a few new hands were hired at higher wages than had formerly been given. But in a few days the newly hired strikebreakers and the old hands who had returned to their jobs were out with the striking coal heavers and all the work on the docks was once again suspended.[55]

The press was almost unanimous in its condemnation of the strike. Niles charged that the "leaders of these 'strikes' are chiefly freshly imported *foreigners*—who despise and defy the law."[56] The *Saturday Evening Post* asserted that "those who refuse to act with . . . [the strikers] they treat with open violence."[57] A lurid account of the strike was printed in the *Philadelphia Gazette.* "One man who attempted to work was assailed by the laborers, and . . . his head was laid open with a stone."[58] They "paraded the streets commanded by a man with a drawn sword in his hand, and [they] have threatened every man with death who dares lift a piece of coal," charged the editor of the *Gazette.*[59] But the *National Trades' Union,* the organ of the unionized workmen, assured its readers, "that the manner in which the workmen on the Schuylkill have conducted their strike, for the ten-hour system, has been grossly misrepresented, in the same way and by the same class of people, as the journeymen of New York have been." It con-

---

[51] The *Saturday Evening Post,* May 20, 1836; *Niles' Register,* XLVIII, June 6, 1835, p. 235.

[52] *Niles' Register,* VI, June 6, 1835, p. 235.

[53] The *Saturday Evening Post,* May 30, 1835.

[54] *Ibid.*

[55] The *Man,* June 8, 1835.

[56] *Niles' Register,* XLVIII, June 6, 1835, p. 235.

[57] The *Saturday Evening Post,* May 30, 1835.

[58] The *Philadelphia Gazette,* June 6, 1835 quoted in *Niles' Register,* XLVIII, June 6, 1835, p. 235.

[59] *Ibid.*

cluded that this deliberate distortion of fact was an endeavor to discredit the struggles of the workingmen and the Trades' Union.[60]

By the first of June, almost every other trade in the city had joined with the coal heavers in demanding the ten-hour day. This was another manifestation of that desire on the part of the wage earners to make of democracy more than just a shibboleth. Previous to this, abortive strikes had been conducted by the journeymen bricklayers and carpenters of Philadelphia and Pittsburgh.[61] But it was the day laborers on the Schuylkill wharves who, "against the tremendous power of wealth and avarice" and even when "the issue . . . was considered doubtful," stubbornly resisted all efforts to break their strike.[62] When joined by the carpenters, the bricklayers, the stone masons, and a dozen other trades, the outcome was inevitable. On June 13, The *Saturday Evening Post* reported:

> The excitement among our mechanics seems to have nearly abated, the object for which the strike was made having been obtained by the acquiescence of the master workmen generally in their request.

In the turbulence and excitement which prevailed in the City during these hectic June days, only brief and sneering remarks greeted the turn out of "that humble but useful class of workingmen, the wood sawyers." They struck for an increase in wages "from forty to fifty cents for oak wood, and seventy-five cents for hickory."[63] More interest should have been directed toward it since it was an early attempt of negro and white workers acting in unison to improve their lot. Instead of sympathy for the efforts of these humble woodcutters, there was only animosity in the derisive accounts of the strike in the local papers. "The woodcutters had a regular turn out, ebonies, mulattoes and whites," caustically observed one paper. "They raised a dust, made a good deal of noise, marched up street and down again, and 'strait were seen no more'!"[64] The conservative *United States Gazette* made no effort to conceal its racial sentiments. "Yesterday," the *Gazette* informed its readers, "there was a turn out among the wood sawyers—some ten or a

[60] *National Trades' Union*, June 6, 1835.
[61] The *Aurora and Franklin Gazette*, June 14, 1827; The *Mechanic's Free Press*, June 27, 1829; The *Allegheny Democrat*, March 24, 1829; The *Pittsburgh Mercury*, May 25, 1831; The *Pittsburgh Gazette*, March 20, 1832.
[62] *National Trades' Union*, October 10, 1835.
[63] The *Pennsylvanian*, June 13, 1835.
[64] The *Republican Standard and Downington Journal*, June 30, 1835.

dozen who claimed affinities with whites and the rest the cullings of a lot of blacks. . . ."[65]

Elsewhere in Pennsylvania the day laborers were on the move. At Norristown, three or four hundred railroad workers struck successfully for the ten-hour day.[66] The laborers and carters employed by the Borough of Reading "left off work, on account of the alleged lowness of their wages." They had been receiving seventy-five cents per day.[67] From Pottsville came word that the boatmen had assembled at Hamburg and had refused to permit any coal boats to pass until their demands had been met. The merchants and miners flatly rejected their request for $1.25 a ton for carrying coal.[68]

The *Miner's Journal*, rabidly opposed to the strike, charged that only a small minority—forty to fifty of the four hundred boats on the canal—supported the strike; that the strikers had resorted to "force and violence" to intimidate their fellow workmen; and lastly, that the civil authorities had "connive[d] at their outrages, and by their culpable apathy [had] afford[ed] encouragement to the strikers."[69] But other accounts contradicted these charges. When the strikers held a demonstration and marched into Pottsville, several hundred boatmen made up the procession.[70] And what violence occurred seems to have been precipitated by the sheriff, who, "with a 'monstrous watch,' charged the column [of marchers], secured several, and put the rest to flight. . . ."[71] Late in July a satisfactory agreement was reached between the boatmen and the coal operators.[72]

In the spring of the following year, rising costs induced the canal hands at Manayunk and the day laborers and the Schuylkill coal heavers at Philadelphia to strike for higher wages. At Manayunk, where unemployment prevailed, the contractors on the canal works cut the wages of their hands to seventy-five cents per day. But the canal workers re-

---

[65] The *United States Gazette*, June 12, 1835.

[66] The *Pennsylvanian*, June 18, 1835; The *Columbia Spy*, June 20, 1835.

[67] The *Chronicle of the Times*, July 21, 1835; The *Berks and Schuylkill Journal*, July 25, 1835.

[68] The *Berks and Schuylkill Journal*, July 11, 1835; The *American Sentinel*, July 7, 1835.

[69] The *Berks and Schuylkill Journal*, July 11, 1835; The *American Sentinel*, July 7, 1835; *Hazard's Register*, XVI, July 1835, p. 12.

[70] The *Berks and Schuylkill Journal*, July 11, 1835.

[71] The *Pennsylvanian*, July 14, 1835.

[72] *Ibid.*

sisted to a man and not only rejected the reduction but compelled the bosses to give them the ten-hour day.[73]

The efforts of the Schuylkill laborers to advance their wages to $1.25 per day met with more substantial resistance. As evidence of good faith and to meet the criticisms of their employers, the coal yard workers, weeks in advance of the strike, made known their intentions. Their employers responded by placing in the newspapers an advertisement for 500 hands.[74] Sufficient workers apparently did not respond to the call, because the employers turned to the courts for aid. A charge of rioting secured the arrest of several of the coal heavers and the mayor placed the bail for three of them at the exorbitant sum of $2,500.[75]

Other trades reacted immediately to this attack on the Schuylkill workers and made the coal heavers' struggle their own. The Trades' Union entered into the fray and for the first time it admitted unskilled workers into its membership.[76] From the far end of the State came word that the Pittsburgh workers had assembled and had protested this unwarranted attack on "our rights and liberties" by the present mayor of Philadelphia.[77] Despite the testimony of many of the respectable coal speculators themselves, the court decided "that there was no evidence of a breach of the peace" during the strike.[78] This vindication of the coal heavers did not assuage the angry wage earners of Philadelphia, and the Trades' Union led a movement for the defeat of Mayor John Swift in the forthcoming election, because of his prejudiced conduct toward the Schuylkill laborers.[79]

Caught up in this general movement for higher wages were the day laborers who were employed by the plasterers and bricklayers. They struck for a minimum wage of $1.25 per day. The Trades' Union, responding to an appeal of these workmen, recommended that its members pay the prices asked. Months later, to the chagrin of that organization, it learned that some of its own members were paying "less than the prices fixed by the Laborer's Society."[80]

---

[73] The *National Laborer*, March 7, 1836.

[74] *Ibid.*

[75] *Ibid.*

[76] The *National Laborer*, May 21, 1836.

[77] The *Allegheny Democrat and Working-Man's Advocate*, Sept. 2, 1836.

[78] The *Public Ledger*, August 25, 1836; The *National Laborer*, August 27, 1836. See also Commons, *History of Labour*, I, p. 377.

[79] The *Public Ledger*, August 25, 1836; The *National Laborer*, Aug. 27, 1836.

[80] The *National Laborer*, July 2, 1836.

Unemployment and the hard times which accompanied the panic of 1837 stayed for a brief time those violent outbursts which had characterized the relations of labor and capital in the previous two years. Isolated and futile strikes emphasized how seriously the depression had struck the ranks of the common laborers. Late in the summer of 1837, a general strike broke out among the workmen on the Susquehanna Canal "for higher wages and more grog."[81] All work was suspended and for a short time it appeared as if the strikers would win their demands. But the resolute stand taken by the contractors and the return of many hands broke the strike.[82]

Two years later, three hundred railroad workers between Reading and Hamburg turned out for an increase in their wages from $1.00 to $1.12½ per day, and for a larger ration of whiskey. One contractor complied with the requests of his workers but on most sections their demands were summarily rejected.[83] The bewildered laboring men looked hesitantly toward the future for a solution to their difficulties.

These unskilled wage earners had fought the good fight. Against tremendous odds they had bent their efforts toward making this Democracy live up to its promise. They were among the first workers to realize the necessity of an organization embracing all workingmen. They had inspired the first successful ten-hour movement in Pennsylvania. And when all else failed, they alone, of all the wage earners, were able to arouse the State Legislature and to compel it to consider the workers' demands. Although many of their dreams were shattered and their high endeavors met with failure, the fault was not theirs. Forces far beyond their comprehension and control conspired to defeat them.

---

[81] The *Harrisburgh Chronicle*, August 23, 1837.

[82] *Ibid.*

[83] The *Public Ledger*, June 12, 1839.

VIII

LABOR AND POLITICS DURING THE JACKSON ERA

THE ASSIDUOUS COURTING of the wage earners by the professional politicians in the decades of the 1820's and the 1830's marked the appearance of a new and unknown quantity in the political affairs of the State and nation. It is true that the partisans of Jefferson made a strong and effective plea for the support of the people but their appeal was "to the 'masses' against the 'aristocracy' of riches" with no specific plea for the support of the wage earners as such.[1] Although the Jeffersonians had not paid special court to labor they had, with their attacks on the Federalist Party and with their success in identifying that party with privilege and the hated British aristocracy, been instrumental in arousing in the hearts and minds of the common man a desire for a greater voice in the affairs of the government which thus far had been denied them.

Nothing was more indicative of the awakening of the American wage earners to their interests as a class than this constant plea for their support, and the contentions of most of the aspirants for political office that not only had they at one time been humble hard-working mechanics, but that they could best serve the interests of the laboring classes in the legislative halls. Democrat and Anti-Democrat vied with one another in proclaiming their lowly origins. In the local elections in Philadelphia in 1828, the mechanics were reminded that Judge Hemphill, a Jackson Democrat, had "served his time to a *Trade*—that he was an apprentice . . . to a wheelwright, and has always proved himself to be the Mechanick's Friend."[2] The *Philadelphia Mercury* attributed the success of Andrew Jackson in the election of 1828 "to the *Farmers,* the *mechanics* and *working people* of Pennsylvania," and there was a large element of truth in this assertion.[3]

If the working people of Pennsylvania were unaware that their interests and their problems were separate and distinct from those of other social classes, the hopeful office seeker was unwilling to let them live in

---

[1] Charles A. Beard, *Economic Origins of Jeffersonian Democracy* (New York, 1949), p. 401.

[2] The *Philadelphia Mercury,* October 4, 1828.

[3] *Ibid.,* November 8, 1828.

this blissful ignorance, but constantly reminded them of the peculiar nature of their difficulties. One has only to read the partisan presses throughout the Jackson era to realize that the politicians were keenly aware of the awakening of labor to its interests as a class, and they were willing to exploit it to the fullest. The Jacksonian Democrats assumed for themselves the role of spokesmen for the working classes but not without protests from the organized wage earners and from the opposing parties.

The *Allegheny Democrat* appraised the victory of the Democrats in a local election in 1825 as a triumph of the labouring classes. "It is with no inconsiderable satisfaction that we have the pleasure to announce to our democratic brethren throughout the state, the complete triumph of principle, democracy, and the rights of the labouring class of citizens ...," declared the editor of the *Allegheny Democrat*.[4] Throughout the next decade the Democratic Party endeavored to identify and link itself with the cause of the working men. The *Pennsylvanian,* the organ of the Jacksonians in Philadelphia, did yeoman's work toward this end. Scarcely an issue of this paper appeared without an appeal to the wage earners as a class to rally behind the Jackson Democrats. It kept them posted on the machinations of the Federalists and was liberal with its political advice to them. Faithfully, it printed the reports of the various trade union meetings and kept the workingmen generally informed on those affairs which it considered of primary interest to this class. In the summer of 1832, when the presidential campaign for that year was getting underway, it warned the workingmen of Philadelphia to beware of the chicanery of the "*tory gazettes* of Chandler and Poulson, who are very anxious as of yore, when they called them [the working men] the *swinish multitude, to save them from their own worst enemies, themselves.*"[5] With the loss of Philadelphia to the Anti-Jacksonians that year, the *Pennsylvanian* admonished the workingmen for their lethargy, and accused them of throwing their votes to their oppressors. "The *Working Men*—Where are they?" this Democratic paper inquired. "Do they remember the screws put upon them by the aristocrats during the closing summer? Are they to throw away their influence and votes upon those that squeeze the life's blood out of their hearts." The *Aurora* accused them of deserting the ranks of their true

---

[4] The *Allegheny Democrat*, October 11, 1825.

[5] The *Pennsylvanian*, July 26, 1832.

benefactors and setting "themselves apart . . . of their fellow citizens" and constituting themselves a third class in society.[6]

The Democratic papers throughout the State like their Philadelphia counterparts made a strong bid for the support of the wage earners, and they too identified their struggles with the struggles of the workingmen. The *American Volunteer* viewed the election of 1836 as a decisive one for the working people of the State. On one side would be arrayed the Bank, "with all its dazzling and corrupting influences—on the other side, the people, the farmers, the mechanics, and laborers, the 'bone and sinew' of the country. . . ."[7] At Harrisburg, the *Keystone* accused the Whig and Bank aristocracy of a desire "to degrade the LABOUR-ING classes, as nearly as possible, to a level with the BEASTS of the FIELD. . . ."[8]

By 1838, when the activity of organized labor had been seriously curtailed by the great panic, some of the Journals began to deprecate this appeal to only one class of citizens, the working class. As early as 1834, the *Farmers and Mechanic's Almanack* had ridiculed this type of electioneering.[9]

> It was all the go, then [this *Almanack* stated] to be considered a *workingman,* and at the time of the election, every sort of professional pride was thrown by, until a more fitting season. "My *great-grandfather* was a *blacksmith*" exclaimed a lawyer in a triumphant voice, at one of the preparatory meetings in Southwark; "I am one of the people", (raising himself up with appropriate dignity). "I ask you to vote *for me* in preference to that *doctor,* who has no plebian blood."

When, in 1838, a call was made for the working men of the City and County of Philadelphia to meet and discuss the question of the resumption of specie payments, the *Public Ledger* heatedly declared[10]

> We are heartily sick of this continual cant about "working men", and shall omit no proper opportunity for reproving it. In a community where all work, it is the excess of arrogance in any portion to claim this epithet as a distinguishing title. . . . Nothing has excited more malignant animosities among bodies of men in this country, than this base cant, introduced by foreign

[6] The *Aurora Semi-Weekly,* July 19, 1834.
[7] The *American Volunteer,* August 11, 1836.
[8] The *Keystone,* November 30, 1836.
[9] The *Farmers and Mechanics Almanack,* 1834, p. 5.
[10] The *Public Ledger,* April 28, 1838.

mischief-makers; and no efforts of ours shall be wanting, to inspire every *American* with just contempt of it.

Even the *Pennsylvanian* which had been anything but restrained in its exploitation of this term now found itself in agreement with the *Ledger*. "It is high time that the term 'workingmen' as a distinctive appellation, were finally laid aside," righteously counselled this rabid Jacksonian organ. "Always objectionable, its day has gone by, and now let it slumber."[11] One can only conjecture as to this sudden about face. It possibly was that the opponents of the Democrats were making more headway among the working classes of Pennsylvania with this appeal, or there was the possibility that in these depressing days when unemployment and misery were the common lot of the wage earners, there was a fear that they might take too literally its previous directive urging them to unite and act in concert to improve their status. The evidences of the growth of a spirit of class consciousness among the wage earners did not come alone from those elements who wished to exploit them. It was manifested in the words and the actions of the working men themselves.

It was no accident that the first labor movement in the United States which culminated in the emergence of the workingmen into politics had its origin in Philadelphia since that city had the necessary aggregation of laborers dispossessed of their tools, and a factory system which made a labor movement natural and inevitable.[12] In addition, the Pennsylvania workingmen were among the first in the United States to enjoy manhood suffrage.[13] The wage earners of Philadelphia possessed a long tradition of militant struggle and some of the earliest conflicts between labor and capital occurred there.

The forces which precipitated the Philadelphia workingmen in 1827 into politics embodies a long list of economic, political and social ills which had plagued them for many years. It was as a consequence of these political and social inequalities that the workingmen felt that they were being deprived of their rights as citizens of a democracy. Since the abstract ideal of equality had failed to be translated into a concrete reality, they felt that "true democracy had been cheated of

---

[11] The *Pennsylvanian*, April 30, 1838.

[12] See Frank T. Carlton, *History and Problem of Organized Labor* (Chicago, 1911), p. 32.

[13] See Francis N. Thorpe, *The Federal and State Constitutions* (Washington, D. C., 1909), V, p. 3096.

any real substantial victory."[14] "We are fast approaching those extremes of wealth and extravagance on the one hand, and ignorance, poverty and wretchedness on the other, which will eventually terminate in those unnatural and oppressive distinctions which exist in the corrupt governments of the old world," complained the *Working Man's Advocate*.[15]

When the city councils and the State Legislature ignored their petitions for more just and equitable legislation, it merely confirmed the workers' suspicions that justice for the laborers did not emanate from those sources. All their efforts to draw the attention of the governing classes to their unsanitary and unprotected dwellings were in vain. In the spring of 1829, the *Mechanic's Free Press* wrote that "the manner in which the memorials of the working people have been first produced in the councils of the City of Philadelphia and secondly in the legislature of Pennsylvania show us clearly that we may expect neither favor nor affection, neither equal laws nor justice from any political party who may ascend into power."[16]

There were other evils more immediate and more tangible which had a desolating effect upon the workingmen. They had seen their unions maligned as conspiracies, and their fellow workmen who struck for higher wages and better working conditions thrown into prison. "If the mechanics combine to raise their wages," wrote Stephen Simpson, author of *The Workingman's Manual*, "the laws punish them as conspirators against the good of society, and the dungeon awaits them as it does the robber. But the laws have made it a just and meritorious act that capitalists shall combine to strip the man of labor of his earnings, reduce him to a dry crust and a gourd of water. Thus does power invert justice, and derange the order of nature."[17]

While the members of the wage earners' unions had been arrested for no other cause "than trying honestly to obtain an advance in wages,"[18] they saw a bill of indictment charging some employing tailors for conspiracy to reduce wages, dismissed by the grand jury. On that grand jury sat two of the tailors against whom the indictment had been drawn.[19] They were convinced that there was little hope for the workingman from the courts of justice.

---

[14] See Commons, *History of Labour*, I, p. 177.

[15] The *Working Man's Advocate*, November 7, 1829.

[16] The *Mechanic's Free Press*, March 14, 1829.

[17] Stephen Simpson, The *Workingman's Manual* (Philadelphia, 1831), p. 86

[18] The *National Laborer*, May 21, 1836.

[19] *Ibid.*, June 11, 1836.

Imprisonment for debt was another of those evils which dwell more heavily upon the poor man than upon the rich. The debts on the whole were small but they had an injurious and degrading effect upon the workingmen. *Hazard's Register* reported that from June 6, 1829 until February 24, 1830, 817 persons were imprisoned for debt in Pennsylvania as follows:[20]

30	for	debts	below	$ 1.00				
233	for	debts	above	$ 1.00	and below	$	5.00	
174	"	"	"	5.00	"	"	10.00	
140	"	"	"	10.00	"	"	20.00	
142	"	"	"	20.00	"	"	100.00	

For 252 of these unfortunate individuals, the debts totaled $663.00 while the costs totaled $448.00, and for 68 others, the debts were $58.00 and the costs were $120.00.

While the poor man languished in prison for some trifling debt, he lost not only his source of income but he was forced to depend upon charity for the necessities of life. Thus indisposed, he often fell into the hands of an unscrupulous creditor and was a valuable pawn during the elections. "The blessed law (if law it is)," grumbled the *Working Man's Advocate*, "gives the monied man an influence in our elections that no other man could possess."[21]

The horrible indignities which this law inflicted on the poor but honest laborer convinced him that it was a vital factor in bringing on his degradation. In an address to the city and county conventions of the workingmen of Pennsylvania the speaker bitterly asked: "How long fellow citizens, shall the fair page of our history be blemished by this foul blot? How long shall it be the policy of our government to add oppression and insult to the wounded feelings of the unfortunate?"[22]

Of all the evils against which the wage earners of Pennsylvania raised their voices in protest, their loudest and most persistent complaint was directed against the highly partial and totally inadequate system of education provided for their children. Private schools for the wealthy were provided, but for the sons of the poor there existed only the detested charity schools.[23] Under such a system only the very poor were taken care of, however inadequately. Thousands of children whose parents were unable to provide a good private education for them, and

---

[20] *Hazard's Register of Pennsylvania*, V, p. 176.

[21] The *Working Man's Advocate*, November 1, 1830.

[22] *Ibid.*

[23] The *Mechanic's Free Press*, July 10, 1830.

whose standing in the community excluded them from taking advantage of the benefits of the poor law, were totally neglected.[24]

As in the case of those other evils against which the wage earners protested, they struggled for social and political equality rather than for economic equality. They feared the degradation of their status in society and felt that their fundamental liberties were jeopardized because of the present unfair system of education. "Lack of education deprives the poor from representation in government," contended the *Mechanic's Free Press*.[25] The workingmen believed that the future of a free and democratic government hinged on this issue. A committee of workingmen investigating the state of public education in Pennsylvania made the following statement which expressed accurately the prevailing attitude toward this problem. "The original element of despotism is a monopoly of talent, which consigns the multitude to comparative ignorance, and secures the balance of knowledge on the side of the rich and the rulers—this monopoly should be broken up and . . . the means of equal knowledge (the only security for equal liberty), should be rendered, by legal provision, the common property of all classes."[26]

It was infuriating for the poor to see public funds expended for the improvement of colleges and universities which obviously did not provide for the education of their sons. "Funds thus expended," lamented the *Mechanic's Free Press*, "may serve to engender an aristocracy of talent, in the hands of the privileged few; but can never secure the common prosperity of a nation nor confer intellectual as well as political equality on a people."[27]

The vigor displayed by the Pennsylvania wage earners in their fight against the inadequate educational facilities for the poor brought upon themselves attacks not only from the conservative local papers but also from papers outside of the State. Their whole program was dubbed "agrarianism" by the *National Gazette*.[28] The *Southern Review* felt that nothing good could result from such a program. "Is this the way to produce producers?" it asked. "To make every child in the state a

---

[24] *Hazard's Register of Pennsylvania*, IV, p. 293. See Stephen Simpson, *Workingman's Manual*, p. 26. See also Joseph McCadden, *Education in Pennsylvania, 1801-1835* (Philadelphia, 1937), p. 6.

[25] The *Mechanic's Free Press*, October 3, 1829.

[26] *Ibid.*, March 6, 1830.

[27] The *Mechanic's Free Press*, March 6, 1830.

[28] The *National Gazette*, as quoted in The *Working Man's Advocate*, August 28, 1830.

literary character would not be a good qualification for those who must live by manual labor," argued The *Southern Review*.[29]

Humanitarians joined in this struggle for school reform, and some of the most prominent names in the State were to be found in agreement with the workingmen. Roberts Vaux, John Sergeant and Governor Wolf, all influential in the affairs of the State, devoted much of their time to the reformation of the public school system of Pennsylvania. But in evaluating the forces responsible for education reform, F. T. Carlton states that "the vitality of the movement for tax-supported schools was derived not from the humanitarian leaders, but from the growing class of wage-earners."[30]

Undoubtedly, of all the injustices and iniquities against which they grumbled, the most pressing were the long hours of work. The accepted working day was from sun until dark, a system according to Helen Sumner, that had been carried over from agriculture. One paper reported that the men worked from 4:30 a. m. to 8:00 p. m. during the hottest months of summer, but during the short days of winter were without work.[31]

If there was any single item which could be designated as the immediate cause for the rise of labor as an organized force in politics, it was this issue of the long working day. An excerpt from the Preamble of the Mechanic's Union of Trade Associations read:[32]

> Is it equitable that we should waste the energies of our minds and bodies, and be placed in a situation of such unceasing exertion and servility as must necessarily, in time, render the benefits of our liberal institutions to us inaccessible and useless in order that the products of our labour may be accumulated by a few into vast pernicious masses, calculated to prepare the minds of the possessors for the exercise of lawless rule and despotism, to overawe the meagre multitude, and frighten away that shadow of freedom which still lingers among us?

Out of this growing demand for leisure time by the workingmen came the ten-hour issue in subsequent political campaigns.

---

[29] Anonymous, "Agrarian Educational Systems," The *Southern Review*, VI, (1828), p. 16.

[30] Frank T. Carlton, "Economic Influences Upon Education Progress in the United States 1820-1850," *University of Wisconsin Bulletin No. 221*, (Madison, 1908) p. 68.

[31] The *Working Man's Advocate*, May 7, 1831.

[32] The *Mechanic's Free Press*, October 25, 1828.

There were many other live issues against which the voices of the workingmen were heard in protest. The hated militia system, which required that every able-bodied male, with the exception of those employed in public service be enrolled in the State militia incurred the wrath of the wage earners throughout Pennsylvania.[33] What purpose was served by this annual collecting of "the depraved and the vicious . . . contributing largely to a continuance of their degradation," queried the *Mechanic's Free Press*.[34] The *Columbia Spy* thought the whole system absurd.[35]

> We were spectators last Saturday [this paper reported] of the *grand annual military farce* performed by those "gallant souls that shoulder sticks, and once a year go out a training"; and were never more fully impressed with the absurdity of our present militia system than on that occasion. . . . But if the training itself is a farce, the accompanying scenes partake more of tragedy when viewed with reference to their effect on public morals. In many of the adjacent taverns, gambling tables are put up and betting on chance from dollars down to paltry coppers is carried on in open day; . . . The kindred vice of drunkenness finds at these gatherings many of her degraded worshipers.

Equally hated by them was the lottery, which, according to one of the spokesmen of the wage earners, "had been the fruitful parent of misery and want to numberless heartbroken wives and helpless children, who have beheld the means of their subsistence lavished in the purchase of lottery tickets."[36] They vented their invective on the chartered monopolies which they charged were insidiously gaining exclusive control of the "wealth creating powers of modern mechanism." At a meeting of the working people of Byberry township it was decided that they would give their support only to those candidates who[37]

> maintain a firm resistance to all *chartered monopolies* whereby a "privileged order of men" accumulate wealth to the detriment of the many—This applies more particularly to banks; but as they do exist the stockholders should at least be made answerable for all "losses" for as they are the only gainers, others should not be the only losers."

---

[33] From the "Acts of the General Assembly of the Commonwealth of Pennsylvania," pp. 231-247 as quoted in Commons, *History of Labour*, I, p. 222.
[34] The *Mechanic's Free Press*, July 10, 1830.
[35] The *Columbia Spy*, May 24, 1834.
[36] The *Mechanic's Free Press*, September 26, 1830.
[37] *Ibid.*, September 18, 1830.

Paper money which in the minds of the working men was closely associated with the banking monopolies was subjected to the scorching criticism of the spokesmen for their cause.[38] John R. Commons very adequately sums up labor's struggle in this period in the following: "In general, the workingmen of this period were ardent champions of all reforms, from temperance and the abolition of prison labour, lotteries, and capital punishment, to the reform of taxation and a simpler and less expensive system of legal procedure, and many of those measures found their first friends in this labor movement."[39] On the masthead of the last issues of The *Mechanic's Free Press* were listed the following planks of the platform of the Working Men's Party of Philadelphia:[40]

> Abolition of Imprisonment for Debt
> Abolition of all licensed monopolies
> An entire revision or abolition of the present militia system
> A less expensive law system
> Equal taxation on property
> No legislation on religion
> A district system of elections

Inarticulate and unorganized, the workingmen of Pennsylvania were no serious threat to the existing order. As long as they conducted their struggles for political and social equality through the various local unions which existed prior to 1827, they were incapable of achieving any of their most cherished reforms.

THE WORKING MEN'S PARTY OF PHILADELPHIA

The year 1827 marked a sharp turning point in the history of the labor movement in the United States. The first signs of labor unrest appeared in Philadelphia in the spring of that year with the publication of a pamphlet describing "the evils under which the working people are laboring and a plan for their efficient removal."[41] It went on to add that the blessings of universal suffrage were useless to the worker as long as he possessed insufficient knowledge to make proper use of it. Scientific inventions and improvements might have been instrumental in reducing the hours of work from twelve to ten, to eight, to six, and so on "until the development of science [had] reduced human labour

---

[38] *Ibid.*, December 13, 1828; see Simpson, *op. cit.*, pp. 88, 89.
[39] Commons, *History of Labour*, I, p. 131.
[40] The *Mechanic's Free Press*, March 19, 1831.
[41] *Ibid.*, June 21, 1828.

to its lowest terms" instead of increasing the many difficulties which beset the laborer.[42]

Not long after the appearance of this pamphlet, the journeymen carpenters of Philadelphia struck in June 1827 for a ten-hour day. Soon the unrest spread to the other labor organizations within the city and, as has been mentioned, resulted in the formation of the Mechanic's Union of Trade Associations. Shortly after the formation of this central trades' union, the *Mechanic's Free Press* appeared on the streets of Philadelphia.[43] It was published by the Mechanic's Library Company of that city and its editorial board was chosen periodically from members of this association.[44] The editorial staff, it was stated, were all mechanics and performed their tasks gratuitously.[45] In September 1828, the officers of this organization were: President, John Parker, a waterman, Vice Presidents, William English, a cordwainer, John W. M'Mahon, a carpenter or weaver, and John Thompson, probably a printer.[46] John Thompson and Edward Haydock made up its editorial staff in the spring of 1831, when this paper changed hands.[47] It would appear then that this paper was conducted by genuine wage earners. This journal, and justifiably so, laid claim to being "the first paper established in the Union specially devoted to the interest of the producing classes." In December 1828, it had 1,500 subscribers and moderately estimated its regular readers as numbering 2,000.[48] Apparently its circulation remained stationary, for subsequent reports in 1829 place it at 2,000.[49] This paper was intimately associated with the Working Men's Party of Philadelphia and with the collapse of that movement this paper lost its identity and ultimately disappeared.

Now, with a paper to speak for them and with an organization to guide them, the working men of Philadelphia prepared themselves for political action. Thwarted in all their attempts to achieve reform

---

[42] Commons, *History of Labour*, I, p. 186.

[43] The date of the first number of The *Mechanic's Free Press* preserved in the Historical Society of Pennsylvania is April 18, 1828.

[44] *Free Trade Advocate*, Nov. 14, 1829, II, p. 315. See also The *Mechanic's Free Press*, Jan. 9, 1830.

[45] The *Working Man's Advocate*, July 16, 1831.

[46] *Desilver's Directory of Philadelphia*, 1828, pp. 145, 149; 1829, pp. 58, 123.

[47] The *Pennsylvania Inquirer*, April 16, 1831.

[48] The *Working Man's Advocate*, Jan. 21, 1832. The *Mechanic's Free Press*, December 27, 1828.

[49] The *Free Trade Advocate*, November 14, 1829; The *Mechanic's Free Press*, July 31, 1830.

through the old and established parties, they decided to push forward their own candidates for the various elective officers in the city government. The *Mechanic's Free Press,* in the summer of 1828, reported: "At a very large and respectable meeting of Journeymen House carpenters held on Tuesday evening, July 1st, at the District Court House ..., the Mechanics' Union of Trade Associations is entering into measures for procuring a nomination of candidates for legislative and other public offices, who will support the interests of the working classes."[50]

The workingmen looked with a jaundiced eye to the important city offices and the State legislative posts which heretofore had been dominated by "ambitious and designing men" who had secured their influential positions through an "injudicious use, or criminal abuse of the elective franchise."[51] They too wanted their share of the elective offices in the city. The city legislature consisted of twenty Common Council members and fifteen Select Council members. Members of the former were elected annually, while the members of the latter served for three years and vacated their seats in rotation so that one-third of them were elected each year. The executive authority was vested in a mayor who was selected at a joint meeting of the two councils.[52]

Why should not the workingmen nominate and elect candidates of their own choosing for the various elective posts in the city? It was a well-known fact, reported the *Mechanic's Free Press,* that "the interest of the labourer had never been efficiently recognized by legislators."[53] The workingmen caught in the swirl and excitement of the election day would blindly support their favorites at the polls only to see a deterioration in their influence as a body and "with it a decline in their rights and privileges."[54] At a general meeting of the mechanics and workingmen of the City and County of Philadelphia, they decided "to take the management of their own interest, as a class, into their own immediate keeping . . . and to support such men only for the City Councils and State Legislature, as shall pledge themselves in their official capacity to support the interests and claims of the Working Classes."[55]

---

[50] The *Mechanic's Free Press,* July 5, 1828.
[51] *Ibid.,* May 3, 1828.
[52] J. Thomas Scharf, *History of Philadelphia* (Philadelphia, 1884), III, p. 1703.
[53] The *Mechanic's Free Press,* May 30, 1829.
[54] *Ibid.*
[55] *Ibid.*

In the fall of 1828, when the nomination of the Jackson and the Anti-Jackson parties appeared in the city papers, there also appeared a list of candidates supported by a new party, the Working Men's Party.[56] This event did not pass unnoticed by the two major parties which previously had monopolized the politics of the State. "The leaders of the two great political parties," The *Mechanic's Free Press* noted, "appear to feel a deep interest in the present effort of the working people to form themselves into a distinct party." "The friends of the Administration . . . have tried every means to divert their attention and draw them within the sphere of its own influence." In one thing both parties agreed: "their dread of our forming a party distinct from and independent of themselves."[57]

The Federalists and the Jacksonians displayed more than a passive interest in this party. When the formation of the Working Men's Party was being discussed in the late summer of 1828, the *Mechanic's Free Press* reported an "attempt made by certain lawyers and speculators, to distract the meetings lately held for the purpose of taking into consideration the propriety of nominating suitable persons to represent our interests in the different legislative bodies."[58] This first attempt of the workingmen "to inquire whether they possess, as individuals or as a class, any right to say by whom they shall be governed," they discovered was to meet with the stern opposition and the destructive efforts of their opponents.[59]

Despite strong opposition, men nominated and supported by the Working Men's Party appeared on the city ticket for four years. From the fall of 1828 until the fall of 1831, candidates were nominated and campaign speeches were issued by the Working Men's Party. Its nominees openly proclaimed their allegiance to the workers' cause and pledged themselves "to promote the interests and support of the claims of the Working People."[60] Working Men's parties soon appeared in other cities throughout the State. Pittsburgh, Harrisburg, Lancaster, Carlisle and other towns in Pennsylvania all witnessed the rise and fall of political organizations which were purported to represent the workingmen.[61]

---

[56] *Poulson's Daily American Advertiser,* September 30, 1828.

[57] The *Mechanic's Free Press,* September 28, 1828.

[58] *Ibid.,* August 23, 1828.

[59] *Ibid.,* August 16, 1828.

[60] See Commons, *Documentary History,* V, p. 76.

[61] The *Mechanic's Free Press,* August 16, 1829.

Then as now the problem of evaluating the impact of the workingmen on politics and assessing his vote has proved both difficult and perplexing. Then as now labor's champions were to be found in various political affiliations and of varying political persuasions. Partisans of Jackson, then and now, have laid the strongest claim to representing the interests of labor and being the spokesmen for labor in our legislative halls. But Professor Ware in his admirable study of the industrial worker has cautioned the student of labor that "care must be exercised in distinguishing between the authentic voice of the worker and that of his advocate or advisor."[62]

As a result of the investigations of John R. Commons and his associates into the impact of labor on the politics of the nation, the year 1827 has been generally accepted as marking the first appearance of labor as an articulate and active force in politics. That year witnessed the full blossoming of the campaign of Jackson partisans to ensure the victory for their candidates in the next Presidential election. Their success is a matter of history. In the election of 1828, Jackson won an overwhelming triumph and the Democratic Party was installed in power for twelve years.

What were the forces that made this victory possible? Numerous historians have sought to delineate the factors responsible for this Democratic triumph. It has been generally recognized that the extension of the franchise to thousands of new voters enhanced the Democratic majority. Jackson's military career, too, has been generally recognized as a factor of major importance in that party's victory in 1828.[63] But to some students the Jacksonian triumph was a victory for the frontier and the West, while to others it was a far more significant and radical departure from the traditional party alignments which heretofore dominated the political life of the nation. According to the latter view, the Democratic party was regarded as representing the interests of the "toiling masses."

---

[62] See Norman Ware, *The Industrial Worker 1840-1860* (New York, 1924), p. xvii. See also Joseph Dorfman, "The Jackson Wage-Earner Thesis," *American Historical Review*, LIV, (January 1949), p. 296.

[63] See John C. Fitzpatrick (ed.), The *Autobiography of Martin Van Buren*, printed in the *Annual Report of the American Historical Association*, (Washington, D. C., 1920), I, p. 449. See Marguerite Bartlett, *Chief Phases of Pennsylvania Politics in the Jacksonian Era* (Philadelphia, 1919) p. 5. Also see John S. Bassett (ed.), *Correspondence of Andrew Jackson* (Wash. D. C., 1926-1933), III, p. iv, and Herman Hailperin, "Pro-Jackson Sentiment in Pennsylvania," *Pennsylvania Magazine of History and Biography*, 50, (July 1926), p. 194.

John Bach McMaster envisioned the Jacksonian victory as a "triumph of Democracy, another great political revolution, the like of which the country has not seen since 1800."[64] And Richard T. Ely, one of the pioneers in the study of American labor history, when commenting on the twelve-year reign of the Democrats, stated, "there can scarcely be a doubt that the Democratic party from 1829 to 1841 was more truly a Workingman's party than has been the case with any other great political party in our country or with that party either before or since."[65] A more recent student evaluating this Democratic triumph asserted that "during the Bank War, laboring men began slowly to turn to Jackson as their leader, and to his party as their party."[66]

Pennsylvania may well be considered as an ideal location for the student of the labor movement in the Jackson era. It was in Philadelphia, the second largest city in the nation, that labor first became vocal. It was here that the first Working Men's Party appeared when the trade unions of the city endorsed the proposition initiated by the central organization to nominate candidates "to represent the interest of the working classes" in the city councils and the state legislature.[67]

To test the validity of the thesis that the Jackson party was the party of the workingmen, two questions must be answered. First, did these Working Men's Parties, the only organizations purporting to speak solely for the working men, manifest during their short existence any preference for the Jacksonian candidates? And secondly, did those communities which had a large wage-earning population align themselves with the Jacksonians in this period? We shall first turn our attention to the Philadelphia scene to determine the nature of labor's political activity there.

Despite the overwhelming popularity of Jackson in 1828, factionalism was the dominant note in Pennsylvania politics, and continued to be so throughout this period. This was particularly true of Philadelphia where the old Federalist Party, long absent from national politics, and moribund in state politics, was still very much alive. The Democratic

---

[64] John B. McMaster, *History of the People of the United States* (New York, 1900) V, p. 518.

[65] Richard T. Ely, The *Labor Movement in America* (New York and London, 1905), p. 42.

[66] Arthur M. Schlesinger, Jr., *Age of Jackson* (Boston, 1945), p. 143.

[67] From The *Mechanic's Free Press*, as reported in The *Working Man's Advocate*, November 11, 1829.

Party had split into two factions, the Administration Party and the Jackson Democrats.[68] To add to the confusion and to still further divide the parties, the Working Men's Party made its appearance on the scene at this time.

In view of the generally accepted notion that the mechanics and wage earners of the cities gave their support to the Jackson Democrats, one might assume that the Working Men's Party would have exerted its influence in behalf of the Democratic candidates whenever possible. But a critical examination of those elections in which the Working Men's Party of Philadelphia participated will disabuse us of this idea. Not only was the *Mechanic's Free Press* repetitious in its denials of association with either of the two older parties, but it was vehement in its castigation of the Democratic Party. "At present our danger," warned this mechanic's journal, "is from our old masters, the Democrats, for as most of us are deserters from their ranks they view us with the same sensation as the mighty lord would the revolt of his vassals: there cannot be so much danger from the Federalists as, generally speaking, we were never inclined to trust them."[69] Although they were warned to keep aloof from either "Adams feelings or Jackson feelings," partisans of Andrew Jackson charged that "the leaders of the administration are also the leaders of these deluded operatives."[70]

The election of 1828 was marked by an eager contest for the votes of the workers. Personalities were far more important than issues in this campaign and the military hero of New Orleans was the most popular person in the country at this time. The national triumph of the Jacksonians was also repeated in the local elections in Philadelphia which swept into office every candidate of the Democratic party for the various elective posts.[71] But one cannot attribute the success of the Democrats to the efforts and the influence of the Working Men's Party. Although the Jacksonians did nominate three candidates for the City Assembly and twelve for the Common Council who were also on the Working Men's ticket, one cannot ascribe their success to the votes gained through their association with that party.[72] The candi-

---

[68] See Philip S. Klein, *Pennsylvania Politics 1817-1832* (Philadelphia, 1940), pp. 324 ff. for the best study of this aspect of Pennsylvania politics. Also see Commons, *History of Labour*, I, p. 195.

[69] The *Mechanic's Free Press*, April 12, 1828.

[70] *Ibid.*

[71] *Hazard's Register of Pennsylvania*, II, p. 224.

[72] The *Mechanic's Free Press*, October 4, 1828.

dates of the Democratic Party won over their opponents by an average majority of one thousand votes while the Working Men's Party polled only an average of 314 votes in the city.[73]

Undaunted by the poor showing in its first attempt, the Working Men's Party immediately made plans for the next election. Political clubs were organized and the workers were advised to "go to the assessor" and "have themselves duly assessed," in order to be "eligible to the right of Franchise."[74] They were cautioned to "LET THE SUBJECT OF RELIGION ALONE—or the death knell of our Associations will soon be sounded."[75] From the *Mechanic's Free Press* came the warning "not to give their strength as a party to any candidate for governor" because of the danger of splitting the Working Men's Party into factions.[76]

While the Party in 1828 failed to play a decisive role in that election when the Jacksonians won, the following year, when many of them were thrown out of office, it held the balance of power in the city. After the results of the election of 1829 were made known, the *Mechanic's Free Press* boastfully declared: "The balance of power has at length got into the hands of the working people, where it properly belongs, and it will be used, in future, for the general weal."[77] In the city elections that year candidates of the Anti-Jackson Party won a decisive victory, and a great part of their success can be credited to the Working Men's Party for the substantial aid it gave to their ticket.

All seats of the City Assembly passed into the hands of the Federalists, who were elected by an average majority of 515 votes.[78] One candidate of the Working Men's Party was endorsed by the Anti-Jackson Party but none was nominated by the Jacksonians.[79] The Working Men's Party polled an average of 860 votes, which gave it an enviable position of power in that election.[80]

In the Select Council, the Jackson Democrats retained a slim majority. Here again the hand of the Working Men's Party is seen. Two of the successful Democratic candidates were also endorsed by this

---

[73] See *Hazard's Register of Pennsylvania*, II, p. 224. Votes for the candidates of the Working Men's Party ranged from a low of 239 to a high of 539.

[74] The *Mechanic's Free Press*, November 29, 1828.

[75] *Ibid.*, August 1, 1829.

[76] *Ibid.*, December 27, 1828.

[77] *Ibid.*, October 17, 1829.

[78] *Hazard's Register of Pennsylvania*, IV, p. 256.

[79] *Ibid.*

[80] *Ibid.*

party, while none of its candidates was represented on the Federalist ticket. The Jacksonians held three of the five seats and succeeded over their opponents by a majority of 482 votes. Candidates of the Working Men's Party polled an average of 870 votes.[81]

It was in the Common Council that the Anti-Jacksonian candidates won their most striking victory. They now held fifteen of the twenty available seats; the Jacksonians held only four, and one seat was held by a candidate of both parties.[82] The Federalists succeeded over their opponents by a scant majority of 363 votes, while the Working Men's candidates drew an average of 862 votes.[83] Eight of the successful Federalist candidates were nominated by the Working Men's Party also, while only one Jackson candidate was endorsed by it.[84] During this one year, the only year in which the Working Men's Party held the balance of power in the city, the Anti-Jacksonians benefited most. Nor did this seemingly tacit alliance between the Working Men's Party and the Federalists escape the attention of the Jackson partisans.

A large meeting of Democratic workingmen of the western wards of Philadelphia charged that "from the nominations made by the workingmen's delegates of the city, on the very eve of the election, it is manifest that the main object was to promote the success of the federal ticket." This gathering resolved to "disapprove of the ticket presented for their support by the delegates of the working men of the city and disavow all connection whatever with the federal party, and disclaim any movement calculated to promote the success of that party at the approaching election."[85] A "Working Man" addressing himself to his brethren in the city counselled them that "the time has now arrived in the city when we ought not any longer be deceived by the title of 'working men's ticket'. Under this specious guise some genuine republicans have been led astray. The ticket formed by the workingmen in the city . . . is chiefly composed of federalists."[86] The *American Sentinel* noted that in the inspectors' election "in most of the wards, the federalists and the political workingmen voted the same tickets."[87] This oft repeated charge aroused the *Mechanic's Free Press*

---

[81] *Ibid.*
[82] The *National Gazette and Literary Register*, Oct. 15, 1829.
[83] *Hazard's Register of Pennsylvania*, IV, p. 256.
[84] The *Mechanic's Free Press*, October 3, 1829.
[85] The *Pennsylvania Inquirer*, October 9, 1829.
[86] *Ibid.*, October 10, 1829.
[87] The *American Sentinel*, October 7, 1829.

to issue a blistering denial to the accusation that the Working Men's Party was "allied to or in correspondence with, Federalists, and anti-masons throughout the State."[88]

Despite the charges that the Working Men's Party was but an echo of the Federalists, it was encouraged by its successes in the election of 1829, and eagerly made preparations for the next year's campaign. Ward meetings were regularly held and there was a determined effort made to build a more efficient vote-gathering organization in the city. But at the same time that it was attempting to consolidate and spread it influence, it was being destroyed by the infiltration of political opportunists into its ranks.

The party was never again to achieve the same degree of success which it attained in the election of 1829. Although its candidates received a substantial number of votes in the election of 1830, it lost the balance of power which it held in 1829.[89] Ten candidates of the Federalist Party were also on the Working Men's ticket.[90] One of the candidates supported by this party was the publisher of the conservative Anti-Jackson *Daily Chronicle,* and another was an attorney.[91]

Prior to the election the *Mechanic's Free Press* had charged that the Federalist Party was made up of lawyers and aristocrats, and that the Jackson Party was composed of bank speculators and office hunters.[92] At the same time it piously claimed that "on the Working Men's ticket we have no attornies: the candidates from first to last have been taken from the ranks of the people, and are pledged to support the Working Men's interests."[93]

The results of the election of 1830 pleased no one but the Jackson Democrats. One Jackson paper boastingly stated that the Democrats had "carried the Senator and eight members of the Assembly, over the united forces of Federalism and Workeyism."[94] Discouraged with the results of the election, the *Mechanic's Free Press* glumly wrote: "The election of 1830 adds another instance of the blindness of the working-men to their own interests and exhibits in bold and striking color how easily the public liberties may be endangered by the supineness of the

---

[88] The *Mechanic's Free Press,* October 31, 1829.

[89] *Hazard's Register of Pennsylvania,* VIII, p. 256.

[90] The *Mechanic's Free Press,* October 3, 1829.

[91] Desilvers, *Philadelphia Directory and Strangers' Guide, 1830* (Philadelphia, 1831), pp. 2, 154.

[92] The *Mechanic's Free Press,* October 10, 1830.

[93] *Ibid.,* October 9, 1830.

[94] The *American Sentinel,* October 13, 1830.

peoples themselves."[95] From the occasional letters which were printed in this paper from various "workingmen," there was an inescapable tone of disillusionment with the character of a number of the candidates supported by this party. One "worker" charged that the primary interests of many of the candidates supported by the Working Men's Party was "to grant bank charters and all kinds of monopolies."[96]

A feeble gesture was made by the Working Men's Party again in 1831. It nominated candidates for the various city posts and proclaimed itself as the sole representative of the true interests of the working classes. No copies of the *Mechanic's Free Press* are in existence to reveal its reaction to this election, but the election returns disclose that the party lost its ability to capture the votes of the Philadelphia workingmen. Discouraged by its poor showing in the election and by its inability to cope with the practices of the professional politician, the Working Men's Party disappeared from the Philadelphia political scene.

Why after such an auspicious beginning did this movement fail? Helen Sumner says that "it did not fail as a result of legitimate internal dissensions based on differences of principle," but that "its failure was due primarily to a combination of purely political causes, namely, the workers' inability to 'play the game of politics' and the all too excellent acquaintance of the old party politicians with the 'tricks of the game'."[97] But the evidence would indicate that it was destroyed by more than the machinations of professional politicians. It was the very nature of the party itself and the candidates which it supported for office that contributed to its downfall. In the beginning it was dominated largely by skilled artisans, but it failed to attract the large mass of unskilled laborers whose numbers alone would have made it a serious political force in the politics of the city and State.

During its four years of existence the Working Men's Party nominated and supported one hundred candidates for the elective offices of Philadelphia. A tabulation of these candidates reveals their occupations according to the official listing as follows:[98] ten workingmen,[99]

---

[95] The *Mechanic's Free Press*, October 12, 1830.

[96] *Ibid.*, March 5, 1831.

[97] Commons, *History of Labour*, I, pp. 125-216. See William R. Hingston, *The Philadelphia Working Men's Party 1828-1831*, unpublished Master's Essay, University of Pennsylvania (1949).

[98] Information regarding the occupation of the Working Men's candidates was obtained from Desilvers, *Philadelphia Directory*.

[99] The *Directory* makes no distinction between master workmen and the corresponding journeymen and therefore makes it impossible to determine whether these were bona-fide workingmen.

twenty-three professional men,[100] fifty-three merchants and manufacturers, eleven gentlemen, and three for whom no occupation was recorded.

Among these candidates there were some men of great wealth and affluence in the city. Charles Alexander, publisher of the conservative *Daily Chronicle*,[101] and Joseph Chandler, editor of the *United States Gazette*,[102] were nominees of the Working Men's Party. There were other men wealthy and important enough to be listed in a *Biography of Wealthy Citizens of Philadelphia*. Elhanan Keyser and John Moss, candidates of this party for the Common Council, possessed fortunes of $150,000 each. Two other candidates, Henry Horn and Henry Troth, were reputed to be worth $50,000.[103]

Despite the protestations of the Working Men's Party of Philadelphia against the abuses of the other two major parties, and despite its support of the many social and political reforms desired by the workmen, this party can scarcely be recognized as a true Working Men's Party. To believe that a party composed largely of merchants and manufacturers and professional men, plus a few persons of considerable wealth, was really devoted to solving working class problems in the interests of the workers would seem to lay a heavy tax on credulity.[104]

Undoubtedly the lack of class consciousness among the workers was a contributing factor which ultimately brought about the disintegration of this party. Although there was a growing sentiment of class solidarity as evidenced by the many appeals directed to the workingmen as a class and by the trade union movement of this period, many laborers felt that their status as such was a temporary one, and were reluctant to identify themselves with a movement which at some future date might be directed against themselves.

Nor can one ignore the role of the employers in the destruction of this political movement. It is impossible to measure with any degree of certainty what effect the attitude of the employing classes had on

[100] In the classification designated as professional men are included lawyers, doctors, teachers, druggists and artists.
[101] Desilvers, *Philadelphia Directory 1830*, p. 2.
[102] *Ibid.*, p. 32.
[103] By a Citizen of Philadelphia, *Memoirs and Biography of Wealthy Citizens of Philadelphia* (Philadelphia, 1845), pp. 4, 18.
[104] Philip S. Foner, *History of the Labor Movement in the United States* (New York, 1947), p. 128 states that "no wage earners were nominated on the Working Men's ticket, due largely to the fact that property qualifications existed for all offices." Neither the Constitution of Pennsylvania, 1790, nor the laws incorporating the city of Philadelphia in 1789, substantiate this point of view.

the political efforts of the workingmen, but one can rest assured that it was a debilitating one. "It was said," reported The *Mechanic's Free Press*, "that several employers had threatened their workmen with discharge and that 'some were driven *through fear of losing their places* to bow to this galling yoke'."[105]

This is the Philadelphia story. Not long after this political movement among the Philadelphia workingmen took root, there were politicians in other communities scattered throughout the State who found it expedient to establish Working Men's Parties. In the early winter of 1830, the *Mechanic's Free Press* enthusiastically reported that the farmers and workingmen at Phillipsburgh "are about attempting to form associations in the neighbouring townships."[106] Shortly after the great success of the Philadelphia Party in the election of 1829, it was reported that the working men of Lancaster were "meeting for the purpose of forming a ticket for select and common council."[107] "The 'workingmen' of the borough of Carlisle," it was revealed early in 1830, "have formed themselves into a society, on a plan somewhat resembling that which is composed of the workingmen in this city."[108] That summer the citizens of Grampion Hills in Pike township, Clearfield County met "for the purpose of forming a Working Men's Society."[109] From Erie County there came a report that there was a movement afoot to organize a new party, "to be called the People's Party."[110] And candidates running under the banners of the Working Men's Party appeared in the fall of 1830 at Pittsburgh, Harrisburg, and in Juniata and Mifflin counties.[111]

THE WORKING MEN'S PARTY OF PITTSBURGH

The Pittsburgh Working Men's Party differed from its Philadelphia counterpart in that from its very inception its only association with

---

[105] The *Mechanic's Free Press*, Oct. 24, 1829. Norman Ware, *op. cit.*, p. 127, when analyzing the failure of the ten-hour movement in Massachusetts, states: "The chief reason for the failure of the ten-hour movement is . . . that the corporations were able to prevent the passing of ten-hour legislation because of their control over the Massachusetts legislature and their political domination of the electorate." If the above was true in Massachusetts it is possible that the employers of Philadelphia exerted a similar influence upon their workers.

[106] The *Mechanic's Free Press*, February 6, 1830.

[107] *Ibid.*

[108] *Ibid.*

[109] *Ibid.*, June 5, 1830.

[110] The *Crawford Messenger*, July 9, 1830.

[111] The *Harrisburgh Chronicle*, September 6, 1830; The *Mifflin Eagle and The Lewistown Intelligencer*, September 8, 1830.

the workingmen was its name. Whereas the Philadelphia organization had grown out of a legitimate trade union dispute and was in the beginning intimately associated with the Mechanic's Union of Trade Associations, the Pittsburgh Party was inspired by professional politicians whose only interest in the workingman was his vote.

On May 29, 1830, a so-called "Working Men's Meeting" was held at the court house in Pittsburgh. Apparently influenced and "encouraged by the success of the workingmen wherever organized," some professional politicians here felt that a similar movement would be worth the experiment. Mr. Thomas Hazelton, who at one time was associated with the Bank of Pittsburgh, was appointed to the chair, and J. B. Butler, the editor of the *Statesman* and a staunch supporter of Henry Clay, and W. B. Conway, the editor of the *American Manufacturer*, were appointed secretaries.[112] Very active in these proceedings and in the later development of this party was Lewis Peterson, owner of the Globe Cotton Mills. The meeting resolved that it was expedient "that a ticket be formed for the county, to be called the 'Working Men's ticket', and that all who approve and concur in these views be respectfully requested to support our men and our principles."[113] Early in June, the *Allegheny Democrat* announced that "a new party [the Working Men's Party] with this title has lately been introduced into this city and county, and bids fair to become respectable both in numbers and the standing of its members."[114]

At this public gathering of "workingmen" a committee composed of some of the most prominent business men and industrialists was selected to "publish an address to the county . . . [expressing] the views and objects of the citizens now assembled."[115] The following individuals made up this committee: Mark Stockhouse, steam engine manufacturer; Isaac Lightner, of the Kingsland, Lightner & Co., and the Jackson Foundry; John Arthurs, steam engine maker; John Irwin, rope manufacturer; John Gallagher, bell and brass founder; Thomas Hazelton, at one time associated with the Bank of Pittsburgh; Alba Fisk, William Leckey, John Sheriff and James Shaw, occupations not known; and N. B. Starr, who, according to a notice which appeared in the *Mechanic's Free Press*, had attempted to ingratiate himself with the Philadelphia Working Men's Party, but was found to be dishonest and

[112] The *Pittsburgh Mercury*, June 9, 1830. In the election of 1828 John Butler had been a supporter of John Q. Adams.
[113] The *Statesman*, June 2, 1830; The *Pittsburgh Mercury*, June 9, 1830.
[114] The *Allegheny Democrat*, June 8, 1830.
[115] The *Pittsburgh Mercury*, June 9, 1830.

an imposter.[116] John Irwin, John Butler and John Sheriff all had been Adams men in the campaign of 1828.[117] This committee was also to serve as the committee of correspondence for the Working Men's Party of Allegheny County.

Its address "to the Farmers, Mechanics, and Working men of the county of Allegheny" was filled with the usual platitudes and abjurations. "All party names and distinctions" were renounced by them. This Party was to "have no connection with religious excitement." They complained that in the past "in the selection of men to legislate for us ... too little attention has been paid to the importance of securing the services of those, whose interests are identified with our own." The workingmen, they charged, had "been too much influenced by feelings arising from party spirit, without sufficiently enquiring into the fitness and usefulness of the candidate."[118]

In addition to laying bare the past errors of the workingmen, they put forth the program which it was expected that those candidates who sought the wage earners' votes would pledge themselves to support. First and foremost would be "the protection of National Industry." And closely identified with this plank in their program was a demand for "a well regulated system of Internal Improvements." They too, called for the "establishment of a general system of education ... and the abolition, as far as practicable, of charters, and monopolies, and the suppression of lotteries in every shape and form."[119]

The subsequent history of this movement discloses not only the confused state of the political parties in Allegheny County but also lays open to question the sincerity of some of the individuals who were responsible for this movement supposedly in behalf of the workingmen. A Working Men's convention was held in Pittsburgh on July 3, at which delegates from the various districts throughout the county were present. General Robert T. Stewart, a former owner of the Sligo Iron Works, and now a salt manufacturer was nominated for Congress, "and ... the nomination for the assembly made by the Democratic Republican Party was concurred in."[120] A few days prior to the Working Men's Convention, the Democratic Republicans had held their convention

---

[116] The *Statesman*, July 22, 1829; The *Mechanic's Free Press*, Dec. 11, 1830; The *Pittsburgh Mercury*, June 9, 1830.
[117] Erasmus Wilson, *Standard History of Pittsburgh* (Chicago, 1898), p. 763.
[118] The *Pittsburgh Mercury*, June 9, 1830.
[119] *Ibid*.
[120] The *Statesman*, June 30, 1830; July 22, 1830; The *Pittsburgh Mercury*, July 7, 1830.

and nominated John Gilmore and James Patterson for Congress and Messrs. Craft, Kerr, Walker and Arthurs for the Assembly.

The immediate effect of the concurrence of the Working Men's Party in the Assembly ticket of the Democratic Republicans was to cause a split in its organization, and charges of fraud were immediately levelled against them. Four members of the Committee of Correspondence, Thomas Hazelton, Thomas Blakewell, John Sheriff and John Irwin, immediately resigned from the Party. In an address "to the Farmers, Mechanics, and Working men of Allegheny County" they explained their reasons for withdrawing from the Party:[121]

> The committee endeavored to impress upon your minds the importance of selecting as candidates for the several offices to be filled, suitable persons, without regard to political distinctions—men who should be unfettered by party prejudices and the engagements—whose exertions should be directed to the promotion of the general welfare, without regard to the advancement of the interests of any political party. . . . We leave to your candid and unbiassed judgement, to decide how far these and the other leading principles of the address were acted upon in the formation of the ticket adopted at the convention of delegates held on the third of this month, by whom we were placed on the committee of correspondence.

The *Pittsburgh Gazette* welcomed the disaffection of these four committee men and stated that they were guided in their actions from a conviction "that some external influence was brought to bear upon and control the selection of this ticket."[122] Moreover, the *Gazette* thought it very peculiar that these two conventions, the Democratic-Republican and the Working Men's, having entirely different objects in view should "select precisely the same men for their tickets."[123] If the fact that these two separate political organizations should select the same persons for their tickets was not sufficient ground for suspicion, the *Gazette* was of the opinion that the identity of the candidates was. It admitted that Messrs. Arthurs, Kerr and Walker were "actually workingmen" but Craft's right to that name was very questionable. Yet in the balloting Mr. Craft was nominated on the first ballot with thirty votes out of forty, while it took seven ballotings to secure Mr. Walker's nomination.[124]

---

[121] The *Pittsburgh Mercury*, July 21, 1830.
[122] The *Pittsburgh Gazette*, July 23, 1830.
[123] *Ibid.*
[124] *Ibid.*

This was the first episode in the development of this so-called Working Men's Party of western Pennsylvania. If there was any doubt before of the genuineness of this movement, the subsequent events should drive them out. A second convention of the Working Men's Party met in Butler on July 22, to nominate candidates to be supported by them for the district composed of Armstrong, Beaver, Butler and Allegheny counties. Lewis Peterson and John McKnight were to represent Allegheny County at this convention, and were instructed to "support General R. T. Stewart, to represent the County of Allegheny in Congress, in conjunction with any one the convention should agree upon to represent the counties of Armstrong, Butler and Beaver."[125] But the latter delegate found it inconvenient to attend, and John B. Butler, the editor of the *Statesman* and a fervent supporter of Henry Clay, managed to have himself accepted as a substitute for John McKnight over the vigorous protests of Lewis Peterson. The *Allegheny Democrat* was vituperative in its denunciation of the proceedings and declared that John B. Butler was "a political schemer, a violent Clay man, one not possessing the least title of the requisites of a political workingman."[126]

This marked a further step in the disintegration of the Working Men's Party. Under the circumstances, Lewis Peterson, the regularly appointed delegate, found it impossible to join his colleagues from the other counties, and in the following letter to "Messrs. A. Murphy, Chairman, Wm. M'Clure and John B. Butler, Secretaries, and the gentlemen composing the meeting of delegates at the court-house, on the 3rd of July," disclosed in great detail the reasons for his action:[127]

> I rose and stated to the convention that I objected to Mr. Butler's admission, on the following grounds: that Mr. B. had expressed himself to me that he would do everything he could do in opposition to the nomination made at the court-house, where he was secretary and where he participated in my appointment to represent the convention at Butler, with special instructions to support General R. T. Stewart: that Mr. Butler had not been appointed at the court-house by the delegates, and that Judge Riddle, Judge Shaler, and Judge Pentland had never attended any of the Working Men's meetings, nor partici-

---

[125] *Ibid.*, August 6, 1830; The *Statesman*, July 28, 1830.

[126] The *Allegheny Democrat*, July 27, 1830.

[127] The *Pittsburgh Gazette*, Aug. 6, 1830. John B. Butler asserted his right to the seat vacated by John McKnight by the authority vested in him through a letter signed by Judge Riddle, Judge Shaler, and Judge Pentland and sundry other citizens.

pated with us on the occasion. The gentlemen delegates from Beaver admitted Mr. Butler as a delegate from Allegheny. I then informed the meeting, that I could not serve in conjunction with Mr. Butler, and should leave them and protest against their proceedings.

Despite the absence of any officially appointed delegate from Allegheny County the convention proceeded with its work and appointed John B. Butler, secretary. Walter Forward of Allegheny and John H. Shannon of Beaver County were unanimously nominated to represent the Working Men's Party in Congress. In an address to their fellow citizens, this rump convention righteously stated that "THE WORKING MEN proscribe no party or class of men, whether political or religious. The ground they take is independent of all parties."[128]

This protestation of political independence of all parties smacked of insincerity, for on that very same day the delegates to the Democratic Convention met at Butler. The *Pittsburgh Gazette* found it disconcerting "that these two parties, professing to act upon directly *opposite principles* and entirely independent of each other, should select the *very same day,* and the same town for holding their conventions," and remarked "that there appears throughout the whole course of the *Working Men's Party,* to be a singular and unaccountable connexion between the movements of this party which professes 'to take ground independent of all parties,' and that other party which professes to be exclusively democratic."[129]

The proceedings of the Working Men's Convention were not without their effects on the gathering of the delegates to the Democratic-Republican Convention. Walter Forward, John Gilmore, and R. T. Stewart were nominated for the consideration of this body. David Lynch, the Allegheny County delegate, spoke passionately against the nomination of Walter Forward as the Democratic candidate. "I had become acquainted with the facts and circumstances in relation to the nomination of Mr. Forward, for the working men . . . ," he revealed, and "I thought that nomination an outrage upon the feelings, the sentiments, and the wishes of the working men of Allegheny County."[130] He apparently was present when Lewis Peterson had denounced the appearance of John B. Butler at the Working Men's Convention. "These facts [that the Allegheny delegation was specifically instructed to sup-

[128] The *Statesman,* July 28, 1830; The *Pittsburgh Gazette,* July 30, 1830.
[129] The *Pittsburgh Gazette,* July 27, 1830; The *Pittsburgh Mercury,* August 11, 1830.
[130] The *Pittsburgh Mercury,* August 11, 1830.

port General Stewart in the convention at Butler] were stated to
Messrs. Adams and Logan by Mr. Peterson, in my presence," David
Lynch disclosed.[131] "I made the convention of which I was a member
acquainted with these artifices, as far as I was acquainted with them;
and I accordingly opposed the nomination of Mr. Forward."[132] It would
appear that there was a very close relationship between the Working
Men's Party and the Democratic Party. In the midst of the charges
and counter charges the Democratic-Republican Convention chose John
Gilmore and James Patterson as its congressional candidates.[133] The
obvious confusion which prevailed did not escape the editor of the
Crawford Messenger. He derisively noted that[134]

> there have been no less than three party conventions—
> the *democratic republican*—anti-masonic—working men
> —all professing to be democratic, yet strange as it may
> appear, the candidates selected for Congress by each, to
> wit:—Harmar Denny, Robert Stewart and John Gilmore,
> are old, staunch and unwavering *federalists*—all however,
> we presume, "dyed in the wool" to the Jackson Faith.

The *Gazette* at this time raised a question which, with the appearance of the Working Men's Party and so many aspirants for office who
professed to be and to support the cause of the workingmen, had con-
founded many. "We know not precisely the line which the working
men wish to draw between those who *are* and those *who are not workingmen*."[135] The same perplexing question had been raised in Philadelphia. The editor of the *Mechanic's Free Press* had been asked by "A
regular bred Mechanic" "for a definition of the term working man."
The editor of this workingman's paper acknowledged "that some difference of opinion exists as to the right of a voice in the meetings of
'Working Men'." "To give a comprehensive definition even of so common a term, is harder than some are aware. Perhaps we shall not be
far from the mark in saying, that 'working men' are those engaged in
productive industry." But the most difficult aspect of this question
remained unanswered: that is, should "the term . . . exclude employers." To this the *Mechanic's Free Press* gave an equivocal but probably correct answer. "Most employers," it contended, "unite in their own
persons two distinct classes of society."[136] To those editors enthusi-

---

[131] *Ibid.*
[132] The *Pittsburgh Gazette*, August 13, 1830.
[133] *Ibid.*, July 27, 1830.
[134] The *Crawford Messenger*, July 29, 1830.
[135] The *Pittsburgh Gazette*, July 23, 1830.
[136] The *Mechanic's Free Press*, September 12, 1829.

astically endorsing the Working Men's Party in western Pennsylvania, the *Gazette* addressed two pleas: "Who are *workingmen?—*Who are *not workingmen?*" But the questions went begging for an answer.

The confusion which was the Working Men's Party in this part of the State did not end with the Butler convention. Those elements of the Working Men's Party sympathetic with the Democratic-Republicans sought to undo the work of the rump convention at Butler. On the 24th of August a workingmen's meeting was held in Armstrong County to take steps to ensure "the success of the workingmen's party." They denounced the attempt made "to force upon the working man, a congressional nomination entirely at variance with their wishes and interests" by "a late convention of *two* individuals at Butler, through the *intrigue and management of a citizen of Allegheny county.*"[137] In addition, they announced "that this meeting have not, *under any circumstances,* sufficient confidence in the political view, integrity and capacity of *Walter Forward and John R. Shannon,* and that they are not such men as are calculated to advance the interests of the working men of this district." Not only did they expressly reject these candidates but suggested that "a working men's convention . . . be held at Butler on Friday the 27th inst., and recommend that the delegates be instructed to support General R. T. Stewart and Hon. John Gilmore," as candidates of the Democratic Party.[138] Thus the way was paved for another Working Men's Convention.

It met on the 27th of August at Butler to select candidates who would represent the true interests of the workingmen. Delegates from Allegheny, Armstrong and Butler counties were present. Lewis Peterson was the delegate from Allegheny County; Philip Clingensmith, from Armstrong; and Robert Carnahan, from Butler were the officers of the convention. The delegation from Beaver County failed to make its appearance. With apparently no opposition, the convention resolved unanimously to "recommend *John Gilmore* and *Robert T. Stewart* Esqrs. to the suffrage of their fellow citizens of the Congressional District at the approaching election."[139] The *Allegheny Democrat,* a pro-Jackson paper, hailed the results of this convention.[140]

> We are happy to see the results of the Working Men's
> Convention. The honest and candid of all parties were

---

[137] The *Pittsburgh Mercury,* September 3, 1830.
[138] *Ibid.*
[139] *Ibid.,* September 1, 1830.
[140] The *Allegheny Democrat,* August 31, 1830.

convinced that this party has been most basely defrauded
in the surreptitious convention held on the 23d of July—
and will acknowledge that it behooved them to avow their
wishes in a manner that could not be mistaken, and by
organs that could be confided in. That convention held
on the 27th instant fully and truly represented the sentiments of the working-men . . . and we . . . therefore expect that Ticket nominated will receive the United Support of the Farmers and Mechanics.

In an effort to clear up some of the confusion which prevailed, and
to demonstrate to the public that this gathering truly represented the
will of the workingmen, a long statement was prepared for the edification of the public. Once again the events surrounding the July 22nd
convention were retraced in detail so as to point out the illegality of
that proceeding. It was charged that the July 22nd convention *"was
not a convention* of delegates of the working men of the district. It
did not express their sentiments, nor were its members the regularly
nominated delegates of that respectable body of citizens."[141] Furthermore they contended that this rump convention had arrogated to itself
the "responsibility of nominating candidates for this large congressional
district," and then proceeded to act "in defiance of the positive instruc-
tions of the convention of delegates for Allegheny County, where twenty
one townships and wards were represented," as well as in the total absence "of all representation from Butler and Armstrong counties."[142]
They pointed with pride to their candidates. The fact that Robert T.
Stewart had formerly owned an extensive iron works and was now engaged in the manufacture of salt definitely identified him with the
working men of the district.[143] Mr. Gilmore's long career of public
service and his experience in legislative proceedings admirably fitted
him for the task of representing the workingmen in Congress.[144]

By October, the political picture had cleared somewhat. Both John
Shannon, a candidate of the first Butler convention of Working Men,
and James Patterson, a candidate of the Democratic Party, withdrew
their names from the list, so that there remained five candidates in the
field.[145] The Democratic and Working Men's ticket, according to the

---

[141] The *Pittsburgh Mercury*, September 1, 1830.

[142] *Ibid.*

[143] *Ibid.*

[144] The *Pittsburgh Mercury*, September 1, 1830.

[145] The *Statesman*, September 6, 1830; September 8, 1830; The *Pittsburgh Mercury*,
September 8, 1830.

Mercury, were identical; that is, Robert T. Stewart and John Gilmore were the candidates. But the *Gazette* and the *Statesman* printed their names with no party designation.[146] Harmar Denny and William Ayres were the candidates of the Anti-masonic Party, and Walter Forward was humorously referred to by some of the papers as being the candidate of the "Worked Men's" Party.[147]

The campaign was desultory with no real issues being discussed by any of the candidates. It was more a campaign of personalities than of issues with the names of Jackson and Clay figuring prominently in the contest. The *Gazette* hinted that Stewart's candidacy was "to aid Mr. Gilmore," since "it is absolutely demonstrable that the success of Gilmore, is tantamount to the defeat of Stewart."[148] John B. Butler, one of the founders of the Working Men's Party and the editor of the *Statesman* was accused by the *Allegheny Democrat* of campaigning "against General R. T. Stewart, the regularly nominated [Working Men's] candidate." It was rumored, too, that Gilmore's friends in Butler and Beaver counties were working against Stewart and for Walter Forward.[149]

When the final returns of the election were in, it was revealed that Denny and Gilmore had won the coveted seats. But Stewart, the original Working Men's candidate, did surprisingly well considering the meager support and the opposition there was to his candidacy. His total vote in the four counties composing the congressional district was 4,071, while John Gilmore received 5,744, and Harmar Denny, 6,296. The other candidate, Walter Forward, who had been branded as a supporter of Henry Clay was given only 3,567 votes.[150] In the City of Pittsburgh where the heaviest concentration of industry was located and where one would expect to find the largest class of propertyless votes, Denny nosed out Stewart by only thirty-one votes. He received 637 votes from the four wards in the city while Stewart polled 608. Gilmore was given only 455 votes and Forward 411.[151] But party labels did not mean as much as the identity of the individual candidates.

---

[146] The *Pittsburgh Mercury,* October 6, 1830; The *Pittsburgh Gazette,* October 1, 1830.

[147] The *Pittsburgh Mercury,* September 8, 1830.

[148] The *Pittsburgh Gazette,* October 5, 1830.

[149] The *Allegheny Democrat,* September 21, 1830.

[150] The *Pittsburgh Gazette,* October 19, 1830; The *Pittsburgh Mercury,* Oct. 20, 1830. Pittsburgh at this time had only four wards and it is impossible to make any statistical breakdown of the areas populated by the working classes only.

[151] *Ibid.*

The Working Men's Party in western Pennsylvania was but an episode in that factional strife which had characterized the politics of the
State since 1816.[152] Its existence was brief and torn by internal strife.
Clay and Jackson partisans were its midwives, and in the ensuing
struggle for the control of the party the supporters of Andrew Jackson
won out. It barely survived one election, but this probably was its sole
excuse for being. A letter to the editor of the *Pittsburgh Mercury* from
David Lynch, a delegate to the Democratic Convention, possibly hinted
at some of the considerations which led to the formation of this party.
"Is it honest of him [John B. Butler]," this ardent supporter of Jackson
asked, "to try to palm a strong Clay man on his subscribers and supporters by throwing the Jackson mantle over Walter Forward, when,
by unforeseen events the next Presidential election might be brought
into Congress."[153] As far as can be determined, at no time during its
short life were there any real wage earners associated with this movement, and their only contribution to the party was its name. Some
abortive attempts were made later to revive "a Political Association of
Working Men" in Pittsburgh but nothing concrete ever developed from
these efforts.[154]

THE WORKING MEN'S PARTY OF DAUPHIN COUNTY

Harrisburg, too, had a Working Men's Party. On September 4, 1830,
a "large and respectable meeting of working men of Harrisburgh assembled ... and organized by appointing Henry Crangle, *President*, Samuel
Bryan and Adam Zimmerman, Vice Presidents, and John Houser, Secretary."[155] The Committee charged that "the tickets which have been
presented by the two parties ... to the voters of the district and
county, have been formed without regard to their welfare and rights."[156]
They suggested that a new ticket be presented to the public which
would represent the desires of this large mass of unforgotten citizens.

The *Chronicle* saw in the organization of this party the work of the
supporters of Henry Clay. "Mr. Clay is endeavouring to turn the Working Men to account in other places; and we will soon see whether it is

---

[152] For a keen and lucid analysis of this aspect of Pennsylvania politics see Philip
Klein, *op. cit.*, p. 353 ff.

[153] The *Pittsburgh Gazette*, September 15, 1830.

[154] The *Working Man's Advocate*, Dec. 4, 1830, May 21, 1831.

[155] The *Harrisburgh Chronicle*, September 6, 1830.

[156] *Ibid.;* The *Working Man's Advocate*, Sept. 11, 1830; The *Mechanic's Free Press*,
Sept. 11, 1830.

VOTES FOR PRESIDENT

	1828[176]		1832[177]		1836[178]		1840[179]	
	Jackson	Adams	Jackson	Wirt	Van Buren	Harrison	Van Buren	Harrison
New Market	369	193	242	329	227	324	359	447
Lower Delaware	384	386	298	510	247	432	358	571
Pine	244	235	164	383	129	357	194	426
Upper Delaware	433	244	281	397	285	323	461	428
Chestnut	278	231	165	305	119	267	180	285
Walnut	183	215	88	300	178	256	105	259
High	263	333	131	360	137	314	185	399
Dock	267	227	143	403	128	394	244	460
North	252	296	223	471	253	628	436	791
South Mulberry	311	188	239	387	251	404	334	537
Locust	368	255	285	397	300	425	443	580
North Mulberry	406	136	409	357	328	397	565	630
Middle	253	121	190	273	177	357	278	511
South	155	171	152	337	141	426	223	578
Cedar	215	104	257	262	228	422	406	751
	4,381	3,335	3,267	5,471	3,028	5,746	4,771	7,653

[176] *Hazard's Register of Pennsylvania*, II, p. 305.
[177] *The National Gazette and Literary Register*, Nov. 5, 1832.
[178] *The Public Ledger*, October 29, 1840. The totals should be 3,128 and 5,726.
[179] *Ibid.*, October 31, 1840.

VOTES FOR GOVERNOR[180]

Wards	1832[182]		1835[183]			1838[184]	
	Wolf	Ritner	Wolf	Muhlen-berg[181]	Ritner	Porter	Ritner
New Market	251	301	256	0	288	240	326
Lower Delaware	307	460	52	94	321	240	468
Pine	187	358	206	78	248	140	451
Upper Delaware	297	368	106	101	226	347	368
Chestnut	186	268	0	68	177	108	353
Walnut	115	260	15	19	177	74	414
High	147	323	52	36	225	132	397
Dock	113	369	0	0	250	150	403
North	248	414	91	0	361	264	918
South Mulberry	272	348	155	0	305	246	495
Locust	292	356	0	208	267	313	475
North Mulberry	425	344	280	0	287	246	550
Middle	207	256	81	0	242	210	435
South	161	315	0	0	256	130	610
Cedar	290	217	0	50	308	216	550
	3,498	4,957	1,088	654	3,938	3,156	7,203

[180] The writer was unable to uncover the actual vote by wards for the gubernatorial election of 1829. Only figures available were those for the Inspectors' election that year.

[181] The Trades Union of Philadelphia in this election supported Congressman Muhlenberg. William English president of the Philadelphia Trades' Union for the March term 1835 and Thomas Hogan, president for the September term for the same year were candidates on the Muhlenberg ticket for the Senate and Assembly respectively. The whole ticket was unsuccessful in the city. See The *Pennsylvanian*, April 3, 1835. See also Commons, *History of Labour*, I, pp. 460, 461.

[182] The *National Gazette and Literary Register*, October 1832.

[183] *Hazard's Register of Pennsylvania*, XVI, October 1835, p. 240. The first total should be 1,294.

[184] The *Public Ledger*, October 17, 1838. The totals should be 3,056 and 7,213.

DEMOCRATIC VOTE AS PERCENT OF TOTAL IN THE PRESIDENTIAL ELECTIONS

Ward	1829 Assessed Valuation Per Person	1828	1832	1836	1840
New Market	$81	66	42	41	45
North Mulberry	121	75	53	45	47
Cedar	188	67	49	35	35
South Mulberry	189	62	38	38	38
Upper Delaware	208	64	41	47	52
Lower Delaware	212	49	37	36	38
Pine	213	59	30	27	31
Locust	217	59	42	41	43
North	274	46	32	29	36
Dock	328	54	26	25	35
Middle	343	67	43	33	35
South	385	48	31	25	28
Walnut	587	46	23	41	29
High	598	44	27	30	31
Chestnut	670	55	36	31	39

DEMOCRATIC VOTE AS PERCENT OF TOTAL IN THE GUBERNATORIAL ELECTIONS

Ward	1829 Assessed Valuation Per Person	1832	[186]	1835[185]	1838
New Market	$81	42	0[186]	47[188]	42
North Mulberry	121	53	0	49	39
Cedar	188	49	14	14	28
South Mulberry	189	38	0	34	33
Upper Delaware	208	41	23	48	48
Lower Delaware	212	37	20	31	34
Pine	213	30	13	53	24
Locust	217	42	44	44	40
North	274	32	0	20	22
Dock	328	26	0	0	27
Middle	343	43	0	25	33
South	385	31	0	0	18
Walnut	587	23	9	16	15
High	598	27	11	28	25
Chestnut	670	36	27	27	23

[185] There were two Democratic candidates in the contest for this election.

[186] Percentage of votes in the city for Muhlenberg, who was the candidate of the anti-bank faction of the Democratic Party and was supported by the Trades' Union of Philadelphia.

[187] Percentage of votes for George Wolf, candidate of the pro-bank faction of the Democratic Party. He was the regular candidate of the Democratic Party.

[188] Percentage of the votes given for both of the candidates who were campaigning for office on the Democratic ticket.

A perusal of the above tables will indicate that the working men of Philadelphia gave their votes far more consistently to the Whigs than to the Jackson Democrats.[189] Moreover, it was prior to the Bank War and not during it that the working class districts revealed any inclination to follow the lead of Jackson and his party.[190] During the first four

---

[189] See Robert T. Bower, "Note on 'Did Labor Support Jackson?: The Boston Story'" *Political Science Quarterly*, LXV, Sept. 1950, pp. 441-444 for a criticism of the conclusions drawn from this approach. To meet the criticism raised in Bowers' article, the writer has utilized the techniques demonstrated therein as a further test of the validity of the above thesis. Below is measured the relative size of the vote as it varies from ward to ward in correlation with the richness or poorness of the wards, disregarding for the present the absolute size of the vote. Modern statistical technique frowns on the use of correlation coefficients as such since they have no meaning in themselves. The writer has therefore included the coefficient of determination which is the square of the coefficient of correlation and tells the proportion of the variance in the dependent variable that has been explained by the independent variable.

Presidential Elections

Year	Coefficient of Correlation	Coefficient of Determination
1828	–.68	46%
1832	–.64	41
1836	–.42	17½
1840	–.34	11½

Gubernatorial Elections

1832	–.39	15%
1835	–.53*	28
1835	+.13**	2
1835	–.35***	12
1838	–.66	43½

   * For George Wolf candidate of the Pro-Bank faction of the Democratic Party.
  ** For Muhlenberg candidate of the Anti-Bank faction of the Democratic Party and supported by the Trades' Union of Philadelphia.
*** Combined candidacy of Wolf and Muhlenberg.

Local Elections—
Working Men's Party

1830	+.22	5%

An examination of the above tables reveals little that is significant in the problem of determining whether the workingmen gave their votes to the Jackson candidates or not. One thing appears certain, that is, it was after 1832 that the support of the workingmen for the Jacksonians waned. On the whole, the findings are inconclusive and it would be rash to suggest that according to the above correlation coefficients the Democratic Party did have the support of the working classes of Philadelphia. See Paul F. Lazarsfeld, "Votes in the Making," *Scientific American*, 183, November 1950, pp. 11-13.

[190] It must be noted that Philadelphia was the home of the Second Bank of the United States.

years of the Jackson era there does appear to be a correlation between economic interests and the ward votes. But even during these years the pattern is shattered by the returns from Chestnut and Lower Delaware wards. Chestnut ward, one of the wealthiest in the city, did not, as might have been expected, cast its support to the candidates of the Whig Party. And Lower Delaware ward voted monotonously for the Anti-Jackson Party, giving at the same time far more votes to the Working Men's Party than did any other ward in the city.[191] Thus it is evident that Jackson and his party were unable, in this vital center of industry and finance, to capture the imagination of the wage earners and organize them politically in its own behalf.

Pittsburgh was the second city of the State and the most heavily industrialized community outside of Philadelphia. It is well, therefore, to examine the fortunes of the Jackson Party there. Were the wage earners here attracted to Jackson as it has been so often contended? In Allegheny County, itself, the Jackson vote was steadily declining. The Democratic Party in the election of 1828 won an overwhelming victory over the followers of John Q. Adams and the opposition party. Allegheny County gave to Jackson 3,866 votes, while Adams received only 1,666 votes.[192] The returns from the election of 1832 revealed that the fortunes of the Jacksonians were on the wane, while those of the Anti-Jacksonians were steadily rising. In that election, Jackson received 3,321 votes, while his opponent, William Wirt, polled 2,985 votes.[193] By 1836, the Democratic Party was the minority party in this county. Harrison, the Whig candidate for President, in that election polled 3,623 votes to 3,074 for Van Buren.[194] And according to the returns from the election of 1840, Harrison received 3,000 more votes from Allegheny County than did his opponent, Van Buren.[195]

It is even more instructive to glance at the fortunes of the gubernatorial candidates during this same period by the returns from Pittsburgh and its environs. This includes the City of Pittsburgh, the borough of Allegheny, Northern Liberties and Birmingham. These were the centers of industry in this part of the State and in all likelihood it was in these communities that the propertyless wage earners resided.

---

[191] *Hazard's Register of Pennsylvania*, VI, p. 268.

[192] *Ibid.*, V, p. 306.

[193] *Ibid.*, X, p. 281; *Niles' Register*, LI, 195, November 26, 1836.

[194] *Niles' Register*, LI, 195, Nov. 26, 1836.

[195] *Hazard's United States Commercial and Statistical Register*, V, Nov. 1841, p. 292. See The *Public Ledger*, Oct. 19, 1840.

In the gubernatorial election of 1829, George Wolf, the Democratic candidate, enjoyed a smashing victory over his opponent, Joseph Ritner.. He polled 1,028 votes to Ritner's 536.[196] Allegheny County gave Wolf 2,077 votes and Ritner, 1,872. The next gubernatorial election coincided with the Presidential contest and, despite that fact, the Anti-Jackson candidate was successful in both the greater Pittsburgh area and in Allegheny County. From Pittsburgh and its suburbs, Ritner polled 1,332 votes, while his opponent received 1,304 votes. The county gave Ritner, the Anti-Jackson candidate, 3,506 votes, and George Wolf, his opponent, 3,094 votes.[197]

Candidates of the Anti-Jackson Party repeatedly won the suffrages of the voters from the Pittsburgh area and Allegheny County in subsequent elections. The governor's election in 1835 confirmed this fact. Although there was a split within the ranks of the Democratic Party, this did not appreciably affect the vote in Pittsburgh and its vicinity. George Wolf, representing one faction of the Democratic Party, received 1,098 votes, while Muhlenberg, representing another faction of this party, captured a mere 196 votes. Ritner, the choice of the opposing party, won easily with a total of 1,463 votes. The breakdown of the county vote was as follows: Wolf, 2,854; Muhlenberg, 378; and Ritner, 3,848.[198] Nor did the returns from the election of 1838 reveal any movement of the voters away from the Whig and Anti-Democratic candidates in this part of the State. Ritner, although losing favor elsewhere in the State, easily bested his Democratic opponent, David Porter. From the greater Pittsburgh area he garnered 2,561 votes to Porter's 1,647. In Allegheny County his total vote was 6,308 while that of Porter was 4,505.[199]

Since Pennsylvania was predominantly an agricultural state it is difficult to evaluate the returns from the other counties throughout the State. But the two charts below indicate the losses suffered by the Jacksonians in the Presidential and the gubernatorial elections during the period under discussion.[200]

---

[196] The *Pittsburgh Gazette*, Oct. 20, 1829; Wilson, *op. cit.*, p. 769.

[197] The *Pittsburgh Mercury*, Oct. 13, 1832; Wilson, *op. cit.*, p. 769.

[198] *Hazard's Register of Pennsylvania*, XVI, Nov. 1835, p. 341. See Wilson, *op. cit.*, p. 781.

[199] Wilson, *op. cit.*, p. 786. See also the *Senate Journal of Pennsylvania*, I, 1838-1839, pp. 42, 43.

[200] See Appendix C for the actual returns from these counties. The data was compiled from the following sources: *Hazard's Register of Pennsylvania*, II, Nov. 1828, p. 306; *Niles' Register*, LI, Nov. 26, 1836; *Senate Journal of Pennsylvania*, 1838-1839, I, pp. 42, 43.

	1828 Jackson-Adams	1832 Jackson-Wirt	1836 Van Buren-Harrison	1840 Van Buren-Harrison
Adams	A	A	A	A
Allegheny	D	D	A	A
Armstrong	D	D	D	D
Beaver	A	A	A	D
Bedford	D	D	A	A
Berks	D	D	D	D
Bradford	D	D	A	D
Bucks	A	A	A	A
Butler	D	D	A	A
Cambria	D	D	A	D
Centre	D	D	D	D
Chester	D	A	A	A
Clearfield	D	D	D	D
Columbia	D	D	D	D
Crawford	D	D	D	D
Cumberland	D	D	D	A
Dauphin	D	D	A	A
Delaware	A	A	A	A
Erie	A	A	A	A
Fayette	D	D	D	D
Franklin	D	A	A	A
Greene	D	D	D	D
Huntingdon	D	D	A	A
Indiana ....⎫ Jefferson ....⎭	D	D D	D D	D D
Juniata		D	D	D
Lancaster	D	A	A	A
Lebanon	D	D	A	A
Lehigh	D	D	D	D
Luzerne	D	D	D	D
Lycoming	D	D	D	D
Mercer	D	D	A	A
Mifflin	D	D	D	D
Montgomery	D	D	D	D
Northampton	D	D	D	D
Northumberland ..	D	D	D	D
Perry	D	D	D	D
Philadelphia City ..	D	A	A	A
Phila. County	D	D	D	D
Pike	D	D	D	D
Potter & McKean .	D	D	D	D (Potter)
Schuylkill	D	D	D	D
Somerset	D	A	A	A

	1828 Jackson-Adams	1832 Jackson-Wirt	1836 Van Buren-Harrison	1840 Van Buren-Harrison
Susquehanna	D	D	D	D
Tioga	D	D	D	D
Union	D	D	A	A
Venango	D	D	D	D
Warren	D	D	D	D
Washington	D	D	D	A
Wayne	D	D	D	D
Westmoreland	D	D	D	D
York	D	D	D	D
Monroe				D
Clinton				D
Clarion				D
McKean				D
	45 5	42 10	32 20	37 19

	1829 Wolf-Ritner	1832 Wolf-Ritner	1835 Wolf-Ritner-Muhlenberg	1838 Porter-Ritner
Adams	A	A	A	A
Allegheny	D	A	A	A
Armstrong	D	D	D	D
Beaver	D	A	A	A
Bedford	A	D	A	D
Berks	D	D	D	D
Bradford	D	D	D	D
Bucks	D	D	A	D
Butler	D	D	A	A
Cambria	A	D	A	D
Centre	D	D	D	D
Clearfield	D	D	D	D
Chester	A	A	A	A
Columbia	D	D	D	D
Crawford	A	D	A	D
Cumberland	D	D	A	D
Dauphin	A	A	A	A
Delaware	D	A	A	A
Erie	A	A	A	A
Fayette	D	D	A	D
Franklin	tie vote	A	A	D

| | 1829 | | 1832 | | 1835 | | | 1838 | |
County	Wolf-Ritner		Wolf-Ritner		Wolf-Ritner-Muhlenberg			Porter-Ritner	
Greene	D		A		A			D	
Huntingdon		A	A		A				A
Indiana		A	A		A				A
Jefferson				D		D		D	
Juniata			A		A			D	
Lancaster		A	A		A				A
Lebanon		A	A		A				A
Lehigh	D		A		A			D	
Lycoming		A		D	A			D	
Luzerne	D			D	A			D	
Mercer		A	A		A				A
Mifflin	D		A			D		D	
Montgomery	D		A		A			D	
Northampton	D		D			D		D	
Northumberland	D			D			D	D	
Perry	D			D			D	D	
Potter & McKean	D			D			D	D	
Philadelphia City	D		A		A				A
Phila. County	D			D		D		D	
Pike	D			D		D		D	
Schuylkill	D			D	A			D	
Somerset		A	A		A				A
Susquehanna	D			D		D		D	
Tioga	D			D		D		D	
Union		A	A		A				A
Venango		A	D			D		D	
Warren	D			D		D		D	
Washington		A	A		A				A
Wayne	D			D		D		D	
Westmoreland	D			D		D		D	
York	D		A		A			D	
Monroe								D	
Clinton									
Clarion									
McKean								D	
	32	17	29	23	15	32	5	37	17

It is interesting to note that it was those counties—Lancaster, Allegheny, Dauphin, Franklin—in which there were evidences of organized labor activity which were the first to desert the Jackson fold. There is only one exception. Philadelphia County which had a very active labor movement remained in the camp of the Jacksonians throughout the period under discussion. From an analysis of the distribution of the votes according to the counties, it would appear that the main support of the Jacksonians in Pennsylvania came not from the industrialized and urban areas with their masses of property-less wage earners, but from the rural districts of the State.

Since it was the followers of Jackson who in this period have been generally recognized as the standard bearers of a program for progressive action, the question might properly be raised as to which factors were responsible for their repudiation. The Democrats under the leadership of Jackson had been embraced by Pennsylvania with a passion which Malcolm Eiselen had characterized as a "mad infatuation."[201] The disaffection of the voters from this party is not readily explicable. Quite obviously the wage earners were not especially attracted to this party, nor did they look up to it as their party and Jackson as their leader.

In searching for an explanation for its lack of success in Philadelphia, the Democratic Party was quick to single out the Second Bank of the United States as a force partially responsible for its defeat. The *Pennsylvanian*, an ardent Jackson paper, declared[202]

> among the cruel acts resorted to by the Bank of the United States, to carry on a ruthless and traitorous warfare against the mechanics and workingmen, was that of sending agents around to all the large manufacturers to urge them to discharge their hands, draw in their business, and thus force the workingmen of the country to come around and support the bank by their votes in order to regain their bread.

A similar charge was made by the *Pittsburgh Mercury*. "The Bank monopolists well know at this season of alarms," wrote the *Mercury* in the depressing days of 1834, "a father's fears for his family outweigh his other considerations and he tamely submits to their mandates."[203]

The most effective charge against the bank, as Catterall pointed out, was that it "subsidized the press." In the summer of 1831, the *Work-*

[201] Quoted in Louis Hartz, *op. cit.*, p. 24.
[202] The *Pennsylvanian*, October 11, 1834.
[203] The *Pittsburgh Mercury*, as quoted in Wilson, *op. cit.*, p. 775.

ing Man's Advocate printed a letter from a "working man" of Philadelphia to the editor of the *Washington Globe* in which it was charged that even the *Mechanic's Free Press*, "the only press [in Philadelphia] that opposed the Bank of the United States," too, had succumbed to the lush printing contracts of the bank, and that since the printing of Mr. McDuffie's defense of the Bank, it, too had been silenced.[204]

> The Bank, [this workingman charged] not contented with the circulation given to the report through the papers, selected or caused to be selected, the only printers who had evinced *hostility* to the Bank—They passed by their friends, and, in the obscurity of an alley, found the hostile printers, who were immediately *employed* on this defence of the bank, for the printing of which they received at one time nearly $2,000. I do not say that *this sum* has muzzled this paper, but *I do say, that no articles have appeared against the Bank, since the Bank printing job was completed.*[205]

After the election in 1832, the *Pennsylvanian* rationalized the loss of the city by the Democrats with a charge that "it is the money of the Bank—directly or indirectly applied—that has for a time, covered our city with disgrace."

But the contention that it was the Bank War which finally brought the workingmen to the side of Jackson and the Democratic Party is an oversimplification which has never been fully explored. It is a fit subject for a monograph in itself. There can be no doubt that the majority of the leaders of the organized labor movement at this time were ardently opposed to banks and chartered monopolies, and especially to the Bank of the United States. In 1838, at a meeting in Philadelphia attended and officered by individuals who had long been prominent in the trade union movement, it was resolved that "we are opposed to a *national bank* under whatever name, disguise or pretence it may be created, believing the civil liberties of the country will be in danger, and the political institutions brought down at the feet of the *money power*."[206]

---

[204] See R. C. H. Catterall, *The Second Bank of the United States* (Chicago, 1903), p. 243. The *Working Man's Advocate*, July 16, 1831. See The *Clearfield Democrat*, March 1, 1834.

[205] Charge printed in The *Working Man's Advocate*, July 16, 1831.

[206] The *Pennsylvanian*, May 4, 1838. Among the signers were Israel Young, William Gilmore, E. A. Penniman, John Farrell and Samuel C. Thompson, all who had long been active in the Pennsylvania labor movement. See also John Ferral to James Buchanan, Dec. 22, 1837 in the Collection of the Historical Society of Pennsylvania.

There was a notable absence from this meeting. William English, who in 1836 had been elected to the Pennsylvania House of Representatives, and had long been a hard-money man, was to be found in the ranks of those who voted for a Pennsylvania charter for the Second Bank of the United States. Moreover when a bill was introduced in the State Legislature to repeal the charter of this bank, his vote was recorded against the bill.[207] Obviously some of his supporters in Philadelphia were much disturbed by his attitude, for the *Keystone* reported that "taunts have been thrown out against Mr. English from a certain quarter in the city because he did not accomplish all the objects desired by his constituents . . . and he has been accused of violating pledges and shrinking from the discharge of his duty."[208]

It is open to question how accurately the leaders of this trade union movement voiced the desires and the sentiments of their following. One thing is certain, there can be no question that they failed, if they were so inclined to deliver the vote of the Pennsylvania wage earners to the Jackson Democrats.

Whatever the cause for the ultimate defeat of the Jacksonians in Pennsylvania, and undoubtedly the questions of the Bank, the tariff and internal improvements figured prominently in this defeat, the fact remains that the wage earners were among the first to drop from the Jackson band wagon. His most consistent support came from the rural and agricultural areas of the State.[209]

---

[207] See the *Pennsylvania House Journal,* I, 1836-1837, April 3, 1837.

[208] The *Keystone,* April 26, 1837. See Arthur Schlesinger, Jr., *op. cit.,* p. 204.

[209] Contrast views of the following in regard to the question of the wage earners and Andrew Jackson: Richard Hofstadter, *American Political Tradition and the Men Who Made It* (New York, 1948), pp. 44-68; Joseph Dorfman, *The Economic Mind in Modern America* (New York, 1946), II, p. 601 ff.; and Arthur M. Schlesinger, Jr., *The Age of Jackson,* p. 505 ff.

IX

THE WAGE EARNERS AND SOCIAL REFORM

THE PENNSYLVANIA wage earners were the pioneers of the American Labor Movement, equally as courageous as those who blazed the trails and broke the sod in the land beyond the Ohio and the Mississippi, but with a much keener insight into the deeper meanings of democracy. They intuitively comprehended the dangers of unbridled business expansion, and marshalled all their energies to ward off its more desolating effects. They were among the first to organize into trade unions and to utilize and perfect collective bargaining techniques which would enable them to acquire a more equitable share of the wealth which they had helped to create. And when these actions proved insufficient they turned to the government for aid, and in their appeal for remedial legislation they developed a philosophy based "on natural law, social contract, and individual right."[1]

The workingmen of Pennsylvania, and the workingmen throughout the United States, had a profound faith in democracy. They were able at one and the same time to campaign vigorously against "monopolies" and appeal for governmental action in their own behalf. Nor were they being inconsistent as Professor Hartz has pointed out in his admirable study of *Economic Policy and Democratic Thought in Pennsylvania*.

The failure or the survival of a republican form of government, in the eyes of many workers, hinged on the development of a system of free public education. Their faith in education was sublime. Through it alone, many wage earners were convinced that a social revolution could be effected, and they vigorously assailed the prevailing system of charity schools as a direct violation of their natural rights.[2]

Whether any significance can be attached to the fact that the first agitation for social legislation in the Pennsylvania Legislature occurred almost simultaneously with the economic recovery following the great panic of 1819, and the waves of strikes which involved thousands of

---

[1] Louis Hartz, *Economic Policy and Democratic Thought in Pennsylvania* (Cambridge, Mass., 1948), p. 203.

[2] See The *Public Ledger*, July 12, 1839. Also see *Pennsylvania House Journal*, II, 1824-25, p. 422 for a Report of the Committee on Education, January 11, 1825. And see Joseph McCadden, *Education in Pennsylvania 1801-1835* (Philadelphia, 1937), pp. 6, 17. See Hartz, *op. cit.*, p. 198.

handloom weavers is a moot question. It was in 1824, that Mr. O'Neill, a member of the House of Representatives from Philadelphia County, introduced a resolution "that a committee be appointed to inquire into the expediency of requiring the proprietors of manufacturing establishments, who may employ children under the age of twelve years, to provide for them the means of instruction at least two hours each day in the rudiments of an English education.[3] The House failed to act on the resolution of the committee and the subject was dropped.

In the decade from 1824 to 1834, the agitation for educational reform increased in intensity. Time and again, bills for establishing a system of free public schools were introduced, but invariably failed to secure the support of the legislators.[4] It was in 1834 that the first effective school law was passed by the State Legislature. The mounting agitation of organized labor coupled with the support given the measure by middle class reformers such as Roberts Vaux and Governor Wolf was probably a decisive factor in the passage of a school bill at this time. John R. Commons, in recognition of the efforts of the workingmen toward this end states: "For our great public school system of today ... we owe a large if unrecognized debt of gratitude to this first effort of the working class to exercise independently its citizenship."[5]

The wage earners of Pennsylvania also threw their weight behind the movement for the repeal of the obnoxious laws allowing imprisonment for debt. Although not alone in this struggle, they fought more energetically than did any other class for the repeal of these laws which stemmed from the days of bonded servitude. From 1818 on, the legislature of Pennsylvania was flooded with petitions demanding relief from these oppressive laws.[6]

---

[3] Cited in J. Lynn Barnard, *Factory Legislation in Pennsylvania: Its History and Administration* (Philadelphia, 1907), pp. 1, 2.

[4] See *Pennsylvania House Journal*, I, 1827-1828, Dec. 11, 1827, p. 41; 1831-1832, II, pp. 8, 684. *Digest of the Ordinances of the Corporation of the City of Philadelphia and of the Acts of Assembly* (Phila., 1834), p. 188. The *Annual Register*, VIII, 1831-1832, p. 251. The *Pennsylvania Reporter*, Jan. 29, 1828. The *Saturday Evening Post*, Feb. 9, 1828.

[5] John R. Commons, *History of Labour*, I, p. 327.

[6] See *Pennsylvania House Journal*, I, 1824-1825, December 13, 1824, p. 35; I, 1829-30, March 15, 1830, p. 628; March 16, 1830, p. 646; March 18, 1830, p. 674; March 20, 1830, p. 694; March 27, 1830, p. 758. The writer has searched through many boxes of petitions in the Public Records Division of the Penna. Historical and Museum Commission for manuscript copies to determine whether they were originating from laboring groups, but was unable to locate any.

In April 1833, the reformist element in the State legislature brought the subject of imprisonment for debt before that body. A House Committee was "appointed to visit and examine the debtor's department of the Arch Street prison in Philadelphia." In its final report the Committee strongly urged that "an act to abolish imprisonment for small debts and for other purposes" be approved. And in June of that year such an act was passed.[7]

Opponents of the measure deluged the legislature with petitions for the repeal of this bit of progressive legislation. The subject of repeal was, in 1835, referred to the Judiciary Committee, and in its final report, it declared:[8]

> the committee can discover no sound reason for inter-
> ference at this time with the subject referred to. . . . A
> law, so humane in its object, so consistent with the best
> feelings of the heart, so well calculated to protect the lib-
> erty and so conducive to the comfort of the labouring
> classes, ought not to be repealed without the very
> strongest evidence that it has operated injuriously to the
> interests of society.

With the passage of this legislation one form of involuntary servitude received a sharp setback.[9] That was indentured servitude, and the workingmen could feel justly proud of their role in the enactment of this legislation.

The mechanics of Pennsylvania had from the earliest day of the Republic sought the enactment of laws which would give them a lien on buildings for labor. By 1803, the Philadelphia mechanics had extracted from the State Legislature a law which subjected those buildings constructed in the Philadelphia area "to the payment of debts contracted by the owner or owners" for any work done or materials supplied by mechanics or others.[10] According to one social historian, Henry W. Farnam, "labor protection in the United States really begins with mechanic's liens."[11]

---

[7] *Pennsylvania House Journal*, 1834-35, II, January 14, 1835, p. 206.

[8] *Ibid.*

[9] Although Karl F. Geiser, *Redemptioners and Indentured Servants in the Colony and Commonwealth of Pennsylvania* (New Haven, 1901), p. 42, says that "with the final abolition of imprisonment for debt the institution of indentured service received its legal death blow, and necessarily died out without any special enactment"; the subject entails much more study. The writer in his researches has uncovered evidence of indentured servitude in the late 1830's.

[10] Henry W. Farnam, *Chapters in the History of Social Legislation in the United States to 1900* (Washington, D. C., 1938), p. 152.

[11] *Ibid.*, p. 154.

The emergence of an organized labor movement in the late 1820's brought with it renewed agitation for the passage of more effective lien legislation for the wage earners. They justified independent political action on the premise that the workingmen could through such means procure for themselves better security in their wages. The *Mechanic's Free Press* denounced the Judiciary Committee of the State Legislature for its failure to heed the petitions of the Philadelphia mechanics.[12]

> It will be seen [this Journal declared] by the report of Mr. Banks, on behalf of the committee on the Judiciary system, to whom was referred the memorial of the Journeymen Mechanics, and other Working Men of this city and county, praying for better security in their wages, that our legislature does not feel that interest in attending to our just claims, which they do in the various schemes brought forward more deeply to oppress us; witness their lengthy deliberations on the subject of additional banks in the city and county. After such evidence as this before our eyes, can we any longer doubt the indispensable necessity of our union, regardless of party names, not only at the polls, but by political societies, to meet at short periods throughout the year.

But the wage earners were not entirely without friends in the State Legislature. In 1829, John Hare Powell, a bitter opponent of Jackson but a favorite of the Philadelphia Working Men's Party, led a movement for the enactment of a law which would make the mechanics privileged creditors "in all cases of insolvency."[13] Mr. Powell argued "that liens are established for the benefit of the money lender, for the protection of the landholder, for the advantage of the tavern keeper, for the house and shipbuilder, the lumber merchant, and the livery stable man . . . ," but not for the wage earners.[14] But his plea fell on deaf ears. This issue cropped up again and again in the State Legislature, but it was not until 1854 that a law was passed which "gave mechanics first preference, up to one hundred dollars, in the property assignments of insolvent corporations."[15]

No issue had captured the imagination of the Pennsylvania wage earners or had the emotional drive behind it as did their demand for the ten-hour day. Through sheer overwhelming force, the Philadelphia

---

[12] The *Mechanic's Free Press*, Feb. 7, 1829. See Hartz, *op. cit.*, p. 192.

[13] See *Hazard's Register of Pennsylvania*, IV, Nov. 1829, p. 333; The *Mechanic's Free Press*, November 21, 1829.

[14] Mathew Carey, *Select Excerpta*, VII, December 10, 1829, p. 347.

[15] Cited in Hartz, *op. cit.*, p. 193.

workers wrested the ten-hour day from the city government in the summer of 1835, and the private employers felt compelled to capitulate in this demand. The government Navy Yard held out for one year, but growing pressure from the Philadelphia workers forced it to accede to the ship workers' demands.[16]

What part the Pennsylvania workers played in forcing President Van Buren's hand in establishing the ten-hour day for all laborers and mechanics employed on public works is impossible to assess.[17] Since 1840 was an election year and it was only then that he issued his celebrated directive, and since the Pennsylvania wage earners were among the most articulate and best organized of all workers in the United States, the facts would suggest that theirs was an important role in this pronouncement. George McNeill, a well known labor leader in the latter years of the nineteenth century, was convinced that it was the agitation of organized labor that induced President Van Buren to issue the famous order, but undoubtedly the political considerations of the moment were far more important.[18]

Thus Pennsylvania labor had, in its struggle for free public education, for the abolishment of imprisonment for debt, for the passage of mechanics' lien laws, and for the establishment of the ten-hour day, met with a moderate degree of success. But in one field of endeavor they met with complete failure. "We have seen in this and other States," complained the *Philadelphia Trades' Union*, "Journeymen mechanics, indicted, tried and imprisoned for combining to protect their interests, whilst capitalists for infinitely worse combinations, have not only escaped the censure of the law, but have been held up as public benefactors."[19]

Charges of criminal conspiracy and the successful prosecution of these charges by embittered employer groups continually blunted and frus-

---

[16] The *Pennsylvanian*, Sept. 5, 1836. See again Prof. R. B. Morris' provocative and penetrating article "Andrew Jackson was no F. D. R." in *Labor and the Nation*, May-June 1949, pp. 38-41.

[17] *Hazard's United States Commercial and Statistical Register*, II, April 1840, p. 268; The *Crawford Democrat*, June 2, 1840; Morris, *op. cit.*, p. 40.

[18] "Organization and agitation on this subject finally attained such magnitude as to warrant the President of the U. S., Martin Van Buren, in issuing a proclamation establishing the ten hour system for all employees of the U. S. Government in the Navy Yards." George McNeill, The *Labor Movement: The Problem of Today* (*New York*, 1887), p. 90.

[19] The *Pennsylvanian*, June 10, 1836.

trated the efforts of the wage earners to achieve their ends through organized and concerted action. The judicial basis for criminal conspiracy rested on the common law which regarded conspiracy as a combination of two or more persons who by concerted action endeavor to accomplish a criminal or unlawful purpose, or if not criminal or unlawful, used such means to accomplish their purpose.

Pennsylvania courts, in this first half of the century, usually accepted the English precedents which had declared that a combination to raise wages constituted a criminal conspiracy. Only in the case of the four journeymen carpenters of Pittsburgh who had been indicted for combining "together in connection with several hundred others, for the purpose of obtaining through menace and by force an amelioration of labour—to reduce the daily period of working to ten hours," was a verdict of "not guilty" returned.[20] But throughout the period under discussion, and for decades afterwards, the trade unions unsuccessfully defended themselves against charges of conspiracy.

The momentous decisions of Chief Justice Shaw of Massachusetts in which it held that labor combinations were legal, unless the indictment proved the use of illegal or unlawful means or ends, had no immediate effect on the attitude of the Pennsylvania courts towards concerted labor activity. Despite the fact that the decision was rendered in 1842, it was to be decades before it was even referred to as a precedent in labor conspiracy trials before the Pennsylvania courts.

Nor had the action of the Pennsylvania legislature, which in 1869 had approved an act that exempted wage earners who combined into trade unions from "prosecution or indictment for conspiracy under the criminal laws of this Commonwealth,"[21] appreciably affected their status before the courts. And although in 1872, the law was so ameliorated as to specifically legalize strike action by trade unions, the Pennsylvania courts still regarded concerted action by the workingmen as criminal conspiracy.

The first important court test of the law was in 1875. The coal miners of Clearfield County struck that year for higher wages. Rioting broke out and there was general disorder in the coal fields. John Siney, president of the Miners' National Association, and Xingo Parks, field or-

---

[20] The *Allegheny Democrat*, August 9, 1831.
[21] Law quoted in full in *Labor Laws of Pennsylvania* (Harrisburg, 1914) pp. 306, 307. Compiled and annotated by Jasper Yeates Brinton.

ganizer, were indicted for conspiracy and inciting riots.[22] The trial attracted universal attention. Lawyers of national repute were brought into the trial, both for and against the defendants. The law of 1872 and the Commonwealth v. Hunt decision were cited in behalf of the defendants, but the prosecution charged that the act of 1872 had not changed the conspiracy laws of the State and the presiding judge was in agreement with the prosecution.[23] Hence, even at this late date, and long after the legal status of trade unions had been fixed by statute, the wage earners of Pennsylvania were to find that for all practical purposes the ancient doctrine of criminal conspiracy still prevailed against them.

The labor movement of the United States owes much to the courageous and sometimes futile efforts of the Pennsylvania wage earners. They were the first to organize for collective action. They were the first to formulate a political program, radical in its day but now accepted as a minimum basis of labor's demands in a capitalist society. They were the first to feel the crushing effects of unsympathetic court decisions and the stinging criticisms of a hostile press. These wage earners were convinced that they were involved in a struggle to preserve democracy. And neither adverse court decisions nor unsuccessful strike actions shattered their faith in the creed which Jefferson had written into the Declaration of Independence.

---

[22] *Annual Report of the Secretary of Internal Affairs, Part III, Industrial Statistics,* 1880-1881, p. 315. The writer must acknowledge his debt to Hyman Kuritz, a graduate student at Columbia University, for giving him access to his materials on Labor Combinations in post-bellum Pennsylvania.

[23] Pennsylvania Annual Report, *op. cit.,* p. 315. For a brilliant discussion of the Commonwealth v. Hunt decision see Walter Nelles, "Commonwealth v. Hunt," *Columbia Law Review,* XXXII, Nov. 1932, pp. 1128-1169.

APPENDIX A

Trade Societies in Pennsylvania in the 1830's

Trade Union	Source
Philadelphia—1834	
Journeymen Cabinet Makers	*Pennsylvanian,* March 4, 1834
Journeymen Saddlers and Harness-makers	*Pennsylvanian,* March 8, 1834
United Beneficial Society of Journeymen Cordwainers (Men's Branch)	*Pennsylvanian,* March 13, 1834
Journeymen Carpenters	*Pennsylvanian,* March 13, 1834
Journeymen Brushmakers	*Pennsylvanian,* March 13, 1834
Schuylkill Falls Society	*Pennsylvanian,* March 13, 1834
United Beneficial Society of Journeymen Cordwainers (Ladies' Branch)	*Pennsylvanian,* March 13, 1834
Blockley Society	*Pennsylvanian,* March 13, 1834
Haverford Society	*Pennsylvanian,* March 13, 1834
House Painters	*Pennsylvanian,* March 13, 1834
Tobacconists' Trade Society	*Pennsylvanian,* March 13, 1834
Journeymen Shell-Comb Makers	*Pennsylvanian,* March 13, 1834
Philadelphia Benevolent and Trade Society of Journeymen Tailors	*Pennsylvanian,* March 13, 1834
Bookbinders Trade Society	*Pennsylvanian,* March 13, 1834
Association of Moulders	*Pennsylvanian,* March 13, 1834
Journeymen Hatters' Association	*Pennsylvanian,* March 13, 1834
Typographical Association	*Pennsylvanian,* March 13, 1834
Association of Journeymen Stone Cutters	*Pennsylvanian,* March 13, 1834
Journeymen Umbrella Makers' Society	*Pennsylvanian,* March 13, 1834
Association of Leather Dressers, No. 1	*Pennsylvanian,* March 13, 1834
Association of Leather Dressers, No. 2	*Pennsylvanian,* March 13, 1834
Philadelphia—1835	
Handloom Cotton Weavers, No. 1	*Pennsylvanian,* May 15, 1835
Plasterers	*Pennsylvanian,* June 8, 1835
Journeymen Bricklayers	*Pennsylvanian,* June 9, 1835
Journeymen Black and White Smiths	*Pennsylvanian,* June 12, 1835
Journeymen Segar Makers	*Pennsylvanian,* June 20, 1835
Journeymen Bakers	*Pennsylvanian,* June 20, 1835
Journeymen Plumbers	*Pennsylvanian,* July 8, 1835
Female Improvident Society	*Reformer* and *Working Man's Advocate,* July 18, 1835
Shoe Binder and Corders Society	*Pennsylvanian,* Dec. 31, 1835

TRADE SOCIETIES IN PENNSYLVANIA IN THE 1830's (Continued)

Trade Union	Source
Philadelphia—1836	
Handloom Cotton Weavers, No. 2	*Pennsylvanian*, Feb. 12, 1836
Journeymen Curriers	*Pennsylvanian*, Feb. 12, 1836
Journeymen Glass Workers	*Pennsylvanian*, March 5, 1836
Journeymen Brass Finishers	*Pennsylvanian*, March 5, 1836
Journeymen Biscuit Makers	*Pennsylvanian*, March 12, 1836
Brewery Laborers	*National Laborer*, April 2, 1836
Whip and Cane Makers	*National Laborer*, April 16, 1836
Carpet and Ingrain Weavers	*National Laborer*, April 25, 1836
Fairmount Trade Association	*National Laborer*, May 7, 1836
Manayunk Trade Society	*National Laborer*, May 14, 1836
Day Laborers	*National Laborer*, May 14, 1836
Chair Makers	*Pennsylvanian*, May 19, 1836
Schuylkill Laborers	*National Laborer*, May 21, 1836
Gilders	*National Laborer*, May 27, 1836
Machinists and Millwrights	*National Laborer*, June 4, 1836
Horseshoers	*National Laborer*, June 11, 1836
United Association of Journeymen Paper Makers	*National Laborer*, June 11, 1836
Blacksmiths	*National Laborer*, June 11, 1836
Cedar Coopers	*National Laborer*, June 18, 1836
Coach Makers, Trimmers and Painters	*National Laborer*, June 18, 1836
Dyers	*National Laborer*, June 18, 1836
Soap Boilers and Tallow Chandlers	*National Laborer*, July 23, 1836
Chester Creek Trade Association	*National Laborer*, July 23, 1836
Paper Stainers	*National Laborer*, Aug. 13, 1836
Norristown Trade Association	*National Laborer*, Oct. 14, 1836
Cotton Spinners	*National Laborer*, Oct. 15, 1836
Pittsburgh—1836	
Journeymen Printers	*Pittsburgh Gazette*, Jan. 12, 1836
United States Beneficial Association of Iron Moulders of the City of Pittsburgh and County of Allegheny	*National Laborer*, Dec. 10, 1836
Journeymen Carpenters	Commons, *Documentary History*, VI, 336
Harrisburg—1836	
Typographical Association	The *Keystone*, Dec. 31, 1836

TRADE SOCIETIES IN PENNSYLVANIA IN THE 1830's (Continued)

Trade Union	Source
Lancaster—1836	
Journeymen Carpenters	*Lancaster Journal,* April 15, 1836
Journeymen Cordwainers	*Lancaster Journal,* April 15, 1836
Easton—1836	
Journeymen Cordwainers	*National Trades' Union,* Mar. 26, 1836
Columbia—1836	
Journeymen Cordwainers	*National Trades' Union,* Mar. 26, 1836
Philadelphia—1837	
Silversmiths	*National Laborer,* Jan. 14, 1837
Ship Joiners	*National Laborer,* Feb. 18, 1837
Framework Knitters	*National Laborer,* Mar. 18, 1837
Glass Cutters	*National Laborer,* Mar. 18, 1837
Furriers	*National Laborer,* Apr. 25, 1837
Pittsburgh—1837	
Journeymen Coopers	
United Beneficial Society of Journeymen Cordwainers (Men's Branch)	*National Laborer,* Jan. 21, 1837
United Beneficial Society of Journeymen Cordwainers (Ladies' Branch)	*National Laborer,* Jan. 21, 1837
Journeymen Tailors	*National Laborer,* Jan. 21, 1837
Journeymen Cabinet Makers	*National Laborer,* Jan. 21, 1837
Journeymen Painters	*National Laborer,* Jan. 21, 1837
Journeymen Black and White Smiths	*National Laborer,* Jan. 21, 1837

APPENDIX B

Year	Place	Trade	Issue	Reference and Comment
1799	Philadelphia	Shoemakers	Reduction of wages and lockout	J. R. Commons, *Documentary History of American Industrial Society*, III, p. 113; approximately 100 men involved; strike lasted 9 or 10 weeks and ended in a compromise.
1803	Philadelphia	Curriers	Higher wages	*Aurora and General Advertiser*, Nov. 9, 1903. On Nov. 30, 1803 Master Curriers are still advertising for hands.
1804	Philadelphia	Shoemakers	Higher wages	*Documentary History*, III, p. 12. Strike was successful— employers agreed to pay $2.75, but after Christmas wages were reduced to $2.50 for cossack boots.
1804	Pittsburgh	Shoemakers	Higher wages	Erasmus Wilson, *Standard History of Pittsburgh*, p. 200 —Strike notice in a Pittsburgh paper December 19, 1804.
1805	Philadelphia	Shoemakers	Higher wages	*Aurora and General Advertiser*, Nov. 27, 1805. Strike lasted 6 or 7 weeks. Unsuccessful and strikers were convicted of a conspiracy to raise their wages.
1810	Philadelphia	Printers	Higher wages	Ethelbert Stewart, *A Documentary History of Early Organizations of Printers*, p. 28. Strike seems to have been a disastrous failure.
1811	Pittsburgh	Shoemakers	Higher wages	*Documentary History*, IV, p. 47.
1812	Pittsburgh	Higher wages	Shoemakers	*Documentary History*, IV, pp. 30, 34. In July they turned out for $2.50 and again in October for $2.75. They were out only 3 or 4 days and the raise was granted.
1814	Pittsburgh	Shoemakers	Against apprentice work	*Documentary History*, IV, p. 36.

SUMMARY OF STRIKES IN PENNSYLVANIA—1800-1840 (Continued)

Year	Place	Trade	Issue	Reference and Comment
1814	Pittsburgh	Shoemakers	Higher wages	*Documentary History*, IV, pp. 30, 31. Strike lasted about 2 weeks. Strikers threatened with charges of conspiracy compromised the dispute and paid the costs.
1814	Pittsburgh	Shoemakers	Higher wages	*Documentary History*, IV, pp. 30, 31. Strike lasted about 2 weeks, Strikers threatened with charges of conspiracy compromised the dispute and paid the costs.
1815	Pittsburgh	Shoemakers	Higher wages	The *Pittsburgh Gazette*, Oct. 14, 1815. Strike lasted approximately 9 wks. Shoemakers were tried on charges of a conspiracy to raise their wages.
1821	Philadelphia	Ship Carpenters	Reduction of wages	*Letters from Commandant of Philadelphia Navy Yard 1815-1821*, December 22, 1821.
1824	Philadelphia	Ship Carpenters	Higher wages	*Providence Patriot*, June 26, 1824 cited in John R. Commons, *History of Labour in the United States*, vol. I, p. 157.
1825	Philadelphia	Hatters	Establish a regular system of wages	*Allegheny Democrat*, Jan. 18, 1825. Establish a regular system of wages to prevent one employer from underselling another.
1825	Philadelphia	Weavers	Higher wages	*New York Evening Post*, April 29, 1825. About 2900 weavers struck for an increase of 25% on their existing prices.
1825	Philadelphia	Cabinet Makers	Higher wages	*Freeman's Journal*, June 27, 1825. They were striking for a 25% increase.
1826	Harrisburg	Tailors	Higher wages	*Pennsylvania Intelligencer*, Nov. 17, 1826. They were given an advance of 10% on their wages.
1827	Philadelphia	House Carpenters	Ten-hour day	*Aurora and Franklin Gazette*, June 14, 1827. Approximately 500 journeymen carpenters were out on strike. The master carpenters met and decided not to employ any men except on the old time schedule.

Summary of Strikes in Pennsylvania—1800-1840 (Continued)

Year	Place	Trade	Issue	Reference and Comment
1827	Philadelphia	Tailors	Higher wages	The *American Sentinel*, Sept. 25, 1827.
1827	Harrisburg	Canal Workers	Stoppage of payment of wages	*Poulson's Daily American Advertiser*, Sept. 25, 1827.
1828	Philadelphia	Bricklayers	Ten-hour day	*Mechanic's Free Press*, May 31, 1828. On July 19, 1828, the bricklayers were still out on strike.
1828	Philadelphia	House Carpenters	Ten-hour day	*Mechanic's Free Press*, June 27, 1828.
1828	Philadelphia	Cotton Spinners	Attempted reduction of their wages	*Mechanic's Free Press*, Dec. 20, 1828. On strike at least 3 mos.
1829	Pittsburgh	Carpenters	Higher wages and ten-hour day	*Allegheny Democrat*, March 24, 1829. Approx. 200 men involved.
1829	Clark's Ferry nr. Harrisburg	Canal Workers	Higher wages	*Pennsylvania Reporter*, April 7, 1829. Approx. 300 men involved. Warrants issued for the arrest of 40 of the strike leaders and 3 were arrested.
1829	Chambersburg	Shoemakers	Higher wages and union shop	*Niles' Register*, XXXVII, Jan. 2, 1830, p. 293. They were convicted on charges of conspiracy.
1831	Germantown and Manayunk	Hatters	Higher wages	*Daily Chronicle*, March 22, 1821. Some of the employers complied with the strikers demands.
1831	Philadelphia	Glass Cutters	Higher wages	*Daily Chronicle*, Apr. 22, 1831.
1831	Pittsburgh	Carpenters	Ten-hour day	*Pittsburgh Mercury*, May 25, 1831. Approx. 200 to 300 house carpenters were out on strike for about 10 weeks. Although charges of conspiracy were brought against them, a verdict of not guilty was returned.
1831	Philadelphia	Hatters	Reduction of wages and a uniform system of wages	*Broadside* dated Oct. 29, 1831. The hatters of Philadelphia worked without a uniform system of wages until January 1836.

Summary of Strikes in Pennsylvania—1800-1840 (Continued)

Year	Place	Trade	Issue	Reference and Comment
1832	Pittsburgh	Carpenters	Ten-hour day and higher wages	*Pittsburgh Gazette,* March 20, 1832. Approx. 200 to 300 house carpenters on strike.
1832	Philadelphia	Marble Workers	Higher wages	*Cooperator,* June 1832 cited in John R. Commons, *History of Labour,* I, p. 382.
1833	Manayunk	Factory Operatives	Reduction of wages	*Germantown Telegraph,* August 7, 1833. Approx. 200 to 300 factory hands on strike because of an attempted reduction of 20% on their present wages.
1833	Philadelphia	Handloom Weavers	Lockout	*Pennsylvanian,* Nov. 2, 1833. Approx. 300 weavers locked out. Strike lasted 4 weeks.
1833	Philadelphia	Cabinet Makers	Employers locked out society men	*Pennsylvanian,* Dec. 24, 1833. Approx. 300 cabinet makers on strike for over 4 weeks.
1834	Nr. Lancaster	Railroad Workers	Higher wages	*Bedford Gazette,* Feb. 7, 1834.
1834	Manayunk	Factory Operatives	Reduction of wages	*Germantown Telegraph,* March 19, 1834. On May 29, 1834 they ret'd to work with an advance of 5% on their old prices but leaders of the strike were discharged.
1834	Blockley	Factory Operatives	Reduction of wages	The *Man,* April 15, 1834.
1834	Philadelphia	Leather Pressers and Finishers	Reduction of wages and introduction of machinery for finishing leather	*National Trades' Union,* Nov. 29, 1834. On Dec. 6, 1834 the employers agreed to give the shavers the prices asked for.
1835	Norristown	Factory Hands	Reduction of wages	*Germantown Telegraph,* April 15, 1835. Reduction would be such as would be tantamount to the actual discharge of those hands now employed. Purpose was to hire new hands from another state. Pressure of public opinion forced employer to desist from this action.

SUMMARY OF STRIKES IN PENNSYLVANIA—1800-1840 (Continued)

Year	Place	Trade	Issue	Reference and Comment
1835	Philadelphia	Coal Heavers	Ten-hour day	The *Man*, May 5, 1835. Approx. 300 coal heavers out on strike for one month.
1835	Philadelphia	Hand Loom Weavers	Higher wages	The *Pennsylvanian*, May 15, 1835. The handloom weavers assembled together resolved to join together in an association called the handloom weaver's association of the City and County of Phila.
1835	Philadelphia	Carpenters	Ten-hour day	*United States Gazette*, June 3, 1835. The master carpenters complied with the house carpenters' demands.
1835	Philadelphia	Plasterers	Ten-hour day	*Pennsylvanian*, June 4, 1835.
1835	Philadelphia	Cordwainers	Higher wages	*Pennsylvanian*, June 4, 1835. Approx. 1500 cordwainers out for 2½ weeks. By June 25, 140 employers had acceded to the demands of the journeymen.
1835	Philadelphia	Hod Carriers	Ten-hour day	*National Laborer*, June 6, 1835.
1835	Philadelphia	Bricklayers	Ten-hour day	*Pennsylvanian*, June 6, 1835. The master workmen agreed to their demands.
1835	Philadelphia	Coal Heavers	Ten-hour day	The *Man*, June 8, 1835.
1835	Philadelphia	Stone Cutters	Union shop	*Poulson's American Daily Advertiser*, June 9, 1835. Stone cutters wanted those employees who did not join with them for an advance of wages 3 yrs. ago discharged.
1835	Philadelphia	Tin-plate and Sheet Iron Workers	Ten-hour day	*Pennsylvania Annual Report, Part III: Industrial Statistics*, (1880-1881), p. 264.
1835	Philadelphia	Seamen	Higher wages	*Saturday Evening Post*, June 10, 1835. Seamen were demanding $18 a month and small stores.
1835	Philadelphia	Leather Dressers	Ten-hour day	*Pennsylvanian*, June 10, 1835.

Summary of Strikes in Pennsylvania—1800-1840 (Continued)

Year	Place	Trade	Issue	Reference and Comment
1835	Philadelphia	Tailoresses, Seamstresses, Binders, Folders, Stockmakers	Higher wages	*Saturday Evening Post,* Approx. 300 to 500 workers out on strike. Some of the workers received the advance requested; the others remained out on strike.
1835	Philadelphia	Masons	Ten-hour day	*Saturday Evening Post,* June 10, 1835.
1835	Philadelphia	Woodworkers, Painters, Trimmers	Ten-hour day	*Pennsylvanian,* June 13, 1835.

Saturday Evening Post, June 10, 1835—Reported the following trades on strike for hours or wages:

Journeymen Cordwainers	Saddlers
Carters	Plumbers
Seamen	Binders and Folders
Weavers and Manufacturers	Block and Pump Makers
Leather Dressers	Bricklayers
Carpenters	Cabinet Makers
Tobacconists	Bakers
Tailoresses	Wood Sawyers
Seamstresses	Coal Heavers
Stockmakers	

Year	Place	Trade	Issue	Reference and Comment
1835	Philadelphia	Black and White Smiths	Ten-hour day	*Pennsylvanian,* June 12, 1835.
1835	Philadelphia	Glass Cutters	Ten-hour day	*Pennsylvanian,* June 12, 1835. Their demands were complied with.
1835	Philadelphia	Bakers	Elimination of Sunday work	*Pennsylvanian,* June 18, 1835.
1835	Morristown	Cordwainers	Higher wages	*Pennsylvanian,* June 22, 1835. Their request was granted on the same day.
1835	Norristown	Railroad Workers	Ten-hour day	*Pennsylvanian,* June 22, 1835. Approx. 300 to 400 workers involved. The contractors agreed to their demands.
1835	Manayunk	Factory Operatives	Shorter hours	*Germantown Telegraph,* June 24, 1835. Arrangements were made with their proprietors that their day's service shall close at a somewhat earlier hour.

SUMMARY OF STRIKES IN PENNSYLVANIA—1800-1840 (Continued)

Year	Place	Trade	Issue	Reference and Comment
1835	Pottsville	Boatmen	Higher wages	*Berks and Schuylkill Journal,* July 11, 1835. Several hundred boatmen were involved. On July 27, it was reported that a satisfactory adjustment of the difficulties had been reached.
1835	Reading	Carters	Higher wages	*Berks and Schuylkill Journal,* July 25, 1835.
1835	Philadelphia	Saddlers and Harness Makers	Ten-hour day and higher wages	*Pennsylvanian,* July 20, 1835. Approx. 200 journeymen involved.
1835	Philadelphia	Oak Coopers	Prison labor	*Pennsylvanian,* Sept. 10, 1835. Passed resolutions protesting prison labor but whether any further action was taken is not known.
1835	Pittsburgh	Shoemakers	Higher wages	*National Trades' Union,* Sept. 26, 1835.
1835	Philadelphia	Handloom Weavers	Reduction of wages	*National Trades' Union,* Oct. 31, 1835. Several hundred involved in this strike.
1835	Philadelphia	Stone Cutters	Reduction of wages	*Pennsylvanian,* Nov. 11, 1835.
1835	Reading	Tailors	Uniform schedule	*Democratic Press,* Nov. 24, 1835. The master tailors promptly acceded to the demands of the journeymen.
1836	Philadelphia	Marble Cutters	Prison labor	*National Trades' Union,* Jan. 23, 1836. Not a strike but workmen hailed to court for damages.
1836	Reading	Cordwainers	Higher wages	*National Trades' Union,* Jan. 9, 1836. Demands acceded to by all but one of the employing shoemakers of Reading.
1836	Philadelphia	Bookbinders	Reduction of wages	*Pennsylvanian,* Feb. 2, 1836. *National Laborer* reported on April 30, 1836 that the strike of ten weeks was over and the bookbinders had won.
1836	Philadelphia	Hatters	Uniform bill of prices	*Pennsylvanian,* Jan. 26, 1836.

SUMMARY OF STRIKES IN PENNSYLVANIA—1800-1840 (Continued)

Year	Place	Trade	Issue	Reference and Comment
1836	Philadelphia	Brass and Stirrup Finishers	Higher wages	*Pennsylvanian*, March 5, 1836.
1836	Philadelphia	Female Shoebinders and Corders	Higher wages	*National Laborer*, March 26, 1836. Approx. 400 out on strike.
1836	Philadelphia	Cordwainers (Ladies' Branch)	Higher wages	*National Laborer*, March 26, 1836. The strike lasted over 11 weeks. It was asserted that over 400 journeymen cordwainers had left the city on account of the strike.
1836	Manayunk	Canal Workers	Attempted reduction of wages	*National Laborer*, March 26, 1836. The strikers won higher wages and the ten-hour day.
1836	Philadelphia	House Carpenters	Higher wages	*National Trades' Union*, April 9, 1836.
1836	Philadelphia	Blank Workmen	Reduction of wages	*National Laborer*, April 9, 1836. They had struck with the bookbinders and won an advance on their old wages.
1836	Philadelphia	Leather Dressers, No. 2	Higher wages	*Pennsylvanian*, April 11, 1836.
1836	Philadelphia	Brewery Laborers	Higher wages	*Pennsylvanian*, April 15, 1836.
1836	Lancaster	Carpenters	Higher wages	*Lancaster Journal*, April 15, 1836.
1836	Lancaster	Cordwainers	Higher wages	*Lancaster Journal*, April 15, 1836.
1836	Philadelphia	Horn Comb Makers	Higher wages	*National Laborer*, April 23, 1836.
1836	Philadelphia	Schuylkill Laborers	Higher wages	*National Laborer*, May 7, 1836.
1836	Philadelphia	Day Laborers	Ten-hour day and higher wages	*National Laborer*, May 14, 1836.
1836	Philadelphia	Chairmakers	Higher wages	*National Laborer*, May 21, 1836.
1836	Philadelphia	Horseshoers	Higher wages	*National Laborer*, June 4, 1836. They succeeded in winning an advance on their wages.
1836	Philadelphia	Oak Coopers	Higher wages	*National Laborer*, June 4, 1836. Won requested increase.

SUMMARY OF STRIKES IN PENNSYLVANIA—1800-1840 (Continued)

Year	Place	Trade	Issue	Reference and Comment
1836	Philadelphia	Leather Dressers	Ten-hour day	*Pennsylvanian*, June 11, 1836.
1836	Philadelphia	Bricklayers	Higher wages	*National Laborer*, June 25, 1836.
1836	Philadelphia	Paper Makers	Higher wages	*National Laborer*, June 25, 1836.
1836	Philadelphia	Blacksmiths	Higher wages	*National Laborer*, July 2, 1836.
1836	Philadelphia	Ship Carpenters	Ten-hour day	*National Laborer*, July 23, 1836. Ten-hour day was granted.
1836	Fairmount	Handloom Weavers	Reduction of wages	*National Laborer*, Sept. 10, 1836. On Oct 1, the strike was reported settled but 3 hands discharged for the active part which they played in the strike.
1836	Philadelphia	Cotton Spinners	Shorter work day	*National Laborer*, Sept. 24, 1836.
1836	Norristown	Female Operatives	Reduction of wages and the speed-up	*National Laborer*, Sept. 24, 1836.
1836	Philadelphia	Gilders	Higher wages	*National Laborer*, Sept. 19, 1836.
1836	Philadelphia	Biscuit Makers	Introduction of new machinery	*National Laborer*, Oct. 1, 1836.
1836	Pittsburgh	Factory Operatives	Ten-hour day	*Allegheny Democrat and Working Men's Advocate*, Oct. 21, 1836.
1836	Philadelphia	Tailors	Uniform scale of wages	*Pennsylvanian*, Oct. 21, 1836. By Nov. 12, between 80 and 100 employers had agreed to the journeymen's requests.
1836	Philadelphia	Marble Workers	Reduction of wages	*National Laborer*, Nov. 12, 1836.
1836	Delaware Co., Penna.	Handloom Weavers	Reduction of wages	*National Laborer*, Nov. 12, 1836. The fact that the workers resisted successfully the attempted reduction was attributed to the resolute stand taken by the female workers.

SUMMARY OF STRIKES IN PENNSYLVANIA—1800-1840 (Continued)

Year	Place	Trade	Issue	Reference and Comment
1836	Philadelphia	Ingrain Carpet Weavers	Reduction of wages	*National Laborer*, Dec. 3, 1836.
1836	Philadelphia	Saddle and Harness Makers	Reduction of wages	*National Laborer*, Dec. 3, 1836.
1836	Harrisburg	Printers	Higher wages	The *Keystone*, Dec. 31, 1836.
1837	Pittsburg	Glass Cutters	Reduction of wages	*National Laborer*, Feb. 4, 1837.
1837	Pittsburg	Carpenters	Ten-hour system	*National Laborer*, Feb. 18, 1837.
1837	Brandywine	Cotton Spinners	Reduction of wages	*National Laborer*, March 11, 1837.
1837	Philadelphia	House Painters and Glaziers	Reduction of wages	*Pennsylvanian*, May 10, 1837. On May 17, it was reported that the journeymen had resolved to discontinue the strike and work for $1.50 per day because of the manner in which every kind of business is depreciating.
1837	Harrisburg	Canal Workers	Higher wages and more grog	*Harrisburgh Chronicle*, Aug. 23, 1837. Most of the hands returned to work at the old prices.
1839	Harrisburg	Printers	Higher wages	*Public Ledger*, Feb. 16, 1839.
1839	Philadelphia	Carpenters	Higher wages	*Public Ledger*, March 22, 1839.
1839	Hamburg	Railroad Workers	Higher wages	*Public Ledger*, June 12, 1839. Approx. 300 workers involved.
1839	Philadelphia	Handloom Weavers	Reduction of wages	*Public Ledger*, Aug. 30, 1839.
1840	Kensington	Factory Operatives		*Public Ledger*, March 4, 1840. Serious rioting — f e m a l e workers most active participants.

APPENDIX C

	1828 Jackson-Adams		1832 Jackson-Wirt		1836 Van-Buren-Harrison		1840 Van-Buren-Harrison	
Adams	1,242	1,461	1,071	1,362	1,186	1,520	1,628	2,453
Allegheny	3,866	1,666	3,321	2,985	3,074	3,623	4,573	7,620
Armstrong	1,133	169	1,437	429	1,528	1,014	1,744	1,260
Beaver	1,253	1,282	1,360	1,388	1,075	2,077	1,710	3,143
Bedford	2,260	780	1,970	647	1,587	1,920	2,446	2,910
Berks	4,583	894	4,472	1,150	4,967	1,584	7,425	3,582
Bradford	1,553	910	1,598	1,221	1,463	1,521	2,844	2,631
Bucks	3,297	3,425	2,681	3,011	3,081	3,289	4,488	4,705
Butler	1,068	610	1,076	641	1,008	1,166	1,805	2,100
Cambria	314	94	444	94	450	554	920	811
Centre	1,998	453	1,961	725	1,809	924	2,242	1,477
Chester	3,835	3,535	2,732	4,286	3,277	3,921	4,882	5,643
Clearfield	393	211	520	207	499	284	812	499
Columbia	1,869	562	1,658	404	1,560	544	2,829	1,325
Crawford	1,117	958	1,470	1,130	1,614	1,232	2,908	2,469
Cumberland	2,113	898	2,150	1,337	1,904	1,696	2,695	2,790
Dauphin	1,974	1,140	1,395	1,348	1,372	1,993	2,187	3,124
Delaware	953	1,164	955	1,423	1,030	1,224	1,335	2,031
Erie	773	945	1,049	1,494	1,312	2,134	2,061	3,636
Fayette	2,945	1,230	2,647	1,176	2,016	1,669	3,035	2,755
Franklin	2,386	1,915	1,979	2,176	2,155	2,575	2,892	3,586
Greene	1,498	452	1,443	338	1,138	915	2,010	1,350
Huntingdon	1,708	1,144	1,510	1,441	1,340	2,628	2,266	3,020
Indiana	926	245	654	583	692	1,169	1,209	1,953
Jefferson			175	105	244	229	592	476
Juniata			579	268	627	596	1,043	966
Lancaster	5,186	3,719	4,061	5,140	4,144	6,250	5,472	9,678
Lebanon	1,439	597	1,094	882	1,168	1,487	1,402	2,369
Lehigh	2,000	516	1,544	933	1,987	1,784	2,451	2,405
Luzerne	1,645	1,435	1,745	1,325	1,705	938	4,119	2,774
Lycoming	1,534	467	1,540	669	2,008	1,415	2,181	1,504
Mercer	1,603	738	1,366	1,214	1,253	1,991	2,336	3,249
Mifflin	1,650	506	784	454	917	748	1,269	1,226
Montgomery	3,341	2,311	3,315	2,507	3,446	2,409	4,869	4,068
Northampton	3,628	889	2,786	1,092	2,378	1,426	3,838	2,846
Northumberland ..	1,669	395	1,464	411	1,421	712	2,187	1,351
Perry	1,060	241	1,021	346	1,107	473	1,970	1,072
Philadelphia City ..			3,269	5,476	3,028	5,746	4,774	7,655
Philadelphia County			6,760	6,433	7,965	6,475	13,303	10,189
Pike	549	74	506	43	358	50	524	135

	1828 Jackson-Adams		1832 Jackson-Wirt		1836 Van-Buren-Harrison		1840 Van-Buren-Harrison	
Potter & McKean .	175	108	253	131	312	135	363	180
Schuylkill	863	220	1,270	482	1,380	687	2,184	1,881
Somerset	1,347	238	778	814	511	1,905	765	2,501
Susquehanna	1,062	694	1,082	868	1,145	856	2,023	1,560
Tioga	850	193	1,035	197	1,027	400	1,721	895
Union	1,697	210	1,057	864	1,143	1,328	1,518	2,423
Venango	769	126	1,117	294	967	600	1,275	855
Warren	340	243	490	194	498	254	929	827
Washington	3,883	1,687	3,125	1,888	2,445	2,805	3,611	4,147
Wayne	531	320	633	367	724	340	1,188	675
Westmoreland	3,917	629	3,419	861	2,878	1,725	4,704	2,778
York	3,645	1,864	3,152	1,452	2,156	2,005	4,382	3,792
Monroe					796	166	1,447	345
Clinton							649	637
Clarion							1,366	648
McKean							275	262
	101,652	50,848	90,983	66,716	91,475	87,111	143,675	144,018
	(89,440	44,563	90,973	66,706	90,875		143,676	143,242)

	1829 Wolf-Ritner		1832 Wolf-Ritner		1835 Wolf-Ritner-Muhlenberg			1838 Porter-Ritner	
Adams	836	106	1,030	1,679	406	1,517	911	1,535	3,310
Allegheny	2,077	1,872	3,094	3,506	2,854	3,848	378	4,505	6,038
Armstrong	1,194	712	1,975	959	1,874	1,099	188	2,781	1,510
Beaver	1,280	819	1,440	1,481	1,066	1,669	354	1,931	2,457
Bedford	1,079	1,113	1,629	1,561	1,581	2,067	46	2,384	2,290
Berks	3,990	2,689	3,758	3,435	1,733	3,022	4,194	7,101	3,215
Bradford	1,219	333	1,685	920	1,504	1,239	406	2,420	2,219
Bucks	4,242	841	3,202	2,862	2,534	3,584	829	4,553	4,147
Butler	870	533	1,204	1,032	1,063	1,315	237	1,653	1,700
Cambria	210	434	598	340	610	694	38	844	762
Centre	1,305	944	1,920	1,016	1,742	1,070	446	2,589	1,467
Chester	2,630	2,703	2,374	4,301	1,792	4,052	1,577	4,527	4,971
Clearfield	256	199	513	288	337	323	290	792	474
Columbia	1,374	355	1,768	829	869	767	1,247	2,616	1,088
Crawford	840	939	1,502	895	878	999	814	2,304	1,957
Cumberland	1,592	799	2,326	1,807	1,492	1,748	1,137	2,743	2,316
Dauphin	1,179	1,587	1,575	2,285	780	2,320	717	1,944	2,843
Delaware	744	267	918	1,291	698	1,240	406	1,263	1,731
Erie	497	1,545	1,170	1,792	164	1,943	1,280	1,565	2,747
Fayette	2,177	1,056	2,440	1,806	1,132	1,708	1,378	2,788	1,984

	1829 Wolf-Ritner		1832 Wolf-Ritner		1835 Wolf-Ritner-Muhlenberg			1838 Porter-Ritner	
Franklin	2,016	2,016	2,234	2,516	1,423	2,207	1,336	2,815	2,560
Greene	980	941	1,009	1,355	365	1,076	997	1,849	1,109
Huntingdon	1,011	1,616	1,657	2,189	1,324	2,555	423	2,761	3,687
Indiana	456	1,044	813	1,106	991	1,524	14	1,262	1,723
Jefferson			249	173	369	246	3	591	421
Juniata			687	692	588	763	211	1,049	863
Lancaster	3,976	5,542	4,124	6,387	4,283	7,018	471	5,503	8,558
Lebanon	850	1,363	1,002	1,906	621	1,968	435	1,553	2,228
Lehigh	1,650	1,455	1,564	1,624	841	1,914	1,204	2,460	2,349
Luzerne	1,994	124	2,064	1,586	618	1,488	1,886	3,132	2,592
Lycoming	903	982	1,729	986	1,159	1,277	935	2,406	1,555
Mercer	599	1,303	1,347	1,553	522	1,686	935	2,326	2,935
Mifflin	1,283	1,041	782	834	909	866	109	1,177	1,109
Montgomery	2,067	1,314	2,972	2,933	1,755	3,003	1,600	4,558	3,748
Northampton	4,060	458	3,376	1,820	3,135	2,560	458	3,634	2,566
Northumberland ..	1,253	879	1,415	1,084	753	883	1,253	2,144	1,164
Perry	1,180	540	1,284	697	706	762	797	1,916	883
Philadelphia City ..	4,350	323	3,558	4,957	1,801	5,043	1,351	3,155	7,203
Philadelphia County	7,043	223	6,263	5,950	6,033	5,591	2,754	7,982	6,187
Pike	653	9	613	71	620	65	88	526	135
Potter & McKean .	241	37	368	37	408	128	56	276	68
Schuylkill	902	347	1,328	754	406	833	1,172	2,271	1,508
Somerset	584	1,520	744	1,855	542	2,031	89	883	2,244
Susquehanna	981	300	1,140	475	873	594	789	1,530	1,264
Tioga	656	174	710	446	868	468	176	1,448	594
Union	764	2,068	1,021	2,131	578	2,185	653	1,595	2,268
Venango	541	752	1,261	406	847	613	467	1,765	828
Warren	436	132	450	218	426	250	225	700	542
Washington	2,207	2,388	2,749	2,889	2,466	3,179	379	3,461	3,528
Wayne	552	47	606	241	744	226	85	1,062	538
Westmoreland	2,585	1,322	3,542	1,549	2,652	2,192	757	4,515	2,315
York	1,855	760	2,357	2,367	1,070	2,665	1,658	4,196	3,257
Monroe								1,223	366
Clinton									
Clarion									
McKean								219	127
	79,219	51,776	91,235	88,186	65,855	94,083	40,637	127,821	122,325
	(78,219	50,866	91,139	87,872	65,805		40,639	130,781	122,248)

See page 201, note 200, for sources. Most of these totals are incorrect, but as in original. The actual totals of the figures are shown in parentheses.

BIBLIOGRAPHY

The following symbols have been used to indicate the location of manuscript collections, newspaper files, etc.:

HSP: Historical Society of Pennsylvania, Phila.

HSWP: Historical Society of Western Pennsylvania, Pittsburgh.

PSL: State Library of Pennsylvania, Harrisburg.

RBL: Library Company of Philadelphia, Ridgway Branch, Phila.

LC: Library of Congress, Washington, D. C.

NA: National Archives, Washington, D. C.

PRD: Public Records Division of the Pennsylvania Historical and Museum Commission.

1. MANUSCRIPT MATERIALS.

*Bakewell—Page Collection—*HSWP.

Canal Papers, Uncatalogued—PRD.

*Captains Letter Book—*NA.

*Denny—O'Hara Papers—*HSWP.

*Frazer Collection—*Uncatalogued—PRD.

*Haldeman Papers—*Uncatalogued—PRD.

*Letters from the Commandant of Philadelphia Navy Yard—*NA.

*Letters from Navy Agents Philadelphia—*NA.

*Miscellaneous Letters—*HSP.

Morris, James B., *Diary of Daily Notes of the Weather together with the events of the Neighbourhood, etc.,* Morgantown, 1837-1842, 3 vols. in the manuscript collections of the Berks County Historical Society.

*Union Canal Company Papers—*Uncatalogued—Berks County Historical Society.

*Van Buren Papers—*LC.

2. MANUSCRIPT ACCOUNT BOOKS EXAMINED.

*Agreement made and agreed upon this 16th day of March 1822 between Nathan Edwards of the one part and Joseph Jones of the other—*Berks County Historical Society.

*. . . ace Furnace Day Book and Journal—*Berks County Historical Society.

*. . . 'borough Forge Day Book—*Berks County Historical Society.

*B . . . ter Brandywine Iron Works—*Offices of the Lukens Steel Co., Coatesville, Pa.

*Blotter and Pay Roll Triadelphia Iron Works—*Offices of the Lukens Steel Co., Coatesville, Pa.

*Bond and Yardley, Contractors Account Book—*Bucks County Historical Society.

*Book Containing Statement of the Supervisor of Roads—*PRD.

*Brandywine Iron Works Ledger—*Offices of the Lukens Steel Co., Coatesville, Pa.

*Thomas Bull Esquires Book—*Berks County Historical Society.

*Simon Cameron Day Book—*Dauphin County Historical Society.

*Charming Forge Day Book—*Berks County Historical Society.

Charming Forge Time Book—Berks County Historical Society.

Calvin Coopers Mill Book—HSP.

Isaac Craig Account Book—Carnegie Library, Pittsburgh.

Dowell Forge Day Book—Chester County Historical Society.

Dowling Forge Day Book—Chester County Historical Society.

Eastern District Penitentiary Commissioners for the Erection of the State Penitentiary —PRD.

Federal Slitting Mill Day Book—Offices of the Lukens Steel Co., Coatesville, Pa.

Federal Slitting Mill Journal—Offices of the Lukens Steel Co., Coatesville, Pa.

John Gillingham, Weaver Account Book—Bucks County Historical Society.

W. H. Glenn—Nailer's Account Book—Chester County Hist. Soc.

Hampton Furnace Day Book—Schwenkfelder Historical Library, Pennsburg, Pa.

Hampton Furnace Ledger—Schwenkfelder Historical Library, Pennsburg, Pa.

Hopewell Furnace Journal—Berks County Historical Society.

Hopewell Furnace Time Book—Berks County Historical Society.

Joanna Furnace Journal—Berks County Historical Society.

Juniata Forge and Mary Ann Furnace—Notebook—Detailed Description of Forge and Furnace, its Buildings and Equipment and subsequent Operation, including Output and Wages. 1 vol.—PRD.

Joseph Kent Carding Account Book—Chester County Historical Society.

John and Moses Lancaster Carpenters' Account Book—HSP.

Moses Lancaster Receipt Book—HSP.

Lehigh Coal and Navigation Co. Journal No. I—Offices of the Lehigh Coal and Navigation Co., Phila.

Mary Ann Forge Day Book—Chester County Historical Society.

Mount Hope Furnace Journal—Grubb Collection—HSP.

Settlement Book—Grubb Collection—HSP.

Spring Forge Day Book and Journal—HSP.

Strawn and Myers—Masons Account Book—Bucks County Historical Society.

William Whitaker's Mill Books—Offices of the Whitaker Co., Phila.

3. NEWSPAPERS.

Allegheny Democrat & Working Men's Advocate—Scattered issues Lehigh University Library and Darling Library, University of Pittsburgh.

The *American Sentinel*—RBL.

The *American Volunteer*—PSL.

The *Aurora and General Advertiser*—RBL.

The *Aurora and Pennsylvania Gazette*—RBL and New York Public Library.

Baltimore American and Commercial Advertiser—LC.

The *Bedford Gazette*—PSL.

The *Berks and Schuylkill Journal*—Berks Co. Hist. Society.

The *Bucks County Intelligencer*—Bucks Co. Hist. Society.

The *Clearfield Democrat*—PSL.

Columbia Spy—Lancaster Historical Society.

The *Crawford Messenger*—PSL.

The *Daily Chronicle*—HSP.

The *Democrat and Farmer's Gazette*—PSL.

The *Democratic Press*—RBL.

Doylestown County Patriot—Bucks County Historical Society.

Free Trade Advocate and Journal of Political Economy—RBL.

The *Germantown Telegraph*—HSP.

The *Harrisburgh Chronicle*—PSL.

The *Register of Pennsylvania* (Samuel Hazard, ed.) 16 vols. Columbia University Library.

The *United States Commercial and Statistical Register* (Samuel Hazard, ed.) 6 vols. New York Public Library.

The *Huntingdon Journal*—PSL.

The *Juniata Telegraph*—PSL.

The *Keystone*—PSL.

The *Lycoming Gazette*—PSL.

The *Man*—New York Historical Society.

The *Mechanic's Free Press*—HSP.

Mifflin Eagle and Lewistown Intelligencer—PSL.

The *Miner's Journal*—RBL and Lehigh University Library.

The *National Gazette and Literary Register*—New York Public Library.

The *National Laborer*—LC.

The *National Trades' Union*—Microfilm copy of transcripts from the Wisconsin Historical Society in the possession of Columbia University Library.

The *New York Evening Post*—New York Public Library.

Niles' Weekly Register—75 vols. Baltimore. Columbia Univ. Library.

The *Norristown Herald*—HSP.

The *Oracle of Dauphin*—PSL.

The *Pennsylvanian*—HSP and RBL.

The *Pennsylvania Inquirer*—PSL.

The *Pennsylvania Intelligencer*—PSL.

The *Pennsylvania Reporter*—PSL.

The *Philadelphia Mercury*—HSP.

The *Pittsburgh Commonwealth*—Carnegie Library, Pittsburgh.

The *Pittsburgh Gazette*—HSWP.

The *Pittsburgh Mercury*—HSWP.

Poulson's American Daily Advertiser—HSP and RBL.

The *Public Ledger*—New York Public Library.

Republican Standard and Downington Journal—Chester County Historical Society.

The *Saturday Courier*—HSP.

The *Saturday Evening Post*—Library Company of Philadelphia.

The *Statesman*—Darlington Library, University of Pittsburgh.

The *Tree of Liberty*—Carnegie Library, Pittsburgh.

The *Union Times and Republican Herald*—Lehigh University Library.

The *United States Gazette*—HSP and Library Company of Phila.

The *Western Press*—On loan to the Public Records Division of the Pennsylvania Hist. and Museum Comm.

The *Working Man's Advocate*—New York Historical Society.

The *Lancaster Intelligencer*—In the Office of the Publisher, Lancaster, Penna.

The *Lancaster Journal*—In the Office of the Publisher, Lancaster, Penna.

4. PUBLIC DOCUMENTS.

State of Pennsylvania.

Pennsylvania Archives, 4th Series— vols. IV and V "Papers of the Governors."

Journal of the House of Representatives, 1800 to 1840.

Journal of the Senate, 1800 to 1840.

Pennsylvania: Annual Report of the Secretary of Internal Affairs, vol. IX, 1880-1881 and vol. XIX, 1892.

Purdon, John W., *A Digest of the Laws of Pennsylvania 1800 to 1837* (Philadelphia, 1837).

Labor Laws of Pennsylvania (Harrisburg, 1941), compiled and edited by Jasper Yeates Brinton.

Report to the Legislature of Pennsylvania containing a Description of the Swatara Mining District (Harrisburg, 1839).

United States Government.

A Series of Tables of the Several Branches of American Manufacturers, 1810 (n.p.n.d.)

Coxe, Tench, *A Statement of the Arts and Manufactures of the United States of America for the year 1810* (Philadelphia, 1814).

Fourth Census of the United States (Philadelphia, 1822).

Digest of the Manufacturing Establishments in the United States and Their Manufactures (Washington, 1823).

Fifth Census of the United States (Washington, 1841).

American State Papers; Finance, II, 11th Congress, 2d Session *Albert Gallatin's Report on the Subject of Manufactures.*

Sixth Census of the United States (Washington, 1841).

Documents Relative to the Manufactures in the United States Collected and transmitted to the House of Representatives in Compliance with a resolution of Jan. 19, 1832 (Washington, 1833), 2 vols.

United States, Exec. Doc. 1, part 5, 50th Congress, 1st Session, 1887, pp. 1027-1108. "Strikes and Lock-outs in the United States prior to 1881."

U. S. House Exec. Doc. No. 308, 22d Congress, 1st Session. "Documents Relative to the Manufactures in the U. S. collected and transmitted to the House of Representatives." 2 vols.

U. S. House Exec. Doc. No. 21, 25th Congress, 3rd Session. "Report on Steam Engines in the United States."

U. S. House Exec. Doc. No. 10, 34th Congress, 1st Session, Vol. 4. "Report of the Secretary of Treasury on capital invested in Manufactures."

U. S. House Doc. Misc. 42, part 2, 47th Congress, 2d Session. Carroll D. Wright, "Report on the Factory System of the United States."

U. S. Senate Doc. 45, 18th Congress, 1st Session, vol. II. "Report of the Secretary of the State with a schedule of Factories incorporated by States laws from 1800 to 1820 inc."

U. S. Senate Doc. No. 645, 61st Congress, 2d Session. "Report on the condition of Women and Child Wage Earners in the United States." vol. IX. Helen Sumner, "History of Women in Industry in the United States."

U. S. Senate Doc. No. 645, 61st Congress, 2d Session. "Report on the Condition of Women and Child Wage-Earners in the United States." vol. X. Andrews and Bliss, "History of Women in Trade Unions."

Bulletin of the United States Bureau of Labor Statistics, No. 604. "History of Wages in the United States from Colonial Times to 1928."

5. TRAVELLERS' ACCOUNTS

Ashe, Thomas, *Travels in America performed in 1806 for the purpose of exploring the rivers Allegheny, Monongahela, Ohio and Mississippi, and ascertaining the produce and condition of their banks and vicinity* (London, 1808).

Bernard, John, *Retrospections of America, 1797-1811* (New York, 1817).

Birbeck, Morris, *Notes on a Journey in America* (Phila., 1817).

Bradbury, John, *Travels in the Interior of America, 1809, 1810, 1811* (London, 1819).

Bristed, John, *The Resources of the United States of America, or, A view of the Agricultural, Commercial, Manufacturing, Financial, Political, Literary, Moral, and Religious Capacity and Character of the American People* (London, 1818).

Brothers, Thomas, *The United States of North America as They Are, Not as They are Generally Described Being: A Cure for Radicalism* (London, 1840).

Cobbett, William, *A Year's Residence in America* (London, 1818-1819).

Cuming, Fortescue, *Sketches of a Tour of the Western Country, Through the States of Ohio & Kentucky* (Pittsburgh, 1810). Reprinted in Reuben G. Thwaites, *Early Western Travels, 1748-1846.* vol. IV.

Fearon, H. B., *Sketches of America: A Narrative of a Journey of Five Thousand Miles Through the Eastern and Western States of America* (London, 1818).

Flint, James, *Letters from America* (Edinburgh, 1822). Reprinted in Reuben Gold Thwaites, *Early Western Travels.* vol. IX.

Gilpin, Joshua, *Journal of a Tour from Philadelphia through the Western Counties to Pittsburgh.* Handwritten copy of the original in the possession of the Public Records Division of the Pennsylvania Historical and Museum Commission.

Grund, Francis, *Aristocracy in America,* (London, 1839), 2 vols.

Hamilton, Thomas, *Men and Manners in America* (London, 1833). 2 vols.

Holmes, Isaac, *An Account of the United States of America, derived from Actual Observation, during a Residence of Four Years in that Republic* (London, 1823).

Johnson, C. B., *Letters from a British Settlement in Pennsylvania.* (Philadelphia, 1819).

Martineau, Harriet, *Society in America,* (New York, 1837), 2 vols.

Melish, John, *Travels in the United States of America in the years 1806 and 1807 and 1809, 1810, and 1811.* (Philadelphia, 1812) 2 vols.

Murray, Charles A., *Travels in North America during the years 1834, 1835 and 1836.* (New York, 1839) 2 vols.

Neilson, Peter, *A Six Year's Residence* (Glasgow, 1830).

Pearson, John, *Notes made during a Journey in 1821, in the United States, from Philadelphia to the Neighborhood of Lake Erie; through Lancaster, Harrisburgh, Carlisle, and Pittsburgh and back to Philadelphia* (London, 1822).

Royall, Anne, *Mrs. Royall's Pennsylvania Travels or Travels Continued in the United States* (Wash., 1829) 2 vols.

6. PRINTED CONTEMPORARY SOURCES.

Carey, Mathew, *A Plea for the Poor* (Philadelphia, 1829).

Carey, Mathew, *Essay on the Public Charities of Philadelphia* (Philadelphia, 1830).

Carey, Mathew, *Brief View of the System of Internal Improvements of the State of Pennsylvania* (Philadelphia, 1831).

Commons, John R. et al., *Documentary History of American Industrial Society* (Cleveland, 1911) 11 vols.

Cramer, Zadok, *The Navigator: containing directions for Navigating the Monongahela, Allegheny, Ohio, and Mississippi Rivers* (Pittsburgh, 1802-1818).

Cramer's Pittsburgh Magazine Almanack (Pittsburgh, 1808-1826) Zadok Cramer, ed.

Desilvers Philadelphia Directory and Strangers Guilde (Philadelphia, 1828-1836).

Harris, Isaac, *Pittsburgh Business Directory*, (Pittsburgh 1837-1840).

Jackson, Andrew, *Correspondence* (Washington, 1926-1933) J. S. Bassett, ed.

Narratives of Early Pennsylvania, West New Jersey and Delaware 1630-1707 (New York, 1912) Printed in *Original Narratives of Early American History* (J. Franklin Jameson, ed. 19 vols.

Jones, Samuel, *Pittsburgh in the Year Eighteen Hundred and Twenty-Six* (Pittsburgh, 1826).

Lyford, W. G., *Western Address Directory* (Baltimore, 1837).

Mease, James, *Picture of Philadelphia: An Account of its Origin, Increase and Improvement in Arts, Sciences, Manufactures, Commerce and Revenue* (Philadelphia, 1811).

Memoirs and Biography of Wealthy Citizens of Philadelphia, By a Citizen of Philadelphia (Philadelphia, 1845).

Proceedings of the Government and Citizens of Philadelphia on the Reduction of the Hours of Labor and Increase of Wages (Boston, 1835).

Richardson, J. D., *Compilation of the Messages and Papers of the Presidents, 1789-1908* (New York, 1909) 11 vols.

Riddle, James, *The Pittsburgh Directory for 1815* (Pittsburgh, 1815).

Riddle, James, *The Pittsburgh Directory for 1819* (Pittsburgh, 1819).

Stewart, Ethelbert, *A Documentary History of the Early Organizations of Printers* (Indianapolis, 1907).

The Trial of the Boot and Shoemakers of Philadelphia on an Indictment for a Combination to Raise their wages, (Phila., 1806). Taken in shorthand by Thomas Lloyd.

Thorpe, Francis N. (comp.), *The Federal and State Constitutions, Colonial Charters, and Other Organic Laws of the States, Territories, and Colonies Now or heretofore forming the United States of America* (Washington, 1909) 7 vols.

Thwaites, Reuben G., *Early Western Travels 1748-1846* (Cleveland, 1904-1907). 32 vols.

Van Buren, Martin, *Autobiography* (Printed in the Annual Report of the American Historical Association, 1918, II.) (J. C. Fitzpatrick, ed.)

Williams, Edwin, *The Politicians Manual* (New York, 1834).

7. GENERAL WORKS AND SECONDARY SOURCES.

Abbott, Edith, "Employment of Women in Cotton Mills," *Journal of Political Economy*, 16, (November 1908), pp. 602-662.

Abbott, Edith, "The History of the Industrial Employment of Women in the United States; An Introductory Study," *Journal of Political Economy*, 14, (October 1906), pp. 461-501.

Ames, H. V., and Shimmel, L. S., "Report on the Public Archives of Pennsylvania," *Annual Report of the American Historical Association, 1900*, vol. 2, pp. 267-293.

The Annual Register—8 vols.

Baldwin, Leland D., "Shipbuilding on the Western Waters 1793-1817," *Mississippi Valley Historical Review*, 20, 1933, 29-44.

Barnard, J. Lynn, *Factory Legislation in Pennsylvania: Its History and Administration* (Philadelphia, 1907).

Barnett, George E., "The Printers," *American Economic Association Publications*, 10, (1909).

Bartlett, Marguerite, *Chief Phases of Pennsylvania Politics in the Jacksonian Era* (Philadelphia, 1919).

Bassett, John S., *The Life of Andrew Jackson* (New York, 1931).

Bathe, Dorothy and Greville, *Oliver Evans: A Chronicle of Early American Engineerng* (Philadelphia, 1935).

Beard, Charles A., *Economic Origins of Jeffersonian Democracy* (New York, 1943)

Berger, Max, *The British Traveller in America, 1836-1860*, (New York, 1943).

Bezanson, Anne, Robert D. Gray and Miriam Hussey, *Wholesale Prices in Philadelphia, 1784-1861* (Philadelphia, 1936).

Bining, Arthur C., *Pennsylvania Iron Manufacture in the Eighteenth Century* (Harrisburg, 1938).

Bining, William J., *The Glass Industry of Western Pennsylvania* (Unpublished Master's thesis, University of Pittsburgh, 1936).

Bishop, J. Leander, A *History of American Manufactures from 1608 to 1860* (Philadelphia, 1861), 3 vols.

Bower, Robert T., "Note on 'Did Labor Support Jackson?: The Boston Story'" *Political Science Quarterly*, LXV (Sept. 1950), 441-444.

Byrdsall, Fitzwilliam, *History of the Loco-Foco or Equal Rights Party . . . with Short Characteristic Sketches of its Prominent Men* (New York, 1842).

Buck, Solon J., *The Planting of Civilization in Western Pennsylvania* (Pittsburgh, 1939).

Carlton, Frank T., *Economic Influences Upon Education Progress in the United States, 1820-1851* (University of Wisconsin Bulletin, No. 221, Madison, 1908).

Carlton, Frank T., *History and Problems of Organized Labor* (Chicago, 1911).

Catterall, R. C., *The Second Bank of the United States* (Chicago, 1903).

Chandler, Charles L., *Early Ship-building in Pennsylvania 1683-1812* (Philadelphia, 1932).

Cheyney, Edward P., "Decision of Courts in Conspiracy and Boycott Cases," *Political Science Quarterly* IV, (June 1889), 261-278.

Clark, Victor S., *History of Manufactures in the United States* (New York, 1929), 3 vols.

Cole, A. H., and W. B. Smith, *Fluctuations in American Business 1790-1860* (Harvard University press, 1935).

Commons, John R. et al., *History of Labour in the United States* (New York, 1918), 2 vols.

Commons, John R., "American Shoemakers, 1648-1895," reprinted in Commons, John R., *Labor and Administration* (New York, 1913).

Commons, John R., "Labor Organizations and Labor Politics, 1827-1837," *Quarterly Journal of Economics,* 21, (Feb. 1907), 323-329.

deVyver, Frank T., *The Organization of Labor in New Jersey before 1860* (Unpublished doctoral dissertation, Princeton University, 1934), 2 vols.

Dorfman, Joseph, *Economic Mind in Modern America* (New York, 1946).

Dorfman, Joseph, "The Jackson Wage Earner Thesis," *American Historical Review,* LIV, (January 1949), p. 296.

Eavenson, Howard N., *The First Century and A Quarter of American Coal Industry* (Pittsburgh, 1942).

Eiselen, Malcolm R., *The Rise of Pennsylvania Protectionism* (Philadelphia, 1932).

Elder, Margaret, "Pittsburgh Industries that used to be," *Western Pennsylvania Historical Magazine,* 12, 1929, 211-225.

Ely, Richard T., *The Labor Movement in America* (New York and London, 1905).

Farnam, Henry W., *Chapters in the History of Social Legislation in the United States to 1860* (Carnegie Institute, Washington, 1938).

Ferguson, Russell J., *Early Western Pennsylvania Politics* (Pittsburgh, 1938).

Fine, Nathan, *Farmer and Labor Parties in the United States, 1828-1928* (New York, 1928).

Fox, Dixon R., *Decline of Aristocracy in the Politics of New York* (New York, 1918).

Freedley, Edwin T., *Philadelphia and its Manufactures* (Philadelphia, 1860).

French, B. F., *History of the Rise and Progress of the Iron Trade in the United States from 1621 to 1857* (New York, 1858).

Geary, M. Theophane, A *History of Third Parties in Pennsylvania 1840-1860* (Washington, D. C., 1938).

Geiser, Karl F., *Redemptioners and Indentured Servants in the Colony and Commonwealth of Pennsylvania* (New Haven, 1901).

Gemmell, Alfred, *The Charcoal Iron Industry in the Perkiomen Valley* (Allentown, 1949).

Groat, G. G., *Attitude of American Courts in Labor Cases* (New York, 1911).

Hailperin, Herman, "Pro-Jackson Sentiment in Pennsylvania, 1820-1828," *Pennsylvania Magazine of History and Biography,* 50, (July 1926), 193-240.

Hartz, Louis, *Economic Policy and Democratic Thought in Pennsylvania 1776-1860,* (Cambridge, Mass., 1948).

Hasse, Adelaide, *Index to Economic Materials in Documents of the States—Pennsylvania, 1790-1875,* (Wash., 1919).

Hazard, Blanche C., *The Organization of the Boot and Shoe Industry in Massachusetts Before 1875* (Harvard Univ. Press, 1921).

Heffner, William C., *History of Poor Relief Legislation in Pennsylvania 1682-1913* (Cleona, Pa., 1913).

Hingston, William R., *The Philadelphia Working Men's Party 1828-1831* (Unpublished Master's thesis, Univ. of Pennsylvania, 1949).

Hofstadter, Richard, *American Political Tradition and the Men Who Made it* (New York, 1949).

Hughes, George W., "The Pioneer Iron Industry in Western Pennsylvania," *Western Pennsylvania Historical Magazine,* 13-14 (1930-1931), 207-224.

Hugins, Walter, "Ely Moore: The Case History of a Jacksonian Labor Leader," *Political Science Quarterly*, LXV (March 1950), pp. 105-125.

Hunter, Louis C., "Financial Problems of Early Pittsburgh Iron Manufactures," *Journal of Economic and Business History*, 2, (May 1930), 520-544.

Hunter, Louis C., "Influence of the Market Upon Technique in the Iron Industry in Western Pennsylvania up to 1860," *Journal of Economic and Business History*, 2 (February 1929), 241-281.

Hunt's Merchant's Magazine and Commercial Review 1839-1870 (New York) 63 vols.

Jackson, Sidney L., "Labor Education and Politics," *Pennsylvania Magazine of History and Biography*, 66 (July 1942), 279-293.

Klein, Philip S., *Pennsylvania Politics, 1817-1832: A Game Without Rules* (Philadelphia, 1940).

Kuritz, Hyman, "Criminal Conspiracy Cases in Post-Bellum Pennsylvania," *Pennsylvania History Magazine*, XIII (October, 1950), 292-301.

Lazarfeld, Paul F., "Votes in the Making," *Scientific American*, 183 (Nov. 1950), 11-13.

Livingood, James W., *The Philadelphia-Baltimore Trade Rivalry 1780-1860* (Harrisburg, 1947).

Luetscher, G. D., "Industries of Pennsylvania after the Adoption of the Federal Constitution, with Special Reference to Lancaster and York Counties," *German American Annals*, 1 (1903) 135-155 and 197-208.

McCadden, Joseph J., *Education in Pennsylvania, 1801-1833 and Its Debt to Robert Vaux* (Philadelphia, 1937).

McGrane, Reginald, *The Panic of 1837*, (Chicago, 1934).

McMaster, John B., A *History of the People of the United States from the Revolution to the Civil War* (New York, 1884-1913), 8 vols.

McNeill, George B., *The Labor Movement: The Problem of Today* (New York, 1887).

Mesick, Jane L., *English Traveller in America*, 1785-1835 (New York, 1922).

Miller, Frederic K., *The Rise of an Iron Community, An Economic History of Lebanon County from 1740 to 1865* (Lebanon, Pa., 1950-1952).

Montgomery, James, *Practical Detail of the Cotton Manufactures of the United States of America and the State of the Cotton Manufactures of that Country contrasted with that of Great Britain* (Glasgow, 1840).

Morris, Richard B., "Andrew Jackson was no F. D. R.," *Labor and the Nation*, (May-June, 1949), 38-41.

Morris, Richard B., "Andrew Jackson as Strikebreaker," *The American Historical Review*, LV (October 1949) pp. 54-68.

Morris, Richard B., *Government and Labor in Early America* (New York, 1946).

Morton, Eleanor, *Josiah White—Prince of Pioneers* (New York, 1946).

Mueller, Henry R., *The Whig Party in Pennsylvania* (New York, 1922).

Nelles, Walter, "The First American Labor Case," *Yale Law Journal*, 41, (December 1931), 165-200.

Nelles, Walter, "Commonwealth v. Hunt," *Columbia Law Review*, (Nov. 1932), 1128-1169.

Pearse, J. B., *Concise History of the Iron Trade of the American Colonies up to the Revolution and of Pennsylvania until the Present Time* (Philadelphia, 1876).

Pessen, Edward, "Did Labor Support Jackson?: The Boston Story," *Political Science Quarterly*, LXIV, (June 1949) 262-274.

Rezneck, Samuel, "The Social History of An American Depression," *American Historical Review*, XL (July 1935), 662-687.

Rezneck, Samuel, "The Depression of 1819-1822: A Social History," *American Historical Review*, XXXIX, (October 1933), 28-47.

Rezneck, Samuel, "The Rise and Early Development of Industrial Consciousness in the United States, 1760-1830," *Journal of Economic and Business History*, IV, (August 1932), 784-811.

Robson, Charles, *The Manufactories and Manufactures of Pennsylvania in the nineteenth centry* (Philadelphia, 1875).

Schlesinger, Arthur, Jr., *The Age of Jackson* (Boston, 1945).

Schramm, Eulalia C., *General James O'Hara: Pittsburgh's First Captain of Industry* (Unpublished master's thesis, Univ. of Pittsburgh, 1931).

Simpson, Stephen, *The Working Man's Manual* (Philadelphia, 1831).

Stevens, George, *History of the New York Typographical Union No. 6* (Albany, 1913).

Stevens, S. K., *Pennsylvania: Titan of Industry* (New York, 1948), 3 vols.

Sullivan, William A., "Did Labor Support Andrew Jackson?" *Political Science Quarterly*, LXII (December 1947), 569-580.

Sullivan, William A., "Philadelphia During the Jackson Era," *Pennsylvania History Magazine*, XV (October 1948), 305-320.

Sullivan, William A., "A Decade of Labor Strife," *Pennsylvania History Magazine*, XVII (January 1950), 23-38.

Swank, James M., *Early Iron Enterprises in Cambria, Somerset, Westmoreland, and Indiana Counties* (Philadelphia, 1900).

Swank, James M., *History of the Manufacture of Iron in All Ages and Particularly in the United States from Colonial Times to 1891* (Philadelphia, 1892).

Swank, James M., *Introduction to a History of Iron Making and Coal Mining in Pennsylvania* (Philadelphia, 1878).

Swank, James M., Progressive Pennsylvania, A *Record of the Remarkable Industrial Development of the Keystone State* (Phila., 1898).

Thurman, Lawrence, *The Cotton Industry of Pittsburgh* (Unpublished master's thesis, University of Pittsburgh, 1947).

Trachtenberg, Alexander, *History of Legislation for the Protection of Coal Miners in Pennsylvania 1824-1915* (New York, 1942).

Trant, William, *Trade Unions—Their Origin and Objects* (Wash., 1915).

Trimble, William, "The Social Philosophy of the Loco-Foco Democracy," *American Journal of Sociology*, XXVI, (May 1921), 705-715.

Trimble, William, "Diverging Tendencies in New York Democracy in the Period of the Loco-Focos," *American Historical Review*, XXIV, (April 1919), 416-421.

Turner, Frederick J., *The Frontier in American History*, (New York, 1948).

Turner, Frederick J., *The United States 1830-1850* (New York, 1935).

Ware, Norman, *The Industrial Worker 1840-1860* (New York, 1924).

Webb, Sydney and Beatrice, *The History of Trade Unionism* (London, 1911).

Witte, Edwin, *The Government in Labor Disputes* (New York, 1932).

Woollen, Evans, "Labor Troubles between 1834 and 1837," *Yale Review*, I, 87-100.

Zahler, Helene, *Eastern Working Men and the National Land Policy 1829-1862* (New York, 1941).

8. LOCAL HISTORIES.

Boucher, John, *A Century and a Half of Pittsburgh and Her People* (New York, 1908), 4 vols.

Bowen, Eli, *The Coal Regions of Pennsylvania, being a General Geological, Historical and Statistical Review of the Anthracite Coal Districts* (Pottsville, 1848).

Day, Sherman, *Historical Collections of the State of Pennsylvania* (Phila. 1843).

Documents Relating to the Manufacture of Iron in Pennsylvania (Published on behalf of the Convention of iron masters met Dec. 1849, Philadelphia, 1850).

Fleming, George T., *History of Pittsburgh and its Environs* (New York and Chicago, 1922), 6 vols.

Futhey, J. Smith, and Gilbert Cope, *History of Chester County with Genealogical and Biographical Sketches* (Philadelphia, 1881).

Gordon, Thomas A., *A Gazetteer of the State of Pennsylvania* (Phila. 1832).

Hagner, Charles, *Early History of the Falls of the Schuylkill* (Phila. 1869).

History of the Lehigh Coal and Navigation Company (Published by order of Board of Managers, Philadelphia, 1840).

Jones, Uriah, *History of the Early Settlement of the Juniata Valley* (Philadelphia, 1856).

Killikelly, Sarah, *The History of Pittsburgh,* (Pittsburgh, 1906).

Letters on the Condition of the Poor, addressed to Alexander Henry, Esq. (By a Citizen of Philadelphia, 1836).

Lytle, Milton, *History of Huntingdon County* (Lancaster, 1876).

Mathews, Alfred, *History of the Counties of Lehigh, Carbon, in the Commonwealth of Pennsylvania* (Philadelphia, 1884).

Mombert, J. I., *An Authentic History of Lancaster County in the State of Pennsylvania* (Philadelphia, 1869).

Rupp, I. D., *History and Topography of Dauphin, Cumberland, Franklin, Bedford, Adams, Perry, Somerset, Cambria, and Indiana Counties* (Lancaster, 1846).

Rupp, I. D., *History of Northampton, Lehigh, Monroe, Carbon, and Schuylkill Counties* (Harrisburg, 1845).

Rupp, I. D., *History of Lancaster County to which is prefixed a Brief Sketch of the Early History of Pennsylvania* (Lancaster, 1844).

Scharf, J. Thomas and Thompson Westcott, *History of Philadelphia* (Philadelphia, 1844), 3 vols.

Smith, George, *History of Delaware County* (Philadelphia, 1862).

Thurston, George H., *Pittsburgh As It Is of Facts and Figures Exhibiting past and present of Pittsburgh Its Advantages, Resources, Manufactures and Commerce* (Pittsburgh, 1857).

Watson, John F., *Annals of Philadelphia and Pennsylvania in the Olden Time* (Philadelphia, 1898).

Wiley, Samuel and Henry W. Ruoff, *Biographical and Portrait Cyclopedia of Schuylkill County, Pennsylvania* (Philadelphia, 1893).

Wilson, Erasmus, *Standard History of Pittsburgh* (Chicago, 1898).

INDEX

A

Abbott, Edith, 40
Adams, John Quincy, 174, 182, 195, 200, 202, 203
Adams, Allen & Company, 21
Albany, 117
Alexander, Charles, 179
Allegheny County, 182, 184, 185, 187, 188, 200, 201, 205
Anti-Jackson party, 160, 175, 193, 200, 201
Anti-Masonic party, 189, 191, 192, 193
Arch Street Prison, Philadelphia, 211
Armstrong County, 184, 187
Artisans, skilled, 3, 75-83; *see also various trades*
Arthur, James, 20
Arthurs, John, 181, 183
Association of Journeymen Hatters, 113
Austria, 24
Ayres, William, 189

B

Bakers, 137, 143
Bakewell, Robert, 25
Bakewell, Thomas, 183
Baldwin, Henry C., 9
Baldwin Locomotive Works, 11, 24
Baltimore, 15, 73, 97, 105, 116, 117, 134
Banks, 3, 167, 181; bank war, 173, 199, 205-207
Baxter, John, 18
Beatty, George, 192
Beaver County, 184, 185, 187, 189
Beaver Falls, 14
Beelen, Anthony, 13
Berks County, iron industry, 9, 10, 11, 16, 17; unemployment, 54
Biddle, Nicholas, 52-53
Birdsborough Forge, 61-62, 68
Blacklist, 36, 37, 121, 138, 146-147
Blacksmiths, 109, 110, 135
Blackstock, William, 36, 37
Blakewell, Thomas, 183
Blockley, 104, 147
Bookbinders, 105; strike, 138-139
Borie and Keating, 19
Boston, 134
Brandywine, 104
Bricklayers, 99, 102, 130, 131, 135, 137, 154; wages, 78

Brooke William, 62
Brothers, William, 192
Bryan, Samuel, 190
Bucks County, 79
Bull, Thomas, 16
Bullick, Dr. John F., 46
Butler, J. B., 181, 182, 184, 185, 189, 190
Butler, 184, 185, 186, 187, 188
Butler County, 184, 187, 188, 189
Byberry township, 167

C

Cabinetmakers, 99; organization, 103, 110, 111, 133
Canals, *see* Pennsylvania Canal, Union Canal
Canal workers, demand for, 29-30, 72; strikes, 120, 151-152, 155-156, 157; wages, 71, 72-73
Caney, John, 116
Care, Henry, 70
Care, Thomas, 71
Carey, Mathew, 31, 49, 52, 60, 72
Carlisle, 171, 180
Carlton, F. T., 166
Carnahan, Robert, 187
Carpenters, 91, 97, 99, 102, 126, 137, 143; conspiracy trial, 132-133, 214; hours, 75-76; national union, 117; strike, 129-130, 131-133, 135, 136, 141-142, 154, 169; union, 102, 110, 111, 146; wages, 69, 76-78, 142
Centre County, iron industry, 12, 13, 16
Chandler, Joseph, 179
Charming Forge, 62
Chauncey, Isaac, 8
Chester County, 1, 10, 81, 92, 97; iron industry, 10, 62
Child labor, 8, 38, 40, 42-47, 55, 56, 150; hours, 44; wages, 44, 47
Cincinnati, 16
Clark, Victor S., 3
Class consciousness, 85-90, 103, 159-160
Clay, Henry, 181, 184, 189, 190, 193
Clearfield County, 180; coal miners' strike, 214-215
Clingensmith, Philip, 187
Coal heavers, strike, 134, 152, 153, 154, 156

Sloan, Robert, 191
Smith, Adam, 35
Smith, John, 63
Social reform, labor and, 209-215
Southwark, 137
Spayd, Christian, 192
Stackhouse and Thompson, 24
Starr, N. B., 181
Steam engines, 23-24; builders, 103
Steam-power, 8, 17, 21
Stewart, Robert T., 182, 184, 186, 187, 188, 189
Stockhouse, Mark, 181
Stone cutters, 99, 137
Strawn and Myers, 79
Strickland, William, 79
Strikes, 37, 95-96, 110, 119-120, 125, 133-134; boatmen, 155; bookbinders, 138, 139; cabinetmakers, 133; canal workers, 151-152, 155, 157; carpenters, 76, 90, 129, 130, 131-133, 135, 141, 169; coal heavers, 134, 152, 153, 154, 156; coal miners, 214-215; cordwainers, 80, 120-121, 122-123, 125, 126, 128, 135, 140, 141; curriers, 122; factory operatives, 35, 38, 145-151; handloom weavers, 149, 209-210; printers, 92, 125, 143; railroad laborers, 155, 157; ship carpenters, 128-129, 143; tailors, 130; woodcutters, 154
Sumner, Helen, 166, **178**
Swift, John, 156

T

Tailors, 99, 137; strike, 130; union, 102, 105, 110
Tariff, 8-9
Ten-hour day, 46, 76, 117, 129, 131, 132, 133, 134, 136-137, 142, 143, 149-153, 166-168, 212-213
Textile industry, 3, 7, 17-23, 36, 59; extent, 22; hours, 38, 44; labor in, 34, 35-36, 37; profits, 23, 57; wages, 38-44, 47; women and children in, 40-47
Thompson, John, 169
Trade unions, collapse, 97, 104, 105; conspiracy, 163; opposition to, 85, 88-91; origins, 36-37, 85-88, 92, 103, 105, 209
Trades' union, beginning, 99-101, 105ff, 129, 148; see Mechanics' Union of Trade Associations, National Trades' Union, Pittsburgh Trades' Union, Trades' Union of the City and County

of Philadelphia, Trades' Union of Pennsylvania
Trades' Union of the City and County of Philadelphia, 112; beginnings, 105, 120; decline, 110, 111; employer opposition, 110; finances, 108; growth, 105-106; jurisdictional disputes, 109, 110; membership, 106-107; purpose, 108; strikes, 108, 110, 133, 135, 138, 139, 156
Trades' Union of Pennsylvania, 104
Triadelphia Iron Works, 61
Troth, Henry, 179
Turnpike roads, 72

U

Union Canal, 73, 79
Union County, 63
Union Rolling Mill, 14
United Beneficial Society of Journeymen Cordwainers, 81, 88, 95-96, 106-107
United Trade Society of Ladies Cordwainers, 101-102
Universal suffrage, 168

V

Valentine and Thomas Iron Manufacturing Company, 16
Van Buren, Martin, 195, 200, 202, 203, 213
Vaux, Roberts, 166, 210
Venango County, 16

W

War of 1812, 7, 20, 76, 77
Ware, Norman, 172
Washington, 117
Water power, 8, 17
Weavers, 1, 20, 36, 126; hours, 38; rents, 33; union, 103, 107, 109, 117; wages, 33, 38-39
Whig Party, 136, 199, 200
Whitaker's Mills, 33, 38, 39, 40-42, 44, 47
Wiley, Samuel, 75
Wirt, William, 195, 200, 202, 203
Withers, John, 66-67
Wolf, George, 166, 196, 201, 203, 204, 210
Wolf, Michael, 63-64
Women in industry, 46, 49-50; organization, 107; wages, 40-42, 49
Wood sawyers, strike, 154-155
Workingmen's Party of Dauphin County, 190-192